Must the Show Go On?

Les Dennis

Must the Show Go On?

This edition first published in Great Britain in 2008 by
Orion Books
an imprint of the Orion Publishing Group Ltd
Orion House, 5 Upper St Martin's Lane,
London WC2H 9EA
An Hachette Livre UK Company

1 3 5 7 9 10 8 6 4 2

A CIP catalogue record for this book is available
from the British Library.

ISBN: 978 0 7528 9096 8 (hardback)
ISBN: 978 0 7528 9877 3 (export trade paperback)

Designed in Swift Light by Geoff Green Book Design
Printed in Great Britain by Clays

www.orionbooks.co.uk

Contents

Acknowledgements

I would like to thank everyone who has helped and encouraged me in writing this book.

My agent, Jonny Geller, for first suggesting the idea and for his continued encouragement. Ian Marshall and his team who took my original sample chapters and had faith enough to believe that, despite my never having written anything before, I could do it.

Thank you also to my family and friends in particular our Marg who was a willing listener whenever I lost my way and my auntie Pat who helped clarify details from my dim and distant childhood.

My main thanks, though, go to my fiancée Claire who has given me so much support when I have gloomily thought that this tale would be of no interest to the reader, as well as patiently deciphering and typing my illegible scrawl. The downside, I suppose, to being with a technophobe! I love you very much.

For my mum and dad – I love the bones of you.

Why must the show go on?
It can't be all that indispensable,
To me it really isn't sensible
On the whole
To play a leading role
While fighting those tears you can't control,
Why kick up your legs
When draining the dregs
Of sorrow's bitter cup?
Because you have read
Some idiot has said,
'The Curtain must go up'!
I'd like to know why a star takes bows
Having just returned from burying her spouse.
Brave boop-a-doopers,
Go home and dry your tears,
Gallant old troupers,
You've bored us all for years
And when you're so blue,
Wet through
And thoroughly woe-begone,
Why must the show go on?
Oh Mammy!
Why must the show go on?

From Noel Coward's 'Why Must the Show Go On?'

Introduction

This book is the tale of a reluctant celebrity. When I was growing up in post-war Liverpool, my heroes were comedians: Ken Dodd, the Goons and the entire cast of *Round the Horne*. The shows that I listened to on the radiogram, while my dad was having his weekly pint in the pub, and my mum was cooking our traditional Sunday roast, inspired me to aspire to a career in show business.

In the early 1960s, when the Beatles took the world by storm, and Liverpool Football Club thrived under Bill Shankly's management, unlike most other boys in the city, I didn't want to form a pop group or play centre forward at Wembley. Instead, I dreamt of following in the footsteps of a young Scouse comedian who had achieved remarkable success as the new compère of Britain's top TV variety show, *Sunday Night at the London Palladium*. Every week we would sit together as a family in front of the TV and watch Jimmy Tarbuck stride on to the stage, make us laugh with his snappy one-liners and introduce world stars like Judy

Garland and Sammy Davis Junior. The fact that he was, like me, working class, the son of a bookmaker and from Liverpool made me think that perhaps comedy was something I could do. I got an act together and started to learn my craft in the working men's clubs in Liverpool and the north-west.

The shy Leslie Heseltine eventually morphed into the TV personality that is now Les Dennis. My constant struggle in life has been dealing with this split personality. Leslie Heseltine doesn't like parties, values his private life and gets embarrassed when he is recognised in the street; Les Dennis is warm, cheerful, gregarious and blossoms in the spotlight. For a while, I managed to maintain a kind of balance between the two. However, in the late 70s, just as my career took off, the private side of my life was rocked by three significant losses. In the space of ten years, I would have to deal with the deaths of both of my parents and my close friend and business partner. Instead of taking stock and allowing myself to grieve fully, I buried myself in my work and pushed my emotional welfare on to the backburner. I went into meltdown and lost sight of the things that were truly important to me. Classically, I embarked on an affair and, as a result, my first marriage collapsed and my relationship with my biological family suffered enormously.

My career, however, went from strength to strength. For more than sixteen years I would host a successful show on prime-time TV. The public perception of me was of an amiable, cheeky chappy but away from the cameras I was anything but and would continue to struggle with the Heseltine/Dennis conflict. Marriage to a younger woman, who was equally as ambitious as me, together with an unhealthy addiction to the newly flourishing celebrity-obsessed culture, had a suffocating effect on the boy from Liverpool who had started out simply wanting to be Jimmy Tarbuck. As one half of a celebrity couple, I welcomed the attention and would do anything to fill as many column inches in the tabloid press as I could. Something had to give and eventually the bad karma I created in my first marriage would come back to haunt me. Marriage number two crashed on to the rocks, and the career that had been successful for so long floundered in the wake. After the debacle that was *Celebrity Big Brother*, an unlikely lifeline in the shape of a soul (and arse) baring appearance in the first series of Ricky Gervais and Stephen Merchants's hit show *Extras* would help me to re-establish myself and restore the balance.

Had I written this book two years ago, I know I would have been more defensive, much more bitter about the press and unable to view objectively what has happened in my private life over the last few years. When the eye of the storm subsided and I came out the other side, I could appreciate how right Nietzsche was when he said, 'That which does not kill us makes us stronger.'

In an interview for the *Observer* I commented, 'Hindsight is a fucker.' Now I see it more as a gift. On this unique and exciting journey I believe we are dealt the same lessons over and over until we learn them. For so many years I believed that the show must go on, but now, having learnt the lesson the hard way, I no longer have that view.

Today I am a much more contented man. I have a happy relationship, which I guard fiercely. No longer am I prepared to turn up to the opening of an envelope. I have rebuilt my relationship with my biological family and in my sister Marg have a rock that helps keep me grounded. My career is still important to me, but my family and friends now take priority.

In this book I want to show how the heady concoction of ambition and success can, if you let it, destroy the fundamentally good values that make you the person you really are. If *Celebrity Big Brother* failed to show the real Les Dennis, then my hope is that here I can set the record straight. Some of the stories I have read about myself over the years have been absurd, and some positively hilarious. I guarantee to be honest and tell the truth, but like any story, it is only my take on it. I have worked with some of the top entertainers and actors in the business and have a wealth of stories with which to pepper the warts-and-all tale.

Comics are renowned, I suppose, for being mournful by nature. There is this story of a man who went to see his doctor. 'I'm depressed,' he said. 'I find no joy in life. Nothing excites me.'

The doctor's advice was, 'If you're depressed, go and see Grock, the brilliant clown. He will make you laugh so much you won't be able to be depressed.'

The man replied sadly, 'I am Grock.'

CHAPTER 1

Extras

It was a blisteringly hot afternoon in the summer of 2004, and with my friend and property adviser, Justin, I was viewing a house in Muswell Hill. I was between homes, having recently sold my house in Highgate, and was eager to find somewhere permanent to live. As we wandered around the property, which I had immediately known was unsuitable, my mobile phone rang and my agent's name, Mandy Ward, flashed on the screen. My career was as unstable as my housing situation. *Family Fortunes* had ended after an amazing sixteen-year run and, following a less than career-boosting appearance on *Celebrity Big Brother*, offers from TV companies were thin on the ground. Any call from my agent had to be returned. I excused myself to the vendors, saving me from the delights of yet another avocado bathroom suite, and wandered into the garden to call Mandy back.

'Hi, Mandy. Sorry I missed your call.'

'Oh, hi, Les. Just a couple of enquiries to run by you. First, the BBC have been on, want to know if you're interested in being a contestant on *The Weakest Link: Nineties Icons*.'

I took a deep breath, considered it for all of a nanosecond and turned it down. 'Don't think so, Mandy. "Nineties icons" sounds like a euphemism for "TV has-beens". Don't think I could bear to hear Anne Robinson say, "Les Dennis, you are the weakest has-been. Goodbye." Anything else?'

'Oh, yeah,' she said. 'Ricky Gervais called. He wants you to give him a call. He wouldn't say what it was about. Just left his number.'

I took the number and quickly called the most successful comedy performer in British television, the man who, together with Stephen Merchant, had created *The Office*, the best TV sitcom since *Fawlty Towers*, and had only recently taken the Golden Globes by storm. My heart was thumping as the phone connected. After two or three rings an answerphone kicked in. 'Hello,' said the voice of David Brent. 'It's Ricky here. Can't take your call right now. Leave me a message and I'll call you back.'

'Hi, Ricky. It's Les Dennis,' I squeaked. 'Mandy asked me to give you a call.' Be funny, I thought. No bollocks. Don't even try. 'Here's my number. Thanks.' I hung up and thought immediately, This is a wind-up. John Culshaw does a great impression of Ricky. Somebody's got him to call and set me up. Before I'd had time to build this thought into an elaborate conspiracy theory, my mobile rang again and this time 'R. Gerv.' came up on the display. I'd already entered his name in my phone – how sad is that! 'Hello,' I said, thinking it was really J. Culsh.

'Hello, Les.' That Reading twang was unmistakable, and although John is good, I knew immediately that this was the genuine article. 'Stephen and I are doing a new series called *Extras* and there's a part for you. Before we write it, though, we need to know if you're interested.'

'Well, Ricky, there's a lot going on right now, so I'll think about it and get back to you' is *not* what I said, I am relieved to say. If he'd been there in person, I'd have bitten his arm off. 'Yes,' I shouted. Oops – be cool. 'Erm, yeah, of course. It would be an honour to work with you guys.'

That unique Gervais laugh. 'You don't know what we want you to do yet. You'd be playing yourself, or rather a twisted, demented version of yourself.'

Oh, I thought, that's honest.

'Think Larry Sanders.'

Immediately I knew what he meant. Lots of American film and TV stars had guest-starred on *The Larry Sanders Show* and had mercilessly sent themselves up. David Duchovny, in particular, had been hysterical in a towel scene in which he'd flirted with Larry, even doing Sharon Stone's infamous *Basic Instinct* crotch shot! Ricky said he would show me the script from day one and promised that I could make changes if there was anything I didn't like. We then made arrangements for me to go in and discuss it further with him and Stephen.

Over the next couple of weeks whenever I told people about the conversation the reaction was always the same: 'Be careful – he could be taking the piss. His comedy can be very cruel and you are at a low ebb.' A seed of doubt had been planted, so when I went to see Stephen and Ricky at their offices in central London, I was still excited, but just the tiniest bit wary. As always, I was ridiculously early, so I wandered up and down the street a few times. I still knocked on their door with ten minutes to spare. No posh foyer, with loads of media receptionists and secretaries. Ricky answered, deli sandwich in hand.

'Hello, you're early.'

Damn.

'We were trying to have lunch before you got here so we wouldn't have to buy you anything.' Typical uncomfortable Gervais joke. He directed me to a nearby café, the one with, as he put it, with 'dodgy chairs' to get myself a sandwich.

When I returned, Ricky ushered me into his sparsely furnished office. There was no art on the wall, and just a couple of sofas. It looked like they had just moved in. Stephen was sat on one of the sofas tucking into his 'dodgy-chair special'. He stood up to meet me and just kept on going. I managed to stop myself from saying, 'My God, aren't you tall,' as I figured a) that's what everybody says, and b) he already knows he is. He spotted my reaction, though, and I'm sure I blushed.

Ricky was wearing a T-shirt from the Kronk Gym. We had both, separately, trained there for our Comic Relief boxing matches – he against Grant Bovey, and me against Bob Mortimer. We spent a few minutes discussing the nobility and stupidity of pugilism, and before I could suggest Stephen should try it because he'd have a great reach and wouldn't get hit much above the waist, Ricky rescued the situation. 'Right, *Extras*. There you are – episode five, "The Man",' he said, pointing to a wall laid out with lots of Post-It Notes with scribbled ideas on them. Where episode five said, 'The Man,' I noticed the others had question marks. 'We want a different high-profile celeb for each episode, so we're still ringing around. The show is not about the celebs; it's about the little people.'

'Except for yours,' chipped in Stephen. He mostly smiled and ate his sandwich but, like a real-life *Creature Comfort* character, threw in the odd important piece of information.

'Oh, yeah.' Ricky laughed and started to get really excited. 'Your episode is all about you, or more importantly, the press perception of you.'

'Like the "Les Miserables" label?' I asked. After that regrettable stint in *Celebrity Big Brother* at a low point in my life and my subsequent divorce from Amanda Holden, the press had seized on the pun of my name to describe my depressed and grumpy state.

'Exactly. It's a chance for you to have a sense of humour about it. Do it properly and the public will say, "What a great sport." For instance, you're in panto, and it's the only job my character's offered, so he takes it.'

Those dissenting voices in my head were saying, 'He's taking the piss.' His comment about the press perception, though, had intrigued me.

He went on to describe other scenarios, some of which didn't make the final cut. 'We're in the pub, and to cheer you up I suggest karaoke. You get up and sing "Maybe I Didn't Love You", but halfway through you break down in tears and run out. I follow you and find you sitting on a wall. "You all right, Leslie?" I ask, putting my arm round you.'

I laughed out loud. 'OK, I'm in.'

'How far can we go?' Stephen asked.

'Go as far as you want,' I said, 'and if I don't like anything, I'll tell you.'

Sandwiches finished, they thanked me and said they'd be in touch.

As I was leaving, Ricky shouted, 'Oh, forgot to tell you – there's a naked scene.'

'A what?' I asked.

'A naked scene, but it's OK – it's all shot from behind, just the odd glimpse of your arse, à la *The Graduate*.' Ricky laughed. 'We'll get you an arse double if you want.'

'Don't think you'll find one as shit,' I replied, and left.

I didn't hear from them for a very long time. I found, bought and moved into the house I presently live in and, for the first time in a long while, began to feel at least physically rooted. I also got a challenging and fulfilling new job. David Babani, the wunderkind producer who runs the Menier Chocolate Factory, a fringe theatre in Southwark, called me and asked me to play the lead in a revival of Anthony Shaffer's comedy thriller *Murderer*. I was very scared, as the role had been played by the wonderful classical actor Sir Robert Stephens and hadn't been done since the 1970s. It was a physically and mentally demanding role, as for two and a half hours I would never be offstage. When David and the director, Adam Speers, offered me the part, I was shit-scared of failing and did everything to get out of it. 'I'm moving into a new home during rehearsals so it's out of the question' was my last, desperate excuse.

'We'll help you move,' said David, and they press-ganged me into it. I'm so glad they did. We opened in early December – two days after my move – and, with a little help from Paul McKenna to deal with opening-night nerves, got excellent reviews from no less than Charles Spencer of the *Telegraph* and even the great Michael Billington from the *Guardian*. It seemed my efforts to reinvent myself as a serious actor were, at last, paying dividends.

It was almost Christmas, though, and still not a word from Stephen and Ricky. My friend Andy Davies, best known as producer and on-air co-presenter to Jonathan Ross on his Saturday-morning Radio 2 show, told me that Ricky had been in and had mentioned that he was writing me a part. I think if I hadn't heard that, I would have begun to think that they had cooled on the idea and opted instead for Bobby Davro! In show business, your availability is checked all the time for lots of exciting projects, most of which fail to come to fruition. Then, on Christmas Eve, a script-sized BBC envelope flopped through my letterbox on to the tessellated hallway of my new home. I seized on it and tore it open. It was a first draft and there on the first page was my name. I quickly flicked through and saw a lot more of my name. I put the script down on the kitchen table and nervously made myself a cup of coffee. I didn't want to read it and discover that it was all a huge mistake.

Coffee in hand, I sat down and read the script. Although it was a first draft, it was almost word for word what we would film the next summer, and despite a couple of moments I felt anxious about, I laughed out loud and knew with certainty that it was the right thing to do. What I was most thrilled about was that, unlike the other episodes, where Ricky had said the A-listers would have cameos, this was a lead part. It was almost a double act between Andy Millman, played by Ricky, and Les (me, obviously!), and had both hilarious and poignant moments. It was a chance not just to prove that I could act, but to show that I could have a sense of humour about the events of the last few years. If I could take the mickey out of myself, perhaps that would at last draw a line under everything.

I looked back at the things that had made me feel uncomfortable, such as contemplating suicide and breaking down in panto, neither of which has ever happened, and realised that they were typical Gervais–Merchant devices – the times in the show when the viewer would be watching from behind a cushion. As Ricky had said in our first phone conversation, I would indeed be playing a 'twisted, demented' version of myself.

I'd lost my mobile phone over Christmas and didn't have Ricky's number to call him. After leaving a message with his agent, Ricky called me a few days later. 'Hello. It's Ricky.' He sounded surprisingly nervous.

'Hi, Ricky. Lost your number, but I've been wanting to call to say I think the script is brilliant.'

Huge sigh of relief from the other end of the phone. 'Thank God for that. We thought there must be a problem. Do you like the scene in the dressing room?' The laugh again. Ricky has an almost childlike enthusiasm that is incredibly infectious.

We discussed the scene and he was off. 'Oh, what about when you call *Heat*? Oh, and the scene in the pub where I get you to do Mavis? Anything you didn't like?'

'No,' I replied. 'You can go further if you like.'

'Ha, ha. Stephen, he says we can go further. Great, Les, we'll call you in a couple of weeks and bring you in for a read-through.'

One of the things I really admire about Ricky and Stephen is that there is no 'our people will call your people' bullshit. For such incredibly busy people, they are completely hands-on. I'd get calls from Ricky just to keep me in the loop about how things were progressing.

One day he called and was really excited. 'Just wanted to let you know who's agreed to do the project: Ross Kemp, Ben Stiller, Samuel L. Jackson, Kate Winslet and one other – oh, yes, Jude Law.'

And me, I thought. What an absolute gift.

A couple of weeks later, when Philip, my son, was driving me back from a meeting in London about Tim Firth's play *Neville's Island*, which I'd appear in at the Birmingham Repertory Theatre when we had finished filming *Extras*, Ricky called and asked if I would come in and do some work on the script with him and Stephen.

'Sure,' I said. 'When?'

'In about an hour?'

'No problem.' Putting my hand over the phone, I whispered to Phil, 'Turn the car round. We're going back.'

Six months on, the offices still looked as if they had just moved in. Over coffee we read the script. I was a little nervous, as I usually prep fully the night before a read-through. An hour's notice doesn't give you much time to consider how you will play a scene. I reminded myself, Remember you're playing yourself. How hard can that be?

After our first stumble through, Ricky slurped his coffee and said, 'Yeah, not bad, but could we try it again, and this time could you be a bit more natural?'

Shit! Thought I was doing that.

Two lines in and this time it was Stephen. 'Great, Les, but a bit quieter, almost throw the lines away.'

I was reminded of the story of Jack Lemmon being directed by Billy Wilder. 'Do less, Jack,' Wilder kept saying.

Frustrated, Lemmon replied, 'If I do less, I'll be doing nothing.'

'Now you're getting it,' smiled the great man.

A couple more tries and I too was obviously getting it because by the time we got to the pub scene Ricky and Stephen were laughing out loud. 'Great. You've nailed it. See you at the cast read-through next month.'

Each of the six episodes was to be read at the American Church on Tottenham Court Road, which meant that all available cast members would be there. Surely not the A-listers, I thought, as a month later I sat nursing an Americano in the Café Nero next door to the American Church. I was ridiculously early again.

My episode would be the first to be filmed (apart from a couple of scenes with Samuel L. Jackson, who was only in London for a short time) and was being read last so that we could rehearse it when everyone else had gone. I was incredibly nervous as my call time approached, so I decided to go to the loo before making my entrance. I didn't really need a wee, but wanted to kill time. As men get older, they start peeing in Morse code and, as the saying goes, no matter how much you shake or dance, a little bit stays in your pants! Big occasion, so I stood and shook endlessly until I felt sure I was safe. As I was doing up my flies, though, I felt a warm trickle down my right leg. No, please not today. I looked down at my jeans, and yes, it looked like I'd pissed myself, which I suppose, technically, I had. 'You bastard, you did that on purpose,' I whispered to my evil willy. What was I going to do now?

Praying that nobody would come in, I spent the next five minutes with my right leg extended up towards the hand-dryer, cursing every ten seconds as it tripped off automatically.

Eventually, having smacked the button a dozen times and got severe cramp in my left leg, I felt confident that the damp patch would merge with the denim and go unnoticed. I glanced at my watch. Shit – one minute to go! I ran out of the gents' and down the corridor. I was met outside the rehearsal room by one of the show's runners. 'Ready?' she asked.

'Yes,' I said, and, with my briefcase strategically held in front of my crotch, entered the room. Huge roar of laughter. Oh, no, they've spotted the wet patch, I thought. Then I realised that they were laughing at Ricky. The cast of episode three, minus Kate Winslet, were round a vast table reading the prayer-meeting scene. I was ushered to a spare chair and given a script so that I could keep up with what was going on. Kate's part was being played by a stand-in, and as I imagined her in the role, I too was joining in with the gales of laughter. Even so, I couldn't help but think, Oh, no. What if my performance is met with stony silence?

Episode three finished to applause and Charlie Hanson, the producer, stood and addressed the room. 'We're not reading episode four today, so we move straight on to episode five. Welcome, Les Dennis, who's playing...er...Les Dennis, Gerard Kelly, who's playing Bunny, Rebecca Gethings, who's playing Lizzie...'

I also met the wonderful Ashley Jensen for the first time, and of course the equally wonderful Shaun (Barry from *EastEnders*) Williamson, whom I already knew. I'd known Gerard for years, too.

We started the read-through. Ricky and Stephen did their agent's office scene, and as my first scene approached, my heart was thumping madly.

Bunny: I promise you, listen, I've done panto before. (To Andy) Aha, Andy Millman, this is Les Dennis.

Andy: Hi. I know who you are.
Les: Good to meet you.
(Andy and Les shake hands.)
Andy: Nice to meet you.
Bunny: (To Les) Andy is playing our gentle genie.
Les: (Frowns, massively disappointed) Oh, no, really? Could Chris Biggins not do it?
Bunny: He was busy.
(Andy looks embarrassed.)
Les: Biggins was busy? Oh, that's a nightmare. What about John Thompson off *Cold Feet*?

There was a laugh from the room and immediately my nerves were settled. We read on and I was feeling confident and elated by the time we'd got to the pub scene with the spoof of Graham Norton.

The read-through finished and a tea break was announced. Ricky came over with the biggest smile on his face. 'I knew that would go brilliantly. It's our favourite episode. It's everybody's.' These were words I would hear him repeat every time he called me. If he likes something, he certainly lets you know.

After the break, everyone who was not involved in our episode left and we started rehearsing. Ricky and Stephen had always said that if I had any suggestions to add to the script, I was welcome to do so. Tentatively, I suggested that the final line of the last scene could be better. Ricky looked sceptical and asked what was wrong with it.

'Erm, well, you've got me saying to the girl, as we are shagging, "I don't really know," as Mavis.'

'Yeah,' he said. 'What's wrong with it?'

I began to wish I'd never brought the matter up. 'Well,' I began nervously, 'what if I was to give her my *Family Fortunes* catchphrase, "If it's up there, I'll give you the money myself"?'

I was used to the volume of Ricky's laugh, but suddenly I felt like I'd been transported to London Zoo and plonked in the middle of the tropical bird aviary. 'Oh, we're having that,' he said, and then quickly added, 'but you're not having a writer's credit.'

All through rehearsals he would suddenly laugh and mutter, 'I'll give you the money myself.'

When we had finished, Charlie, the producer, said, 'Thanks, everyone, see you next Monday in Wimbledon.'

Gerard Kelly and I headed for lunch and a catch-up. We hadn't seen each other since panto in Glasgow in the 1994–5 season, so we had a lot to talk about. Amanda had been in the panto with us and it had been shortly before we married. I discovered recently that Gerard had been concerned that Ricky and Stephen were going too far with my story and had said so to them. At the time, over lunch, he said the words that everyone would utter to me when the episode aired later in the year: 'It's very funny...very *brave*...but very funny.'

On the first day of filming we did the scenes with Simone, the blonde actress that I had (fictionally) become involved with. By coincidence, Simone was played by a dear friend, Nicky Ladanowski. I hadn't suggested her for the role; apparently, she'd gone along to read for another part and Ricky and Stephen had looked at her, then at each other and said, 'Simone.' Nicky and I had worked together in the weirdest play, *Cherished Disappointments in Love*, a Finnish comedy. When I had first read it, I hadn't a clue what it was about, but I thought that if Janet Suzman was doing it, it must be good. To my amusement, on the first day of rehearsal she had admitted, 'Haven't got the foggiest what it's about, darling, but I like to take risks.' We opened at the Soho Theatre on 12 September 2001, so as it happened, hardly anyone saw it. Nicky and I, though, became firm friends.

The first day of filming went well. The Gervais–Merchant working method is remarkably relaxed. They would both block the scene, and if Stephen wasn't in it, he would direct what they'd agreed from behind the camera. Ricky is a terrible corpser and would spoil take after take by laughing out loud at what he found funny. The relaxed atmosphere was infectious and we would suddenly all be guilty of laughing like drains. On other productions you would get a bollocking for being unprofessional, but here it helped towards the creative process.

Ricky also had a little trouble not talking directly to the camera in a few scenes. In *The Office*, because it was a mockumentary, David Brent was always playing to the camera and at first Ricky would do it with Andy Millman. 'Shit, I just looked at the camera again.' We would always keep to schedule, though, and no scenes were dropped because of time. We would finish every day at 4 p.m. Usually you're lucky if you get away by 7 p.m.

One morning in the make-up wagon, Ricky was a little pissed off because Jude Law, who was due to do the last episode of the series, had pulled out at the last minute. The storyline had been written around him, so I think Ricky had good reason to be miffed. It was fascinating listening to him and Stephen brainstorming to find a replacement.

'Don't suppose you have Leonardo DiCaprio's number, Les?'

'No, sorry. I've got Lionel Blair's, though.'

'Ha, ha.' That laugh again.

We got through the panto scene without any problems until Ricky came on in his genie outfit. The whole theatre – extras, cast, crew included – collapsed in laughter and when he spoke it was worse. At the end of every line he would do this weird, guttural sigh that was absolutely hilarious. 'Ooh, I'm used to squeezing into tight holes. No pain, no gain. Humnooh!'

'What is that you're doing?' I asked between takes.

'Cyril Fletcher,' he replied. 'Remember on *That's Life* Esther

Rantzen would hand over to Cyril, who would say, "Thank you, Esther. Humnooh!"'

I was sorry I'd asked. With that extra knowledge I could hardly complete a take without laughing.

The naked dressing-room scene was looming. Oh, God, how will we get through that? I thought. I arrived at work the next day knowing that I would have to strip off not only in front of Ricky, but also a whole crew, cameras, lighting, sound, make-up, even wardrobe. They had to be there to dress Ricky and provide me with the gaffer-taped cricket box that would be strategically placed to save Ricky from getting an eyeful of, as he called it, 'Les's offal'. If you've seen the scene, you'll probably be amazed to know that I worked out intensively for weeks before the day of the shoot. Count yourself lucky that you weren't subjected to an even flabbier middle-aged body! If I had held my stomach in and tried to preserve some kind of physical dignity, it would have gone against the truth of the scene. My character is a broken man, having just been told by Andy that Simone is having it off with one of the stagehands. When I slump in the chair as the runner tells us there is five minutes to showtime, rather than suck my stomach in, I decided to let everything hang out – everything, that is, apart from the cricket-box offal.

On the first take, everything was going well until the moment when I removed my towel and the cricket box sent Ricky into fits of laughter. 'Sorry,' he said. 'So unprofessional. Quick – let's go again.' Same point, same thing. 'No. Sorry. Again.'

When somebody laughs at a particular moment, every time you get to it, you expect it to happen again. This time it didn't. Unfortunately, that set me off and I ruined the take. On take four we got through that moment, but when we got to the point where I was drying my crotch, saying, 'She likes to video us and we watch it back together and sometimes I can't believe it's my arse going up and down,' thrusting my hips to illustrate, the whole thing broke down. Ricky and I couldn't speak for laughing and the entire crew were shaking behind the camera. Any nerves about having them watch me strip off were long gone, and we were enjoying the serious business that is comedy. Eventually we pulled ourselves together and got the scene in the can.

My last day of the shoot was the following Monday, and was the only one that wasn't at Wimbledon Theatre. Instead, we were at a small pub where we could do the Graham Norton–Mavis Riley and the 'pissed-up slapper' scenes, including the final bedroom scene.

Acting is a weird business – you can meet an actress over lunch and an hour later be fumbling together (or at least acting it) under a duvet. The room Kate Smith and I were filming in was tiny, and during rehearsals Ricky couldn't control his laughter. 'I'll be OK during the take – don't worry.'

We started to film, and when I said to Kate in a seedy, mid-sex croak, 'If it's up there, I'll give you the money myself,' it was as if we were back in the aviary at London Zoo.

'Ricky,' Stephen said sternly. 'Sorry, mate, but you are going to have to leave the room.'

Like a naughty schoolboy, still giggling, Ricky had to be escorted out. He was made to stand silently in the hallway as we completed the scene.

The first assistant director announced, 'That's a wrap for Les and Kate.' I went back to the make-up and wardrobe unit in the car with Ricky, the only time we had really been alone together. He thanked me again, said he'd let me know when the cast screening and wrap party would be, and I was driven home. Our business is full of climaxes and anticlimaxes. You go from the excitement of a film or TV production to a quiet TV dinner at home, watching other people's work. It's very strange, but the six days I was on that shoot were some of the funniest and happiest of my career.

The screening was held at the BAFTA Theatre on 11 June 2005. My episode wasn't being shown, as it wasn't ready, and we were treated to the episodes with Kate Winslet and Ben Stiller. Apart from the cast and crew, there were lots of comedians there to see the preview. David Walliams and David Baddiel were sat behind me in the screening room, and I sat with Nicky (Simone) Ladanowski. Both the expectation and excitement were huge. Will it be as successful as *The Office*, or will Ricky and Stephen, who both seemed a little nervous, fall foul of second-album syndrome? The Ben Stiller episode was shown first, and although there was plenty of laughter and sharp intakes of breath, I, and I suspect a lot of others in the room, felt a slight sense of disappointment. With hindsight, it was difficult to just jump into the show. We were used to seeing Ricky as David Brent and it would take a few episodes to grow to love the relationship between Maggie and Andy. As Ricky had always said, *Extras* is about the little people, not the celebs, but we didn't know the little people yet. The Kate Winslet episode seemed more accessible and within minutes the laughter in the screening room was much more natural. When it had finished and we were wandering across Piccadilly to the wrap party, it was clear from the comments that everybody believed that they had another success on their hands.

As transmission of the series got closer, I grew more excited – not least because in every interview, when asked whose performance most surprised him, Ricky always said me. 'Les Dennis is a very funny man, both onstage and off, and I can't wait to see the public's reaction to him.' After three years in the wilderness I felt that maybe this was the opportunity I needed to reboot my dimming career.

Before the series was aired, I was sent a copy through the post. I sat nervously looking at the package, just as I had when the script had been sent, fearful of watching it in case I had made a dreadful mistake. I decided to watch it on my own. With all Ricky's stuff you watch it from behind a cushion. When you are in it, you watch it from behind a sofa in the next room. Despite the cushion factor, I loved it and couldn't wait to show it to family and friends. I had moved into a small rented flat while my house was being renovated, so that evening my friend James invited some people over to watch it on his big telly. After much laughter, head-burying and gasps, most people gave it two thumbs up. My friends Bill and Amanda, though, were very quiet over dinner afterwards.

'You didn't like it, did you?' I asked.

'Oh, yeah,' they said unconvincingly. 'It's well acted and' – here we go again – 'very brave. But if we're honest we didn't like to see you portrayed that way, because that is not the Les we know.'

I argued that that was the point but they still seemed unsure. Maybe I had misjudged the whole thing and Bill and Amanda's reaction would be how the public would see it. A week later, at Andy Davies's fortieth-birthday bash, we watched it again (me, through the banisters on the staircase) and this time, encouraged by others' positive reactions, Bill and Amanda laughed louder than anyone. When it was actually shown on TV, I was onstage in Torquay. I was hosting the live stage version of *Who Wants to Be a Millionaire?*, so as my naked arse was aired across the nation, I was sat, doing my best Chris Tarrant impersonation, asking some hapless contestant, 'Is that your final answer?'

I came offstage to find my mobile full of messages. Everyone, it seemed, had loved the show. Thank God.

The next day, alone in a hotel room, with no one to share the success, I woke to the best reviews of my career. I wandered into town to have a coffee, and as I was leaving the café, a neatly turned out, very middle-class mother and daughter stopped me and said, 'Congratulations, Mr Dennis. We loved the show.' I thanked them, and as I was walking away, it dawned on me with increasing horror, Oh, no, they've seen my arse! Until then I hadn't fully realised the implications; I had just got on with the artistic process.

A couple of weeks later I was in Liverpool with Andy Davies when a woman stopped me at the bottom of Bold Street. She looked concerned and compassionate as she asked, 'Are you all right now, lad?'

'Yeah,' I replied. 'What do you mean?'

'You know, after that documentary about your life.'

I roared with laughter – she thought it was for real. Life would never be quite the same again!

CHAPTER 2

In My Liverpool Home

I was born Leslie Heseltine, at home on 12 October 1953. Home was 83 Chesterton Street, Garston, and I was the third of five children. Our Marg was first, in 1947, and then came our Roddy, in 1951. Then, after me, our Ken, in 1955, and last the baby, our Mandy, in 1958. Garston is a working-class village in the south of Liverpool and is situated on the banks of the Mersey, just inland from the Irish Sea.

When I came along, my parents were still grieving the loss of Roddy, who died of pneumonia, aged just eight months. He died in hospital after a fitful illness. With modern medical technology, it probably wouldn't happen today. Though I didn't know him, his death would have a profound effect on me, as when I was born everyone said, 'My God, he's the spit of Roddy,' and, 'Winnie, you have been given him back. What a gift.' I grew up believing that I had to be my mum's good son and that I had big shoes to fill. I still have a photo of my mum, our Marg and a baby that I think is me but might be Roddy. Mum carried the grief of our Roddy's death with a heavy heart but tried not to let us see it.

Let me explain the 'our' syndrome. In Liverpool, we preface all of our relations' names with the word 'our'. Whether it is a sister, brother, uncle or auntie. My two sisters, Marg and Mandy, become 'our Marg' and 'our Mandy'. My auntie Pat is 'our Pat' and on it goes. Parents, though, are 'mine'. Even when talking to our Ken, Mandy and Marg, she is 'my mum' and he is 'my dad', and it is the same for them. Clear? Good.

My mum, born Winnie Grimes, was a strong, fiery, working-class woman. She was the eldest of seven children. There was her, then John, Charlie, Jim, Peter, our Pat and Bernie. Peter died when he was thirteen in a horrific road accident. He lost control of his bike and collided with a bus, a bus that his brother Jim was actually travelling on. As we were growing up, my mum would resist letting us have bikes and could never, despite her love of classical music, listen to the opera *Peter Grimes*, which was her brother's name.

Winnie was a wonderful mother, strong and loving but also, when she needed to be, a strict disciplinarian. She had to be, as we could each wrap my dad round our little fingers. My mum wanted the best for her family and would always work hard to improve our quality of life. To do so, she toiled long hours in factories. First, the bobbins works, then Millners, then when we moved to Speke, the Metal Box and in her later years at Lucas Aerospace. Still she managed to look after all four of us without us ever feeling like latch-key kids.

In her heart, though, she always dreamt of a life on the stage. As a young girl, she had sneaked backstage at the Liverpool Empire where Carroll Levis, a kind of pre- and post-war Simon Cowell, was auditioning for new talent. The signature tune to his radio show began, 'Paging Carroll Levis. Paging Carroll Levis.' My mum found her way past the stage-door man and wandered the corridors shouting those very lines. To her surprise, Carroll Levis himself came out of his dressing room and asked what she thought she was playing at.

'Sorry, Mr Levis,' she replied, suddenly timid and shy. 'I didn't think you'd be in. Just a joke.'

'Right, young lady,' he said. 'Come back this afternoon and let's see if you have the singing voice to match your confidence.'

Excited, she ran all the way home, a good three miles, only to be told by her mother, 'Not for you, my girl. You start at the bobbins works on Monday.'

Because she had had her ambitions thwarted, I think she saw in me, despite my almost chronic shyness, a strong desire to perform, and so became my champion. She wasn't a pushy show-biz mother; she just gave me that extra shot of confidence to believe that I could stand in front of a crowd of people and entertain.

My dad, Leslie Heseltine, couldn't have been more different. He was always known in Garston as 'the quiet man' or 'Rusty', because of his red hair. Nobody had a bad word to say about him, but he was, I think, a bit of a dark horse. His early life is shrouded in mystery. We know he was brought up in Garston by a Mrs Martha Goulden, who we believe was an auntie, though on his certificate of service in the Royal Navy, dated December 1940, he entered her as his mother. She absolutely doted on him. Where the name Heseltine comes from, we don't know.

We know my dad was an accomplished sportsman, a champion swimmer, and to this day I have a book printed in the 1920s called *Swimming for Schoolboys*, which has photos of him, aged about eleven, demonstrating various dives and strokes. Other treasured possessions are his football contracts. He played for Liverpool Schoolboys, South Liverpool, Tranmere Rovers, Blackburn Rovers and, on 31 January 1935, signed a contract with my beloved Liverpool FC. The contract reads, 'The CLUB hereby agrees that the said CLUB shall pay to the said PLAYER, the sum of £1/10/- per week from 31 January 1935 to 4 May 1935. The said PLAYER is to receive an extra £1 per week when playing in the first league team and the usual bonuses for wins and draws as allowed by the Football League.' A far cry, then, from the huge fees paid to players today. I don't know how many games he played for the first team that year, but the club finished the season a less-than-distinguished nineteenth in Division One. He was, by all accounts, a good inside left, though whether he played with passion and loyalty could be in doubt, as when he was a young man, my dad was a staunch Evertonian. He actually stood in the boys' pen when the legendary Dixie Dean scored his record-breaking sixtieth goal of the 1927–8 season.

There is little known of my dad's war effort except for one story. He was a gunner on a naval minesweeper and one day, while on duty, a plane that wasn't British was flying low, coming very close, too close for comfort. As kids, I remember us asking, 'Was it German, Dad?'

'No, it was a bloody Yank showing off.'

'What did you do, Dad?'

'I fired a bloody warning shot.' My dad couldn't speak a sentence without saying 'bloody' (sometimes even splitting words to in-bloody-sert one!). 'Not close, but near enough to scare the bloody idiot. Eventually he flew off.'

'Did you get into trouble, Dad?' we wanted to know.

'No. The captain hated the bloody Yanks and gave me an extra tot of rum.'

He could have been a decorated war hero but we would never have known. His naval records show that he was awarded a silver A/S M/S Badge on 10 October 1942. He hardly ever talked about his past and certainly never about his successes.

After the war my dad worked on Garston timber docks as a

checker. I have known a lot of dockers over the years and somehow can't imagine him as one. He was very quiet and unassuming, whereas most dockers are loud and boisterous, using Scouse humour to get them through the long days. Most had nicknames. One fellow was known as the 'Diesel-Fitter', so called because he would look through the stuff coming into the port and say, 'Deez'll fit the wife, and deez'll fit the kids.' Another was called 'Little Red Riding Hood' because he went home to his grandma's for his dinner.

My dad did tell us once of a practical joke he played on one of the lads. This bloke would go every day and do a number two behind the timber stack because he couldn't be bothered to make the long walk to the gents'. 'Just off for a Tom Tit,' he'd say. One day, fed up with this, my dad and his mate (he would never have done it on his own) sneaked up behind him and carefully slid a large shovel underneath, quietly taking the offending turd away. When the bloke had finished, he looked round to inspect and, to his horror, there was nothing there. When telling us the story, Dad would beam and say, 'His bloody face was a picture. Me and Bunny would laugh all day.'

In his spare time, Dad was working illegally as a bookie's runner. A friend of his, William Kay, had received compensation for an accident and would, once it was legalised, set up his own betting shop. In the meantime, he recognised in my dad a man who was as quick with mental arithmetic as Carol Vorderman, and who was therefore a valuable asset for his new dodgy business. If my dad had set up his own, he too could have been a rich man, but he was not ambitious and was always content with his lot. This lack of drive would later infuriate my mum and would only make her strive harder to be forever upwardly mobile. During this time, though, she would be embarrassed, as my dad ended up spending the odd night in the cells of Bridewell Prison. He was a bookie's runner but obviously sometimes he didn't run fast enough.

My mum met my dad at the Mona Pub, where she was working as a barmaid. Their dates would take place at the Majestic Club, where, after a few drinks, my mum would get up and sing with a trio. Her party piece was 'My Yiddishe Momma', a strange choice for a girl who had had a strict Catholic upbringing, but she had always had a sense of drama and the tear-jerker appealed to her.

After a brief courtship, my dad had asked her, without an ounce of romance in his soul, 'Shall we get married, then?'

Could have been worse: he could have said, 'Shall we bloody well get married, then?'

Always the joker, my mum asked, 'All right, but who'd have us?'

That was it; they married on 27 January 1951. Marg had been born in 1947, out of wedlock, and, indeed, not to my dad. In fact, she has no idea and no desire to know who her father was. Our Marg is an amazing woman, the matriarch and, since my mum died, the driving force of our family. My mum had had her illegitimately at a time when that would have been scandalous so my maternal grandparents had agreed to support her only if they could pretend to the world that she was theirs. For someone who was brought up at first believing that she was her mother's sister, she is incredibly well adjusted and extremely wise. When we were older, our parents sat us down and told us the facts. Our Ken and Mandy were shocked, but I wasn't. I had somehow always known.

Marg and I fought quite a lot when she hit her teenage years and one evening she slapped me across my back. I didn't have a shirt on, so it sounded worse than it was. The drama queen in me made me overact like an Argentinian footballer in the penalty box. The easy-going, mild-mannered man that was my dad was momentarily transformed into an angry, glowering monster. 'Don't you dare hit him,' he said, with hand raised.

'It's OK.' I jumped up. 'It wasn't that bad – I was acting.'

There was a kind of Mexican stand-off between him and Marg. He never, ever hit any of us but would always raise his hand as if he was going to.

Our Marg looked him directly in the eye and said, 'You're not my father and you never will be.'

The words cut me to the quick. Yes, we can all say those things to our parents in moments of anger, but something told me it was deeper than that. The tension subsided, but a few months later Marg went to live with my auntie Pat and her family. Marg has always said, though, that she could never have had a better father, and at family gatherings will always tell stories of him with a huge smile on her face. 'I loved the bones of him,' she will say. That's what my dad used to say about all of us: 'I love the bloody bones of you.'

I never knew my paternal grandparents, though I did once catch sight of my dad's father. I have a vivid memory of sitting on the lower deck of a bus at Garston Depot and the only other person was an old (at least to my young eyes), hunched man in a flat cap sitting a few seats in front. My mum whispered to me, 'That man is your grandfather.' She didn't go and speak to him or encourage me to do so. A couple of stops later he got off the bus and that was the last I saw of him. I know now that he was seen as a low-moralled lothario. According to my auntie Pat, any woman in Garston who walked on the same side of the street as him would end up pregnant.

I hardly knew my maternal grandparents either, as they both died when I was very young. According to the stories I have of him, my maternal grandfather, Tommy, was a stern, tyrannical patriarch. From what I've been told, he makes me think of the father in D. H. Lawrence's *Sons and Lovers*. Indeed, my mum was very like the mother in that brilliant novel, wanting the best for her sensitive young son, Paul. It is a favourite book of mine and I identify closely with Paul Morel: like him, my desire for self-improvement and my snobbery would, later on in life, cost me dearly.

I have two memories of my granddad, one of which is of him sitting in vest and braces in front of a roaring fire in my grandparents' house in York Way. I can still hear the sound of sizzling saliva as he coughed and spat on to the red-hot coals. Even at my tender age I remember thinking, That's disgusting. I'll never do that when I'm a man. My other memory of him is watching him in full regalia and feathered beret, playing the bass drum, marching proudly up Window Lane at the front of the Woodcutters' band. The Woodcutters was the working men's club at the end of Chesterton Street. It is still standing amid the desolation that is, sadly, modern-day Garston. Only recently I did a concert there, together with other Liverpool performers, to help with regeneration of the area. As a small child, I went to a Christmas party at the Woodcutters and then on to see Tommy Steele in *Jack and the Beanstalk* at the Empire. That, together with the sight of my showman-like granddad beating his huge bass drum, sowed in me the first seeds of a desire to entertain.

I have only one vivid memory of Tina, my grandmother. When I was very young, she developed breast cancer and had to have a mastectomy, a startlingly horrific procedure at any time, but I fear more so in the mid-1950s. She came to convalesce with us at the prefab we had moved into in Speke, a post-war overspill suburb in Liverpool. One day, as she lay in bed, she played peek-a-boo with me and I remember giggling gleefully. I have dim memories also of an open coffin in the front parlour of York Way and a lively wake afterwards. Children then were seen and not heard, so whatever emotions I felt had to be heavily suppressed. Cancer of one kind or another would later claim my granddad, my mum and my uncles Charlie, John and Jim. No wonder I've never smoked.

Of the Grimes clan, John and Jim were the characters. One evening Jim came running home from school shouting, 'Mac McGregor's got a box of figs.' Apparently, some young Scot he knew had been sent the exotic fruit and Jim wanted the whole family to know. Nobody seemed interested, though, so, to get their attention, he kept saying it: 'Mac McGregor's got a box of figs.' To this day if someone in our family says something over and over, somebody else will say, 'Yeah, and Mac McGregor's got a box of figs.'

When I came to Liverpool in 1994 to appear on *This Morning* with Richard and Judy and announce my engagement to Amanda Holden, we stayed at the Redbourn Hotel in Woolton. The family came over to meet my bride-to-be and we had a drinks do in the front reception room, which was stuffed with beautiful antiques. My niece Steph's husband, Tony, was sat on a magnificently carved chair. I pointed to it and said to my uncle Jim, 'That's a Chippendale.'

Jim looked impressed and, holding his hand out, said, 'Are you, lad? Pleased to meet ya.'

I laughed like a drain. He thought Tony was a member of the famous group of strippers and wasn't the remotest bit interested in the almost priceless piece of furniture.

Just after the war years there was extreme poverty across Britain and no more so than in Liverpool. The house in Chesterton Street was a typical terraced house, very similar to the houses in *Coronation Street*. The bath was in one of the three bedrooms upstairs, while the toilet was out in the yard, which led on to a back jigger, or alley. They were notoriously damp houses, so not in the least conducive to rearing a newborn baby. In the hours before Roddy died of pneumonia, a strange incident happened in the house. My mum often told the story, though if we had only heard it from her, we probably would have taken it with a huge shovelful of salt. She was a master storyteller and could weave wonderful tales, expertly embroidering a dull fact into a compelling drama. I can remember evenings spent peeling potatoes for chips and listening to my mum's versions of Bram Stoker's *Dracula* and the Alan Ladd movie *Shane* – the originals weren't a patch on Winnie Heseltine's versions. My dad, though, also swore blind that what happened the day Roddy died was true. They were about to set off for Garston Hospital for visiting time when a voice suddenly called out, 'Winnie?' They opened the door but there was nobody there. Again the voice, which they didn't recognise, called 'Winnie?' My dad looked upstairs and my mum looked in the back yard. Nobody. The voice again: 'Winnie?' They checked the neighbours on both sides and no one was home. They never did get to the bottom of it. When they got to the hospital, they were met by a nurse who told them that Roddy had died an hour earlier. Heartbroken, they asked to see him. He lay peacefully in a cot, and someone had placed a flower in his tiny hand.

Burying her grief, Mum determined that the same would not happen to us. She would have made an excellent political lobbyist because, after Ken and I were born, she pestered the council until they agreed to move us to the prefab in Speke. Whole estates of prefabricated houses were built across the UK to provide accommodation for those made homeless by the war and aid ongoing slum clearance. They were aimed at families, and ours had an entrance hall, two bedrooms, an equipped kitchen with pantry and, luxury of luxuries, a bathroom and separate toilet. For ease of build, construction materials were usually steel, aluminium, timber and, in our case, alarmingly, asbestos. There was a decent-sized garden, probably the first grass I'd ever seen and a unit similar to an Anderson shelter as a cold store. The roof to the single-storey dwelling was made of corrugated steel, and the outside walls were painted a bright yellow.

I remember my early years being happy there. Our next-door neighbour was Mrs Sharp, a white-haired, rather stern lady in spectacles who, underneath, had a heart of gold. She shared her home with Tom, the lodger. Looking back, they were probably living 'in sin', but 1950s society required the euphemism of 'lodger'. He was a lovely man, an ambulance driver, who one day miraculously cured a sty I had developed, with what seemed to me to be magic potion. It was probably no more than antiseptic eyewash.

Speke, in those days, was all fields and bluebell woods. Speke Hall, one of the finest Tudor homes in England, dating from 1490, was nearby. The only signs of urban growth in the 1950s were the prefabs and Speke Airport, now John Lennon Airport. Our house was 11 Tombridge Way and we could play out safely without our parents worrying. I had a friend across the way, a little girl called Elizabeth. I couldn't pronounce her name, so instead called her 'Little Bit'. One day I was out front with Little Bit when her mum, who tried to pretend she was posh, leant out of the window and shouted, 'Elizabeth, your lunch is ready.'

What exotic surprise, I thought, is lunch? In working-class Liverpool, lunch didn't exist: it was breakfast, dinner and tea. 'Supper' was a word we never used, and if we had, would have consisted of a cup of watered-down cocoa and, if we were lucky, a Jammy Dodger or a custard cream.

The next day as we played my mum, always one to keep up with the Joneses, leant out of the window and shouted in her poshest voice, 'Leslie.' Uh-oh, I thought. I was only called by my full Christian name when I was in trouble. 'Your lunch is ready.'

I wonder what it is, I thought. Imagining a huge present tied with a giant bow, I ran in and looking round the kitchen asked, 'Mum, where's my lunch?'

'There,' she said, pointing to a plate of beans on toast, 'on the table.'

'That's not my lunch,' I said, hugely disappointed. 'That's just my dinner.'

While we were in the prefab, we got our first television. It took pride of place in the corner of the living room and I can remember watching the Hanna-Barbera cartoons *Yogi Bear* and *The Huckleberry Hound Show*. According to our Marg, our Ken's first words were 'Tide clean', from the TV advert for Tide soap powder. We watched spellbound, even enjoying the white dot that disappeared, slowly fading to black, when the set was switched off. Little did I suspect that this magical box would become such an important tool in my chosen career later in life. I loved *Whacko!* with Jimmy Edwards, *Pinky and Perky* and *Lenny the Lion*. Terry Hall with Lenny was the first ventriloquist I ever saw and I was fascinated.

Kenny Lynch recently told me a story about Terry Hall. They were working in summer season together and one evening between shows (summer shows were twice-nightly at 6.10 p.m. and 8.40 p.m.) Kenny was passing Terry's dressing room and could hear a huge row going on. He knocked tentatively on the door, and when Terry answered, Kenny asked, 'Is everything OK?'

'No,' Terry replied. 'It's him – he won't stop arguing,' and pointed to Lenny the Lion, his dummy, which was propped up carefully on a chair.

'Right,' Kenny said, backing away. 'Well, I'll leave you to it,' and got out of there as quickly as he could. Ventriloquists, or 'vents', are a strange breed. They often resent that audiences love the doll more than them and sometimes have a kind of schizophrenic relationship with their wooden and cloth partner.

There is another story that is attributed to the great comedian Ted Ray. He was doing a week on the Moss Empire circuit and was sharing a dressing room with a 'vent'. When he arrived, the vent, who was onstage rehearsing, had already laid out his props and make-up. His doll was on a hook on the door and the make-up was on the dressing table. Like many variety acts, he had covered it neatly with a towel. While his roommate was doing his sound check and band call, Ted couldn't resist checking what make-up he used. He quickly looked under the towel and carefully replaced it. The vent returned from his rehearsal and was hardly in the room when the dummy said, from the hook on the door, 'He looked under your towel.' Echoes of Anthony Hopkins in the movie *Magic*. Aged four, though, as I watched Terry Hall, I was simply transfixed by the monochrome lion talking to me from the magic box in the corner of our living room.

When our Mandy was born on 6 May 1958, the prefab seemed overcrowded. Marg, who was approaching puberty, had to share a small bedroom with our Ken and me, while the baby was in with my mum and dad. My mum, who had given up work for a while, began to get restless and, once again in lobbyist mode, pestered to get us a bigger house. Our time there, though, was idyllic.

We didn't have much money, but Christmases were wonderfully exciting. While some kids at school would boast about needing a pillowcase to house their presents, most others in post-war working-class Liverpool would get very little. On Christmas mornings, apart from one main present, which one year was a now politically incorrect gollywog, we would wake up to find Father Christmas had been. We would fumble at the bottom of our beds to discover that we each had one of my dad's work socks (thankfully washed) stuffed with an apple, a tangerine (no such thing as satsumas then), a couple of nuts in their shells and two or three shiny new pennies. Imagine today's generation of children being content with that.

Hiding what few presents they could afford in such a small

house was virtually impossible for my parents. One year on a Saturday afternoon, a couple of weeks before the big day, our Marg, annoyed because she had been left to look after two boys when she wanted to go out with her friends, went hunting and found the hidden treasure – two jack-in-the-boxes, one each for me and our Ken, and the traditional tin of Quality Street. With surgeon-like precision, she removed the sellotape from the lid in one long strip and carefully stuck it to the metal door of a kitchen cupboard. We watched, wide-eyed, as she removed all the green triangles, her favourites, giving us one each to keep us from snitching when my mum got back. She also let us play with the jack-in-the-boxes, which played 'Pop Goes the Weasel', as she carefully taped the tin back to look like new. The tin and the toys were put away safely, and my mum returned shortly after with the baby. All was well until our Ken, too young to understand the honour of not squealing, suddenly jumped up from behind the sofa singing 'Pop Goes the Weasel'. Our Marg was punished and sent to her room. Well, our room.

Our parents were incredibly generous considering the small salary that was coming into the house. My mum couldn't work with three young children to care for, so, until she could, we lived off my dad's wage. Betting was now legal so he worked full time for Billy Kay, who had done incredibly well for himself since investing his compensation cheque. He had a couple of betting shops and in the summer months he and my dad would drive round Speke knocking on doors and taking bets. His was the first car we'd been in. A beautiful navy-blue Humber with dark-brown leather upholstery, it even had a radio. I can still remember hearing *The Archers* theme play as we drove sedately around the estate.

My mum liked the place to look good so our furniture was up to the minute and would usually come from Lewis's or

Sturlas in the old Swan district. She became expert at signing my dad's signature on hire-purchase agreements and, although he knew, he would turn a blind eye. There was never any danger of these stores not being paid. My dad was a stickler for paying bills, never letting anything get to final-demand stage. As a young man, he had been a gambler but once he was behind the counter he gave up apart from the odd flutter on the Grand National or, his favourite, the Derby. 'It's a bloody mug's game,' he'd say.

In September 1958, a month before my fifth birthday, I started my education at Stockton Wood Infant School. The school badge was really cool – an embroidered Spitfire plane flying over the River Mersey. In recent years I have endeavoured, along with Mike McCartney, who attended the school with his younger brother, Paul, a decade or so before, to obtain one of those badges, but to no avail. Coincidentally, the McCartney boys would also be pupils at my next school, Joseph Williams, and then I went to Quarry Bank, where John Lennon had been the most famous old boy.

I have little memory of my time at Stockton Wood except for a really traumatic event that happened on my very first day. The teacher gave us building blocks to play with, and as play got more and more boisterous, I swung round and, block in hand, collided with another child. He cried and told the teacher that I had hit him deliberately. I still have a strong sense of outrage about that day because I know it was an accident. The teacher, though, in some Dickensian workhouse display, made an example of me, stood me on a table at the front of the class and whacked me across the back of my legs with the offending block. I was mortified, even to the extent that I wouldn't dare ask to go to the toilet when I needed to. Consequently, I soiled my trousers and had to be cleaned up by the teacher in the small bathroom at the back of the nursery classroom. She delivered me to my mum at the school gates. 'I'm afraid Leslie has had an accident.' Needless to say, I never did it again.

In 1960, for our Marg's thirteenth birthday, my parents bought her a Dansette record player, red and cream with the name emblazoned across the front. My mum had a terrible habit of buying presents that she herself would like to receive. Our Marg was a huge Cliff Richard fan so the first record they bought her? 'Move It'? No. 'Living Doll'? No. 'Come Fly With Me' by Frank Sinatra. My mum's favourite.

A few years later, when I was taking my 11-Plus, I saw in the window of the Dale Street pet shop a beautiful pair of ground squirrels. I was mad about animals, always nursing some baby hedgehog or a blackbird with a broken wing. 'Mum, can I have them? They are beautiful.'

'If you pass your exams,' was her reply.

I worked hard and nervously waited for the post on the day of the results. I had passed. Great news for my education choices to come, but more importantly, I could have the ground squirrels which I had already named in my head as Chip and Munk. 'It's not practical,' said my mum. I was totally crestfallen. The next day she turned up with a Kodak Brownie camera, which – surprise, surprise – she had wanted for a while. There is a picture of Ken and me taken on a Sunday trip to North Wales, sat on the wall of the marble church in St Asaph. I looked suitably pissed off. I didn't even get to take the photos, only to be in them.

Meanwhile my mum had continued to pester the council, arguing that it was no longer suitable for our Marg, now aged thirteen, to share a room with two small boys, and in October 1960, as US presidential candidate JFK first suggested the idea of the Peace Corps, Cassius Clay, later to become Muhammad Ali, won his first professional fight and Harold Macmillan first made his 'Winds of Change' speech, the wind was certainly changing for the Heseltine family, as we moved onwards and most certainly upwards into 58 Thornton Road, Childwall.

CHAPTER 3

A Stream Where Youngsters Meet

Childwall, pronounced 'chilled wall', not 'child wall', is three or four miles inland from Garston and Speke, and was for us like moving to Knightsbridge. In the 1086 Domesday Book it is referred to as 'Cilennelle', meaning 'a stream where youngsters meet', which seems appropriate as both *Hollyoaks* and *Grange Hill* are now filmed there. It is dominated by the Childwall Fiveways, a large roundabout that is one of the busiest in Liverpool. It is one of the city's most sought-after suburbs, with plenty of greenery and mostly detached and semi-detached houses.

Our house, a modest three-bedroom post-war council property, seemed like Buckingham Palace to us. It was pebble-dashed with grey and white chips, and had a dining room with a door, not quite a French window, but close, leading into the back garden. There was also a front garden and a bay window. It felt like a supreme luxury, and compared with the tiny prefab, there seemed to be acres of space. It was the home we would live in until we grew into adults, the house my mum would die in and the house that Ken and his wife, Debbie, would bring their children up in. Debbie and Ken split up a few years ago, but she continues to live in the house, so it is still in the family.

When we moved, in 1960, we were really excited, not least because of its easy access to Bowring Park, which we always referred to as 'the back fields'. What joyous times we had playing football there with our new friends and – would you believe it – Mum and Dad too, my dad showing the skills that made him valuable to Liverpool FC, and my mum displaying quite a nifty left foot in front of the goal. One night she must have been playing prior to going out, because she headed the ball while her hair was in rollers and the game had to stop for a while because the pins had pushed into her head, breaking the skin – perhaps one of the most bizarre football injuries ever recorded. Some of the neighbours would tut at my mum's involvement, but she didn't care. She loved those evenings as much as we did.

Our Ken was a brilliant player and could have had a career in the game had he been more focused and less wayward as a youth. I was never very good and felt a sense of frustration because I wanted to please my dad so much. I remember playing in a school game once and hitting the bar with a good right-footed volley. I turned round to see if my dad had seen the shot but he was talking to another parent. I was gutted. I think that's maybe why I turned to showbiz, so that I could at least please my mum.

Football allegiance in our family has always been a bit odd. My dad, as I have said, was a passionate Evertonian as a young man and he tried to instil the same passion into our Ken and me. One evening after school, together with his friend and colleague Desi Whitfield, he took us to watch a game at Goodison. First we had tea, fish and chips with a slice of lemon (how posh) at the Kardomah on Church Street, which was similar to a Lyons Corner House, and then we went to see the match.

Alex Young was an exciting centre forward, and the team included Brian Labone. For some reason though, probably because my dad had been on Liverpool's books, I secretly wanted to support them. In fact, my memory of that night is imprinted with the plaice and chips with lemon at the posh café, rather than the game. When Liverpool won the FA Cup in 1965, with that glorious header from Ian St John proving to be the winner against Leeds, that was it.

'Sorry, Dad, I'm a Liverpudlian.'

'No, you're not. You're a bloody turncoat.'

He'd lost me to the Reds then, but worse humiliation was to come to him. My mum had a huge crush on Denis Law and had always had a fondness for Manchester United since that fateful night in Munich in 1958, when eight of their players were among the dead in a dreadful air crash. Her art of storytelling enthused our Ken and when he saw those amazing diving headers and overhead kicks of Denis Law's, he was hooked. So, not only did my mum and Ken, two Scousers, support a 'Manc' team, but because they were so passionate about Mr Law, they supported Scotland as well.

'You can't. You're bloody English.'

'My mam's maiden name was McLeod,' she would retort, 'so that makes me half Scottish.'

'I don't care – it's bloody embarrassing.'

My dad always cared too much about what other people thought, a trait I'm sorry to say that I've inherited in bucketloads. His attitude eventually, though, was if you can't beat them, join them, and because of his devotion to my mum, he too quietly carried a torch for Busby's Babes. A few years later, when I was looking for a stage name – Leslie Heseltine taking up too much room on the chalkboards of the local working men's clubs – even I was drawn into my mum's world. 'What about Les Dennis?' she suggested. 'It's almost Denis Law backwards.' So I was newly christened.

One of my biggest regrets is that my mum and dad weren't there the evening that Michael Aspel surprised me with the 'big red book' on *This Is Your Life* in 1997. Midway through the show, the story about my name change was related and Michael said, 'Please welcome Denis Law.' I was thrilled and honoured to meet the great man, but our Ken, not the biggest talker anyway, was rendered completely speechless. To this day he supports Scotland, even when they play England.

Going to watch Liverpool play at Anfield during the Bill Shankly and Bob Paisley years was a huge thrill. Great players like Roger Hunt, Ian St John, Tommy Smith and my favourite, Peter Thompson, set the ground alight with excitement. Then later, of course, Kenny Dalglish, Stevie Heighway, John Toshack and Alan Hansen. For me, though, the main attraction was the electric atmosphere and humour of the world-famous Spion Kop. I've been to many grounds over the years, and of course any crowd of enthusiastic fans is exciting, but there is something unique about the Kop that lifts the hairs on the back of your neck as you enter the ground. Since the dreadful Hillsborough tragedy, the ground has seating throughout, but the exceptional atmosphere still exists. In the 1960s and 1970s, though, it was quite extraordinarily magical. Many thousands of fans packed the stand but you never felt threatened or crowded. They would think as one, and some of the songs and jokes were truly inspired.

When Leeds came to play Liverpool in 1967, their keeper, Gary Sprake, made a famous gaffe as he went to throw the ball to his defender. Somehow he lobbed it, not to the waiting player but over his shoulder into his own net. Des O'Connor was riding high in the charts at the time and within seconds the Kop was singing, 'I let my love fall into careless hands, careless hands that can't hold on to love.'

Nowadays, fixtures are called off if you can't see the corner flag from the Liver Building, but then you would sometimes watch a game in thick fog. One time when a cheer went up at the Anfield Road end, suggesting a goal had been scored, the Kop sang, 'Who scored the goal? Who scored the goal? Ee-aye-addyo, who scored the goal?'

My good friend Colin McKeown told me that they would sometimes sing something that had nothing to do with the game. In the early 1980s *Roots*, the hit mini-series about the history of slavery, was gripping the nation every Saturday night. The iconic and sympathetic character that everybody loved was Kunte Kinte, and, in the episode the week before a match, he had died. At half-time the Kop sang, 'Kunte Kinte's dead. Kunte Kinte's dead,' to the same 'ee-aye-addyo' tune but this time more solemnly and respectfully.

My favourite memory is of standing on the Kop one winter's evening watching a dull mid-week fixture. At half-time, the score was a boring nil-nil. Just before the players came out for the second half, a pigeon flew down from the Kemlyn Road stand and landed just inside the centre circle. All eyes were on it as it walked slowly towards us. As it reached the penalty area, the Kop went deathly silent. It inched closer and closer and to a man the Kop were willing it to do what they wanted it to do. Yes, it's going to. Then it did! It crossed the line into the goal. The Kop exploded as if Liverpool had won the treble. It was an hilarious moment.

*

Our Ken and I transferred from Stockton Wood Infant School to Joseph Williams Primary, and then our Mandy joined their infants class in the autumn term of 1962. Joseph Williams was set in the middle of the Childwall Valley council estate and it was there that I made my stage debut. Like most first appearances, it was in the Christmas nativity. Our teacher, Miss Gossage, cast it and I was desperate to play Joseph. Instead, that role went to a big, rather blustery boy called Jimmy Niblock. He was less than enthusiastic and protested in a thick Scouse accent, 'Ah, eh, miss, I don't wanna be in it. All me mates'll laugh at me.'

'I'll do it, miss,' I said excitedly.

Miss Gossage laughed loudly. 'No, Leslie. With your beautiful blond hair, you have to be an angel.'

And so it was that I, the only boy amongst four girls, had to play a guardian angel. I didn't even get to play Gabriel. *That* honour went to a tall, skinny girl in our class called Jennifer Heap. So, reluctantly, both Jimmy Niblock and I took roles that neither of us wanted to play. I think it put him off for life, but obviously something about the experience made me want to try again.

I hated having blond hair. My nickname at school was 'Light Bulb'. When my mum took me with her to the hairdresser's, all the women would coo and pat me on the head, 'Oh, what beautiful hair. What a shame it isn't on a girl.'

I always felt that I had to be my mum's good boy and fill Roddy's shoes, but our Ken was able to be the rebel and was forever being told by neighbours he'd upset, 'Why can't you be more like your elder brother? He's lovely.' I wasn't, of course. I just felt I had to play it. Because of this conflict, our Ken and I fought like cat and dog. My mum started work before 8 a.m. so my dad usually took us to school. Racing started later in the day, so he wouldn't have to leave home until around ten. Our Ken could play my dad like a violin. Just as we were leaving the house, he would fall on the floor, screaming, saying he wasn't going.

'Come on, kid. Stop acting the goat. You've got to bloody go.'

Ken would remain on the floor, bawling, until my dad resorted to bribery and gave him threepence. Our Ken, who knew exactly what he was doing, would suddenly stop crying, dust himself down and, clutching the shiny coin, put his hand in my dad's and go obediently to school. Because I still had some of my pocket money left (our Ken's would go within the first hour) and because I didn't kick off, I wouldn't be treated to the extra money. I was silently incensed, though – so much so that one day I took a half-crown, which was school-dinner money, from the mantelpiece when no one was looking. I was, however, a lousy thief, because that evening I was caught at the ice-cream van buying lollies for all the kids in our road. Great for them, but I ended up being sent to my room with no tea.

One Saturday morning in early summer, Ken and I were fighting about something and I pushed him out into the back garden. I locked the dining-room door, picked up his precious new football and a kitchen knife, and held the ball in front of him as if I was going to burst it.

'You wouldn't dare,' he mouthed from behind the glass.

Suddenly the devil in me took hold and I plunged the knife into the ball, which immediately deflated before his eyes. Filled with rage, he ran round to the kitchen door, fully intending, I believed, to kill me. I quickly dropped the ball and knife, unlocked the dining-room door and ran out into the garden. It was like a scene from *The Keystone Cops*. He chased me around the garden, up the side passage and into the front garden, where luckily the front door was open. I ran in, heavily pursued by Mad Dog Ken, and as I attempted to close the door, he pushed to keep it open. He missed the wooden frame, though, and instead crashed through the plate-glass window. I remember the utter shock on his face, then the blood, and then my panic. My parents were out – what were we going to do? Luckily, our neighbour opposite, Mr Wally, was an ambulance driver and was home. Ken survived with minor injuries, although they didn't look it at the time. His left arm was lacerated, and his lip was badly cut. He still has the scars today, as he loves to remind me.

Before we got a car, Sundays were always the same. My dad would cook eggs and bacon, cursing as the lard in the pan coughed and spluttered. 'Ooh, you barrrstard bloody thing,' he would shout, diving backwards in case he was hit by the scalding-hot fat. Then he and Joe Nolan, another neighbour from across the road, would go for their Sunday pint at the Roby pub. Sunday dinnertime and Friday evenings were my dad's time for the pub. While he was out, I would help my mum cook the Sunday roast. Ken and Mandy would be out playing in the road, so this was my time alone with her. I loved the ritual of preparing the only meal of the week that we were all guaranteed to sit down and eat together. I would peel the potatoes and, if we were having lamb, bring the mint in from the garden. None of us had green fingers and the back garden was, to say the least, an overgrown wilderness. Mint, though, grew in abundance and today I only have to tear a leaf and smell it to be instantly transported back to those Sunday mornings in the early 1960s.

While my mum made the mixture for the best Yorkshire puddings I have ever tasted, we would both listen to the *The Light Service* on the radiogram. *Two-Way Family Favourites* was a show dedicated to people whose loved ones were posted abroad with the armed forces. They would send messages to husbands and wives serving in Cologne, Hamburg and Cyprus – places that sounded incredibly exotic to my young ears. Then came the comedy shows – *Round the Horne*, *The Navy Lark*, *The Clitheroe Kid* and, in his own show, wonderfully observant comedian, Al Read. These guys became my heroes, and somewhere deep inside me the desire to experience that intoxicating drug, laughter, began to grow.

After the dinner, my dad, full up with the Sunday roast and Higson's best bitter, would say to my mum, 'Bloody lovely that, kid. Think I'll go and rest my eyes for a bit.' He never admitted to sleeping; it was always 'resting my eyes', even though the walls would be vibrating within ten minutes from the loudest snoring I have ever heard.

After our evening tea we'd have our one bath of the week, emerging with fingers wrinkled like dried prunes because we'd stayed in so long. Then we would gather in the front room round the family shrine, the telly. Sunday TV didn't start until early evening, so we would listen to *Sing Something Simple* with the Mike Sammes Singers, there being no rush to switch on and watch *Songs of Praise*. The excitement would be building, however, as the time for *Sunday Night at the London Palladium* approached. The first host I remember was the wonderful Bruce Forsyth.

Bruce, like the Queen, has always been there in my life and is, I think, one of our greatest entertainers. He has an amazing gift for communicating with an audience and must have more recognisable catchphrases than any other comedian. Even then, in the days when he had a shock of dark hair, no moustache, just that huge, jutting chin, he would thrill you as he looked directly down the lens and say, 'I'm in charge.' The show was pure old-fashioned variety – the Tiller Girls, acrobats, ventriloquists, magicians, exciting new comedians, and there was always a big name at the top of the bill, usually from America. Frank Sinatra was probably the only star they didn't ever secure. Sammy Davis Junior, Judy Garland and Tony Bennett were all introduced by Bruce, and subsequently Norman Vaughan.

The highlight of the show in the Bruce years was Beat the Clock, which was probably the first game show that he ever did and was a kind of forerunner to the *Generation Game*. He would invite two contestants out of the audience to join him and, in his brilliant way, which only he could get away with, would berate them and push them around – 'Over here, dear, for goodness' sake' – as they competed in various silly and often hilarious tasks. As the credits rolled and each artist who appeared on the show stood waving to camera behind revolving waist-high spangly letters that spelt out the show's title, that desire inside me to entertain was crying out like the plant in *Little Shop of Horrors*: 'Feed me. Feed me now!' Little did I know that the chance to tread the boards was just round the corner.

CHAPTER 4

Hi-de-Hi!

One morning, having seen us off to school and before going to open Billy Kay's betting shop in West Derby, my dad was opening the post. He would later tell the story, 'There was one letter there I was about to throw away. I thought it was another bloody circular and then I noticed it said, "Littlewoods," on the envelope. I tore it open thinking Winnie's forged my signature again for another hire-purchase account. Couldn't believe me eyes. It read, "Mr Heseltine, we are pleased to inform you that you are a winner with Littlewoods pools." I nearly bloody fainted.'

Every Saturday my mum had told us, 'We are going to win the pools.' And every week we had watched her check her coupon while watching Final Score on *Grandstand*. Every week, though, we had been disappointed. This was the first week that Mum hadn't checked, and though Dad hadn't won enough to make us rich, it was, to us, life-changing money: £620! This was 1961 and my dad probably earned about £15 a week, if he was lucky. He had won roughly a year's wages. With my mum's encouragement, we decided not to save it but to, as Cilla put it in the song 'Oh You Are a Mucky Kid', have a splash. I remember coming home from school to luxurious fitted carpets in the living room, hall, stairs and landing, and art on the wall – three horses galloping across an open plain and one of those dodgy kitsch 1960s paintings of a small boy with a tear running down his face that was in nearly every working-class home in Britain.

The most bizarre purchase was a G Plan cocktail cabinet. My parents hardly ever entertained and never drank at home, so why did my mum want it? All I can think is that she was heavily influenced by movies like *A Star Is Born* and *Days of Wine and Roses* in which a cocktail cabinet was a household must. However, instead of martini glasses, olives and bottles of vermouth, ours was just a dumping ground for all the household rubbish that we accumulated, the only booze being a bottle of Stone's ginger wine that sat unopened from one year's end to the next.

There was still enough money left over for us to have our very first family holiday. Summers were usually spent at home playing on the back fields, with the occasional day out at New Brighton, Merseyside's answer to New York's Coney Island. We were going for a whole week to stay at Butlins holiday camp, which was perched on the edge of the North Wales peninsula in Pwllheli. We had never been away from home before and as the day of departure approached we got more and more excited. My mum took us to a seamstress she knew, who made up summer shirts for Ken and me, and summer dresses for Mandy. I remember a royal-blue Hawaiian shirt with sombreros printed on it and my favourite one, which was covered with images of Fred Flintstone and Barney Rubble. They were neatly folded and placed into our new suitcase days beforehand, and for the remaining nights, until that Saturday in July, we found it hard to sleep. After what seemed like a lifetime, the morning arrived.

We were gently woken just before six, bathed, dressed (sombreros for me) and given breakfast. A black cab arrived and the driver didn't need to knock. We were all, apart from Marg, who was not relishing the holiday, sitting watching out of the window for him.

'He's here, Dad.'

'OK, kids. Winnie, have we turned the immersion off?'

'Yes.'

'Cancelled the papers and milk?'

'Yes. Shut up and get in the cab.'

We were already in, this being our first trip in the type of taxi we had seen in countless shows and films on the telly. About ten minutes later we arrived at Crosville Bus Depot on Edge Lane. The cases were transferred and we, along with our fellow holidaymakers, boarded the shiny cream and blue chartered coach, or chara, which would take us through the Mersey Tunnel into the beautiful North Wales countryside and would arrive some four and a half hours later at the military-style holiday camp. For us kids, the journey seemed to be interminable, even though my mum kept pointing out things of interest. The beauty of Snowdonia, the marble church at St Asaph (where in a few years I would be snapped looking miserable with the 11-Plus Kodak Brownie) and the bubbling mountain springs were wasted on us. We did perk up at first sightings of cows and sheep, but very soon they too lost their allure, as they seemed to be in every field. Once you've seen one sheep, you've seen them all.

After a brief break at a café in Betws-y-Coed, where my mum commented on the deliciousness of the tea (she would always say that the water in Wales made the tea taste better), we were assured that we were on the final leg of the trip. We travelled past Portmeirion, where the cult TV series *The Prisoner* had been filmed, through Criccieth, and we could sense the sea. The road got windier and windier, and the cliché 'Are we nearly there,

Dad?' was replaced with 'Are we nearly there, coach driver?' He would patiently shout back, 'Not long now. You will see the chairlift first, leading to the beach.'

On every bend we would say, 'There it is. Oh, no, it's a pylon.' Then, in the distance, we spotted the tiny cable cars wending their way magically towards the shimmering Irish Sea. Ten minutes later we were, at last, at our destination.

After a brief stop at the security gate, we drove through on to the wide new avenues towards the cluster of 1950s buildings that we have all see in reruns of David Croft and Jimmy Perry's nostalgic sitcom *Hi-de-Hi!*

'Let's go to the fair,' our Ken shouted impatiently.

'We've got to check in at reception first and get settled into the chalets,' replied my mum.

Our Marg's eyes rolled heavenward. She was fourteen and had no friends with her. Our cousin Stuart was with us, so Ken and I had a mate. Mandy was only three and would be content to stay with Mum and Dad. Throughout the week Marg would be told, 'Cheer up and go off and make friends.' She hated the holiday and wouldn't come in subsequent years. The camp was split into four houses and we were placed in the House of Windsor. My parents picked up the keys and we were taken by a young, clean-cut man in a red blazer and white flannel trousers to a row of neatly ordered but tiny single-storey huts that reminded us of prefabs smaller than our own had been. Immediately we felt at home. The young redcoat pointed to ours and left us to settle in, saying, 'See you later. The boating lake is just over there and will be open again after the first sitting of lunch.' Lunch. That word again. We had two chalets: one for Mum, Dad and Mandy, the other for us. 'Wow, bunk beds. Bagsie me on top.'

Dinner, or lunch, was served in the huge dining building in two sittings. We were on first sitting, and every mealtime we would make our way to the table we had been allotted, which was bang in the middle of the room. The clatter of cutlery and crockery was almost deafening as the waitresses rushed around plonking stainless-steel jugs of tomato or vegetable soup on to the tables. In their rush, they would often drop and break plates, and every time it happened, a good-natured cheer would echo throughout the room. The food was ordinary standard fare, one step up from school dinners, but we loved it, especially my dad. Mealtimes were one of the highlights of his week. We would come off the fair or from one of the two swimming pools to find my dad near the front of the queue, itching to eat. For us, though, it was an inconvenient interruption in our endless days of play.

On that very first day, having finished our meal, we headed straight for the boating lake with my dad. As we stood in the queue for a rowing boat, our Ken, who was fascinated by the ducks, leant over to try and stroke one. Splash! He was in. Panic ensued, with my dad on the edge of the water, shouting, 'You bloody stupid idiot.' Quickly and expertly, like he'd done it a thousand times before, the attendant fished him out and plonked him dripping wet safely at our feet. My cousin Stuart and I laughed loudly, but then grumbled because instead of getting into the next boat, we had to go back to the chalet to get Ken dried and changed. It became an annual tradition. If our Ken didn't fall into the lake some time in the week, we felt like we hadn't had a holiday.

Like the others, I loved the outdoor daytime activities, but for me the best and most exciting events were the evening variety shows. There was a resident troupe of performers who, together with the redcoats and visiting guest artists, put on shows twice nightly. I loved them and looked forward to them all day. If we were on second sitting for our evening meal, I would go without food and queue to watch the show a second time. It was like watching *Sunday Night at the London Palladium* every night, only live. The thrill I felt as the lights went down and the orchestra struck up with the overture was like nothing I had ever experienced. I had started doing a little act for family and friends, and had felt the rush when they laughed and clapped, but the reaction to the entertainers on that stage in the Gaiety Theatre was something that I too wanted to experience. On the Sunday show, there would, as a surprise, be a well-known act at the top of the bill. I saw Tommy Trinder, Billy Dainty, Ken Platt and the act that for me as a young boy changed my life, Peter Cavanagh. He was the country's top impressionist well before Mike Yarwood came along and I absolutely loved his act. He would turn his back on the audience, take a mortarboard hat and stick-on handlebar moustache from his props table, turn round and, to a burst of spontaneous applause, Jimmy Edwards, the headmaster from *Whacko!* would be standing there onstage. If I didn't know who Peter Cavanagh was doing, I would turn to my mum and ask, 'Is it like him? Is it like him?'

'Yes,' she would whisper. 'Shut up and watch.'

His big finish was Field Marshal Montgomery. This was the early 1960s and the British obsession with the war had not yet subsided. I didn't have a clue, but the audience again applauded wildly. 'Mum, is it like—'

'Yes. I am trying to watch.'

That was it. I was hooked. As we exited with the thronging, ecstatic audience, I said to my mum, 'That's what I want to do when I grow up.'

'Well,' she said, 'there's a children's talent show on here. They're holding auditions on Tuesday afternoon. Let's work on a short spot.'

Over the next couple of days we got an act together, consisting mostly of impressions stolen from Peter Cavanagh's repertoire. I had yet to learn that you don't take material from other comedians. Then, on the Tuesday, we registered to stand in front of a panel of judges and perform, in the hope of getting through to the talent show on the Friday afternoon. I fell at the first hurdle, though, as nerves overcame me and lack of props meant that when I turned round, supposedly transformed into Jimmy Edwards, I was just a little boy doing an impression that the judges didn't recognise. Like the hopefuls who fail on *The X Factor*, I was absolutely devastated. Fighting back tears, it was of little consolation when my mum said, 'Don't worry – we can try again next year.'

That was my first stage rejection, and although it was heartbreaking, as I would continue to do throughout my professional career, I bounced back and tried again.

CHAPTER 5

What Swinging Sixties?

Something exciting was beginning to happen on Merseyside. Marg's first job was at a posh boutique in Bold Street called Nanette's. She would come home and tell us not so much about the job but how she spent her dinnertimes. Like dozens of other teenage girls, she would go in her break to a dingy, dark cellar club in Matthew Street called the Cavern. Once a stronghold of traditional jazz, in the early 1960s the Cavern was transforming into a meeting place for Merseyside youth and a hotbed for new and exciting talent.

'Who did you see today, Marg?' we'd ask.

'The Swinging Blue Jeans, my favourites, the Big Three and a new group, the Beatles.'

'Were they good?'

'Yeah, not as good as the Big Three, but they have this guitarist, John, who is really funny. He kept saying to the lads from the shipping offices, "Shut up, you with the suits on."'

One time, she told us she had been asked to dance by the

drummer from the band Rory Storm and the Hurricanes. His name was Richard Starkey. He would later replace Pete Best in the Beatles, using the name Ringo Starr. At one of those lunchtime Cavern sessions, the screaming girls were joined by a shy young record shop owner called Brian Epstein and suddenly Liverpool was the coolest place on earth.

I first heard the Beatles' songs played at the Silver Blades Ice Rink in Edge Lane. Our traditional Sundays began to incorporate afternoon visits to the rink, which would be packed as Paul McCartney's voice warbled the beautiful ballad 'Till There Was You'. Scousers were everywhere. At *The Royal Variety Performance* that year, 1963, Ken Dodd had the Queen laughing with jokes like 'I love classical music like Handel's "Largo". I never drink anything else.' The Beatles, though, stole the show. John Lennon showed he could charm the most hard-bitten, stuffy audience when he said, 'You in the cheap seats, clap your hands. The rest of you, just rattle your jewellery.' Frank Sinatra and Tony Bennett had dominated the radiogram in our small dining room in Thornton Road, but now the album *With the Beatles*, with its iconic black-and-white photo of the Fab Four, sat on the top of the pile. Other Liverpool bands also began to fill the charts. The Swinging Blue Jeans, Billy Jay Kramer and the Dakotas, Gerry and the Pacemakers. Even the hat-check girl from the Cavern, Priscilla White, had number-one hits using her new name, Cilla Black.

That year almost every teenage boy in the city asked for a cheap guitar for Christmas, and Hessy's music store did a roaring trade. They quickly sold out of guitars and Bert Weedon's *Play in a Day* guitar manual. I, though, was more interested in the flourishing career of the young man some had dubbed the fifth Beatle. Jimmy Tarbuck was beginning to make a name for himself following his appearance on *Comedy Bandbox* earlier that year. He looked like a Beatle – he had the same mop of dark hair and the same sharp 1960s suits, the only difference being that he wore a waistcoat and fob watch. As the Beatles stormed the world, he stormed Britain. By 1965, after several guest spots, he was asked by Val Parnell, the show business impresario, to host *Sunday Night at the London Palladium*. I had watched Bruce hosting, never really believing that a career in show business was possible for a working-class boy from Liverpool, but when Tarby came along, I began to think that perhaps it was not beyond my reach. Like me, he was from south Liverpool and was the son of a bookmaker. What was more, in September 1964 I had begun my secondary education at Morrison Rose Lane Secondary Modern in Allerton, the very school that he had attended the previous decade.

Also, that summer I had had my first success when I had come third in the junior talent competition at Butlins. After that awful rejection in 1961, I had worked on my act with my mum, and with a spot that included impressions of Freddy 'Parrot-Face' Davies, *Steptoe and Son* and Pete and Dud, I had at last impressed the judges. I was beaten to first and second place by a Shirley Temple lookalike, singing, 'How Ya Gonna Keep 'Em Down on the Farm?' and a tutu-wearing ballerina, but I didn't care, as I had my third-place certificate and my little silver-plated cup. To me, it was a great victory and I felt, for the first time, that I was on my way.

One of my new mates at Rose Lane School, Les Roberts, was a good footballer and one day in our first year we made an agreement: if he ever got to Wembley, he would get me tickets, and if I ever got to the Palladium, I would do the same for him. In 1978, when I did my first week at the Palladium, supporting the brilliant, tragic young star Lena Zavaroni, I tried in vain to get in touch with Les, but I had lost contact with him and couldn't track him down.

*

Marg had started to date a young man from Kirkdale, Tony O'Neill. We all liked him instantly. He was a great laugh, very funny and, more importantly to us at the time, had a car. It was a Morris Oxford Countryman with a huge bench seat, ivory steering wheel, column change gearbox and wood-framed windows. We used to be so excited, as all seven of us would pile in and take Sunday trips into North Wales or to the Wirral.

As Marg and Tony were getting serious enough to get engaged and had set their wedding for 19 March 1966, my mum and dad allowed them to go on holiday together. They were going for a week on a coach trip to stay, in separate rooms, in a small guesthouse in London, or so my parents thought. They were actually going in Tony's car to Criccieth in North Wales to stay in a two-berth caravan. Before our Marg headed off, supposedly to the coach station, my mum said, 'Don't forget to send us a postcard.' Damn, our Marg must have thought, how are we going to get a card to them with a London postmark? In the middle of their lovely week in the Welsh mountains, they had to drive, leaving at 5 a.m., all the way down the A5 to London, buy, write and send postcards home just to prove that they had been there.

When they came back from their holiday, Tony would have us in fits of laughter as he told us stories about their trip. 'Oh, yeah, we went to Buckingham Palace. Liz and Phil spotted us in the crowd and invited us in. Young Charlie went down the chippy and we all had a fish supper.' Little did we know as we laughed that not only had they not visited the Queen, but apart from the mad dash to post the cards, they had spent no time at all in the capital city.

One day my mum decided that she wanted a car of her own. 'Don't be bloody stupid, Winnie. You can't drive and we can't afford one,' argued my dad. He knew he was fighting a losing battle, though, as when my mum decided she wanted something, she moved heaven and earth to get it. She bought a small wooden moneybox and one evening wrote on it in blue biro, 'Mum's Car Box.' We all laughed. How was she going to save enough pennies and sixpences to afford even the most dilapidated old banger? 'You'll see,' she said. 'You'll all be laughing on the other side of your faces soon.' She was right. Incredibly, she got together £400, and one Sunday afternoon we went to Harry James's used-car centre on Edge Lane and bought a second hand, duck-egg-blue Austin 1100, registration plate 940GLV. Isn't it funny what you remember?

'Very nice, but who's going to bloody drive it?' asked my dad.

'Me,' she said. 'I'll take lessons.'

She started a course with Hugh Watters, a local driving instructor, and possibly the bravest man in the world. My mum was a terrible driver, and on many evenings in my teens, having been driven home by her from our Marg and Tony's, I would breathe a huge sigh of relief, thanking God we were still alive. She failed her first, second and then her third test. In the meantime, our Pat had passed first time.

'How did you do that?' asked my mum, most disgruntled. 'You can't even spell.'

'They didn't ask me to spell in the test,' laughed our Pat.

After failing the fourth time, my mum began to give up hope. The Sunday before the fifth test, Tony nervously agreed to sit with her so that she could get some last-minute practice. With Tony beside her, and Marg and my dad in the back, we waved them off from the front living-room window. She switched the engine on and engaged first gear to drive them round the block. Mirror, signal – Oh, no, she forgot that the manoeuvre part involved pulling out into the road. Instead, she hurtled six yards, hugging the kerb, and crashed head on into our next-door neighbour Mr Jones's brand-new Ford. Before she had time to think, my dad had jumped out, blushing like a Belisha beacon, and run into the house shouting, 'Bloody hell,

Winnie, that's bloody embarrassing. You will never pass your bloody test. Sell the bloody thing.' That was like a red rag to her and later that week she arrived home jubilantly clutching her pass certificate. Tony always said that they gave it to her for good attendance.

My dad could be extremely uncommunicative and my mum would get frustrated. One time, to attract his attention, she set fire to the bottom of the newspaper while he was reading it. 'Winnie, you stupid bloody woman, what are you doing? You could set the house on fire.'

'Aha, at least you're talking to me now!'

Another time, she craftily cut the power cable for the TV. The crafty bit was that it led from the wall under the carpet to the TV, so to all intents and purposes it still looked plugged in and should be working.

'This bastard thing won't bloody work,' my dad said, and being the most technically inept person in the world, other than myself, he spent half an hour banging it to try and make it work. My mum just wanted a bit of attention.

When my mum and dad rowed, it would go on for days. I would get off the bus on my way home from school and pray as I walked across the back fields that they had made up. I hated it when they didn't talk because I would become their go-between. My mum would say to me, 'Tell your father that his tea is ready.'

I would walk the few feet into the front room and say, 'Dad, your tea's ready.'

My dad would play the same game: 'Tell your mother I'm going for a pint with Joe.'

'Mum, my dad is going for a pint with Joe.'

The silences between them were unbearable and slightly ridiculous. Then suddenly, after days of this, one morning I would come downstairs to go to school and my mum would warmly say something to my dad and he would reply. When did this happen? I would wonder. And why didn't anyone bother to tell me! Like the boy in L. P. Hartley's novel *The Go-Between*, I would feel cheated and very angry, yet relieved that the silences had stopped.

I was probably thirteen when, after an evening of the silent treatment, I went to bed and read in my room. I'd been off school for a couple of days with a cold or something but was feeling well enough to go in the next morning. I remembered that I would need a note from one of my parents explaining to the teachers why I had been absent. I'll go and get it now, I thought, in case I forget in the morning. I went down in the dark: the light bulb on the landing must have needed changing for most of my childhood. I opened the living-room door and it was still dark. That's funny, I thought, as I fumbled for the switch. Suddenly the room was flooded with light and I immediately wished it wasn't. My mum and dad were on the sofa in a state of half-undress *doing it*! I stood there frozen with shock as my dad jumped up and my mum reached for a cushion to cover herself. I ran back into the darkness of the hall and legged it up the stairs and back to bed. I lay there, my heart beating, not knowing what to think. I had recently felt the first pubescent stirrings and had talked with other boys at school, so I kind of knew what they were doing. I knew people did it; I just didn't think my parents did it.

A couple of minutes later there were footsteps on the stairs and my mum came into my darkened room. She lay next to me on the bed and held me tightly. I could hear that her heart was beating as quickly as mine. She didn't say anything for ages and I remember thinking, Don't do anything to me! Eventually she said quietly, 'I think you need another day off school tomorrow.' That was it – no chat, no talk from my dad about the birds and the bees. No, that would have been, in his words, 'too bloody embarrassing'.

The next morning, when my mum had gone to work, and Ken and Mandy had gone to school, Dad came up to my room and said with a hint of unease, 'Here's your comic, kid. It came with the paper.'

I was, I think, quite traumatised by the event. For weeks I went to bed early and prayed that I would get to sleep before my dad came in from work. The lighter evenings meant that because of night racing he would be kept later at the office and wouldn't arrive home much before 9 p.m. I would hear his colleague Desi's car pull up and my dad shout, 'Thanks, Des. See you tomorrow.' I would tell myself not to, but eventually would have to look out of my bedroom window to the living-room bay window below and my heart would sink if the light went off. Oh, no, they're doing it again!

I felt that my parents were aliens. Should I tell our Marg? Should I try to have it stopped? I think my confusion was heightened because of the role I had played as a go-between all those times when I had had to mediate between them and those mornings when they had suddenly spoken to each other with affection. Of course, that's what had happened the night before.

Because of that experience, I can have, I think, an issue with intimacy. Not sexual intimacy; I'm talking about intimacy in public. I'm sure it is very frustrating for anyone I am in a relationship with when I inwardly freeze at the sign of any public affection. Holding hands, I will always be the first to slip my hand out. I have a fear that everyone is looking at us and is about to shout, 'Get a room.' My dad always thought that people were looking at him, judging him. It's something I have inherited, and ironically, because people recognise me, it is very often true. People *are* looking at me. What did Philip Larkin say? 'They fuck you up, your mum and dad. They may not mean to, but they do.'

CHAPTER 6

Quarry Bank and the Walls of Jericho

In the autumn term of 1967, as I entered the fourth year and my fourteenth birthday approached, our school underwent a radical change. Together with Quarry Bank Grammar School for Boys and Calderstones High School for Girls, Morrison merged to create Quarry Bank Comprehensive. I moved from the Rose Lane building to the imposing Tudor-style mansion that had been Quarry Bank Grammar, one of Liverpool's leading schools. Its motto was '*Ex Hoc Metallo Virtutem*' – 'From this rough metal we forge virtue', although in Douglas E. Winter's biography of Clive Barker, it suggests it means 'Out of this rock you will find the truth.'

There had been a few notable old boys. The TV and stage actor Derek Nimmo, the news journalist Peter Sissons, football manager Joe Royle and, most famously, John Lennon. He had, since those early stories related by our Marg, become a hero to me. Suddenly I was at the same school he had been to, wearing the same black blazer, with red and gold stag's-head badge and black and gold striped tie, that he had worn when he had studied, or rather rebelled, a decade or so earlier. We even inherited the same headmaster. William Ernest Pobjoy was, for his time, quite a radical, liberal-thinking man who abolished corporal punishment well before the rest of the nation. He had, against the odds, got Lennon into art school and introduced sixth-form cellars, where he and the teachers would turn a blind eye – or I should say nose – to the smell of cigarette smoke, as it wafted upwards at break and lunchtime. At assembly he would often read from *Playboy*, or let older students perform scenes from Samuel Beckett's *Waiting for Godot*.

Even more radical and exciting was the merger with Calderstones High School. The renowned and respected girls' school was directly adjacent to Quarry, separated only by an imposing red stone wall, built with materials from the nearby quarry in Woolton. During the summer months before I started there, a part of the wall had been knocked down. It was like the walls of Jericho.

On that first day of term, we were mingling for the first time in school hours with members of the opposite sex. Concentrating on academic matters was increasingly difficult as lovely young things walked around in shorter and shorter skirts. Mr Pobjoy was even relaxed about uniform rules.

With the new school came new teachers. Art was my favourite subject, and I seemed to be able to draw well. Alan Plent was an exciting and inspiring tutor, and I think if I hadn't gone into show business, I might have considered art college. Ken Othen was a relaxed and funny man who fired my interest in English literature. With dark hair and a full beard, he looked not unlike D. H. Lawrence, from whom he would read. Sometimes, if the class was getting a bit bored, he would ask me what new impressions I was working on. I was gaining a reputation as the class entertainer.

'I've got a few new ones, sir: Hancock, Norman Wisdom, Mick Jagger.'

'Great. Come and give us a few.'

I would stand at the front of the class and perform my act in the second half of double English literature. My mates would laugh and Mr Othen would chuckle away. He not only gave me a love of D. H. Lawrence but also a platform to try out what would be my future profession.

My mum continued to push for us to achieve the things we wanted from life. Mandy is like my dad and, I think, has always preferred to take things at her own pace. Ken was a frustrated young man who showed great aptitude for football but didn't know how to harness his talent. He had a difficult few years and resorted to petty crime. He was lousy at it and always got caught. One year at Butlins he had stolen some matchbox toys from the department store, and then, when he was older, he nicked a couple of real cars and did a bit of joyriding. My mum decided she could fix things and that his problem was the company he was keeping at school. He had been placed, after junior school, at Sefton Park Secondary Modern, which at that time had a less than respectable reputation. She went into lobbyist mode again and wrote to the Liberal MP Trevor Jones, who was later knighted. My parents were staunch Labour supporters, but Winnie wrote an impassioned letter to Mr Jones and one Sunday afternoon he came to tea. Bone-china crockery, which I didn't know we had, came out of the back of the cocktail cabinet, and salmon and cucumber sandwiches were prepared. Our Sunday evening bath came forward an hour or so, and we awaited the arrival of our VIP guest. Over a sedate tea my mum pleaded Ken's case, while my dad valiantly tried to eat his sandwiches without making a mess and drink his tea without slurping. Trevor Jones promised to do his best to have Ken moved to a better school and, as he shook hands with my parents, asked a favour in return. Would they be prepared to canvass for the Liberals at the upcoming elections?

'Of course,' said my mum in her poshest accent. 'It would be an honour.'

When he had gone, my dad said, 'Winnie, it's bloody embarrassing – we're Labour supporters; we can't change parties now.'

'Let's see if Ken gets into a good school.'

True to his word, Mr Jones not only got him into a good school but into one of the best in the city. Ken began his next term at the Bluecoat, which was Liverpool's answer to Eton. Most pupils boarded, but some were local day boys. In his posh new uniform, our Ken looked, on that first day, like an accident waiting to happen. True to her word, Mum supported the Liberals at the next local election. Our window displayed a 'Vote Liberal' poster and we delivered leaflets door to door for Trevor Jones. I was as embarrassed as my dad though when, at general election time, the posters were replaced with ones saying, 'Vote Labour,' and as we suspected, it all ended in tears when our Ken was expelled from the Bluecoat a couple of years later for some petty misdemeanour, or, in their words, not 'fitting the school's criteria'.

The cloud of post-war austerity and thrift had given way to 1960s consumerism. We already had a car, and to confirm the delusions of grandeur nurtured in me by my mum, I one day asked for a piano. On one *Sunday Night at the London Palladium*, I had seen the brilliant concert pianist and humorist Victor Borge. His trademark was to repeatedly announce his intent to play a classical piece and then get distracted by the audience, telling them, for instance, how useful Chopin's 'Minute Waltz' was as an egg-timer. His other brilliant routine was his 'phonetic punctuation', in which he would recite a story with full punctuation – comma, full stop, exclamation mark and so on – as onomatopoeic sounds. I was totally captivated and announced to my parents that I wanted to learn to play the piano.

Once again, against the flow of their salaries, they managed to save enough money. One day I came home from school and immediately saw in the dining-room mirror the reflection of an upright piano. The G Plan table and chairs and the radiogram had been pushed out of the way to accommodate this exotic walnut instrument that, as yet, nobody could play. I was thrilled. Every week I would go for lessons with a little old lady who lived in a terraced house off Wavertree Road. My mum would come with me, and they would chat while I made heavy weather of the scales.

It soon became apparent that I was not the child prodigy that Mr Borge had been, and on summer evenings, as my friends were playing in the street, I would resent having to practise. If you had timed eggs to my version of 'The Minute Waltz', the pan would have burnt out its bottom. At one such torturous practice session, it eventually dawned on me that it was actually the funny bit of Mr Borge's act that I wanted to do and so the piano was placed in the buy and sell section of the *Liverpool Echo*. A week or so later a van arrived and my dad and our Tony struggled with the piano and manoeuvred it into the garden, up the entry and out to the proud new owner. They looked like Laurel and Hardy in *The Music Box*. My dad huffed and puffed all the way, muttering under his breath, 'Bloody stupid idea. I said you'd never play the bloody thing.' Unlike my mum with the car, his comments didn't spur me on to stick with the piano lessons, but they did harden my resolve to become a comedian.

Apart from a fortnight in the Isle of Man when I was fourteen, our annual holidays were still spent at Butlins in Pwllheli. We went mainly so I could pursue my quest to win the tacky cup that was first prize in the talent competition, but also to watch our Ken fall headlong into the boating lake. The junior talent show gave way to the more competitive adult version, which I became eligible for when I was fourteen. It was run by the *People* newspaper and was the biggest of its kind in the UK, boasting a final at the prestigious Palladium and a whopping £1,000 for the winner.

In the summer of 1969, when I was fifteen, my mum decided that we needed a change of scene and we headed off to the Butlins camp at Filey, which stood resiliently on the windy East Yorkshire coast, just below Scarborough and Bridlington. The competition changed dramatically. Instead of ballerinas and Shirley Temple wannabes, I was up against comedians, vocalists and groups ranging in age and ability. The prize and kudos of winning the biggest talent show in the country attracted lots of professional and semi-professional entertainers in much the same way as *The X Factor* does now. Wearing a blue mohair suit that my mum had bought on her Sturla's account, a shiny bowtie and my dad's size-nine brogues, I entered the weekly heat with my spot of impressions and jokes. My big finish (stolen from Sammy Davis Junior) was a skit of Jerry Lewis singing 'Lulu's Back in Town'. Whether it was the impressions or my dad's shoes, I don't know, but something worked that night and I beat off the considerable and much older opposition to win first prize – a tinny cup and a place in the area final at Pwllheli when the season ended in September.

The euphoria of the win was overshadowed when my dad suffered an unexpected heart attack a few weeks later. I remember that we had to move a bed into the living room for his period of convalescence and he wasn't allowed to go with me to Pwllheli for the next stage of the competition. I also remember my mum suggesting that the moving of the piano had brought on the heart attack. Although she would never have wanted me to, I have to some extent always carried a feeling of guilt that my ambition was in some way responsible for his ill health.

I therefore travelled to Pwllheli alone that September, and when I should have been starting the autumn term of my O-level year at Quarry Bank Comprehensive, I was playing truant for a week and following my Tarby dream. Tarby had even been a redcoat at Butlins. Because I was on my own, I would have all my meals on a table with the other area finalists and the camp's resident comedian, who was the then unknown Frank Carson. I would go on to work with Frank many times over the years and he is a lovely man who is never off stage. On that dining table in 1969, he was always funny, encouraging and friendly.

Other acts on the bill that week hoping to make it to the Palladium were Stan Boardman and the sharp-suited double act the Harper Brothers. I didn't win first prize that year; in fact, I would return every year to Butlins until I went professional in 1973 and never got any further than the area finals, but I did gain an invaluable amount of stage experience and quite a few free holidays. A couple of years later, however, Stan would go on to win the £1,000. The Harper Brothers, on the other hand, ditched the smart one-liners in favour of a more knockabout style. One half of the duo traded his sharp suit for an oversized baggy one with red braces and they went on to have enormous success in the 1980s under their new stage name, Cannon and Ball.

The school plays at Quarry Bank were of a very high standard and were dominated by the same group of players. Clive Barker, Dave Fischel, Malcolm Sharp and Phil Rimmer not only played in the organised productions but also wrote and performed their own avant-garde pieces. They gained a reputation as an exciting and quirky group of young artists. Clive was most definitely the driving force. He walked around the grounds of the school with an air of confidence and a blue silk scarf thrown stylishly round his neck. Two very attractive girls, Judith Kelly, who had long, straight, Saxon-blonde hair, and Lynne Webster, who had similar, though more strawberry-blonde hair, and huge blue eyes, would often be seen in conversation with him at breaktimes. When all the other girls were wearing miniskirts, Jude, as she preferred to be called, and Lynne would be in the new, more fashionable maxis. As a group of people, they certainly stood out from the crowd.

At the start of 1970 Bruce Prince, our English teacher, put a notice on the board advertising auditions for the spring school production of Nikolai Gogol's *The Government Inspector*. At the bottom he had written, 'Newcomers welcome.' I wanted to apply but was nervous of going on my own. Most of my mates were more interested in football, and trials for the school team were coming up. I never did any better than the B team, but then when players of the standard of Steve Coppell, later to play for Manchester United, England and now manager of Reading, and Brian Barwick, present head of the FA, were making the first team, what did I expect. I managed to coax a few of my friends away from football practice to come along to the audition for moral support.

We headed off through the walls of Jericho into the Calderstone building and up to the assembly hall. Through the side doors I could make out a group, including Clive Barker and co., talking to Mr Prince, scripts in hand. Looks like it's cast, I thought. Suddenly I was pushed, along with Les Roberts, through the doors and into the room. The others ran off and Les and I stood nervously staring at the arty company. Some looked disdainful, but Bruce Prince welcomed us with enthusiasm: 'New blood. Fantastic. Welcome.'

Clive, scarf still stylishly in place, said, 'Yes, you are just in time. We're casting and it's quite a large cast, so, indeed, welcome. Here, have a copy of the text.'

Poor Les – he was a good footballer and would certainly have preferred to be elsewhere. He read, though, and got a part as a servant. I read a scene with Jude, and Bruce seemed pleased. Later, I would be cast as the postmaster, a comic role with two important and funny scenes.

The Government Inspector is a satire on the state of corruption in nineteenth-century Russia. In a small town the mayor and his cohorts learn they're going to be subject to an undercover visit from a government inspector. They mistake a penniless conman for him and fall victim to their own greed and stupidity. Dave Fischel played the lead role, but the night unquestionably belonged to Clive and Jude, as the pompous mayor and his self-important wife. I loved the experience – not sure about Les – and, when our short run was over, felt the pain of anticlimax. I had made friends, though, with Clive, Jude and other members of the cast. Together with Doug Bradley, Anne Taylor and Phil Rimmer, we would meet in the Easter holidays to visit art galleries and the cinema.

So began an important and valuable phase of my education. Jude, who was very much a leader, didn't stay within the circle for long, but I learnt more about art and literature from the others than I would get from any school curriculum. In the following year's production, *Dry Rot*, I was cast alongside Clive in an hilarious farce by John Chapman about a gang of crooked bookies who, in order to be near the racecourse, are staying at a country hotel run by a retired colonel and his wife. Jude played Beth Barton, love interest for my slightly dim character, Fred Phipps. It was a roaring success and suddenly I gained a new popularity at school – my first taste of the fame drug. Jude's friend, the alluring, slightly standoffish Lynne Webster, plus other cast members – Sue Bickley, Lyn Darnel and Julie Blake – joined our group, and we began to call ourselves just that – the Group. Lynne didn't actually perform and so tried her hand at stage management but it wasn't where her talents lay.

In the previous term we had performed one of Clive and Phil's epic productions *The Holly and the Ivy*, an improvised and rather solemn Arthurian fantasy, which shocked some teachers and parents as it dealt with a homosexual romance between its two main protagonists. Rehearsals would take place every lunchtime at the Morrison hall, and in breaktime Clive would play Noël Coward LPs and a very old rendition of 'This Is My Lovely Day' on a wind-up gramophone. At that time most people of his age were listening to T. Rex, James Taylor or Pink Floyd.

One day after school I was there when Lynne and Clive got into a passionate discussion about C. S. Lewis, J. R. R. Tolkien and other authors I'd never heard of. I felt intellectually inadequate as the conversation would be peppered with quotes and references to H. P. Lovecraft, Ray Bradbury, Edgar Allan Poe to name but a few.

They would tease me about my intellectual shortcomings. I remember feeling huge embarrassment when at Lynne's house, which became the Group's main meeting place for a while, she said, 'Les used the word "facetious" out of context.'

'That's right,' joked Clive. 'He said, "These pancakes are really facetious."'

I was mortified. They sound now as if they were being cruel. They weren't; it was just their adolescent pretentious banter. Instead of running away, I learnt from them, and Clive in particular was very encouraging.

With the school we visited Stratford, where we saw a wonderful production of *Twelfth Night*. I was spellbound, particularly by an actor called Emrys James, who was a magical Feste. Ever since that night I have held an ambition to one day play that part. Alan Plent, our hippy art teacher, took our class to London to visit the National and Tate Galleries. At Lime Street Station, he was really anxious that nobody should miss the train, and only when he was sure that everyone was on board did he go to get a newspaper. He missed the train.

On that trip, Clive introduced me to a new and fascinating world of art – he was a huge fan of artists like Hieronymus Bosch, and his fascination with horror was evident even then. While my footie mates were out clubbing in the evenings, I instead went with the Group to watch plays in the West End. It was a joyous time and I developed a crush on Lynne. Little did I know, Lynne would be the woman I would marry. In a rare entry in my diary, on 15 April 1971, I wrote, 'London. Great day. Mr Plent missed the train. Pushed L. Webster in front of a bus. Went to play with Robert Morley.' Obviously I didn't push her too far in front of the bus or she wouldn't be here today, and neither would our son, Philip.

If Clive had had his way, I don't think Philip would be here either. His one rule for the Group was that our relationships should remain platonic. He even discouraged us from having boyfriends and girlfriends outside the circle, promoting a pact of celibacy. Most of us, if not all, were still virgins, but the level of sexual tension between us was almost palpable. Jude and Dave Fischel had partners, so I think that's why they annexed themselves from us, only joining again for actual shows.

Clive, who was a year older than us all, left Quarry Bank in the summer of 1971. He was a brilliant artist and had secured a place at the Liverpool College of Arts. He went instead to Liverpool University, at first studying philosophy but then switching to English literature. In his spare time he was writing an outline for a farce, heavily influenced by *Dry Rot*, with a large dollop of Joe Orton thrown in. We would later improvise and perform it at the Liverpool Everyman.

At the weekends I continued to pursue my ambition to achieve a career as a stand-up. My mum got me an open-mic spot at the Norgreen Social Club, where a colleague of hers at Lucas

Aerospace was the entertainments secretary. In between the booked comedian, Liverpool's legendary Bert Cook, I did a ten-minute spot of impressions. I did well and can remember Bert saying, as he came on for his second set, 'There you go, ladies and gentlemen, a young man obviously on the first rung of the ladder to success.'

At the end the compère came up to our table, where I sat with my mum and dad. 'There you are, son, your exies.'

'My what?' I asked.

'Your expenses,' he explained, as he thrust two crumpled pound notes into the palm of my hand.

I was doing a Saturday job at the time in a DIY shop, H&J's, in the city centre. For a long day lugging boxes of ceramic tiles up and down stairs, I was paid £1. Wow, £2 for ten minutes, I thought. This could be good!

Thanks to a club owner, Jack Jeffreys, who took me under his wing, I managed to get an agent. Dorene Gillespie, the wife of local comedian Stuart Gillespie, ran a small but competent agency called Dorene Entertainments. They took me on and I started to do bookings around the social and working men's clubs of Liverpool and the north-west. My first professional gig – for what, to me, was the staggering fee of £7 – was on a Sunday night at the Melling Rate-Payers Club, on the outskirts of Liverpool. My mum and auntie Pat came with me for support and to calm my nerves. I was really scared because the club wanted two twenty-minute spots and until then I had only ever done about fifteen minutes in total. Talk about baptism by fire!

In my first spot, the nerves got the better of me and I rushed the jokes, getting through them so quickly that I had to use most of the material I was saving for the second spot. Because I was so young, the audience cut me some slack and I walked off-stage to reasonable applause. The trouble was, I now had hardly anything for my second spot. My mum, my auntie Pat and I sat in the dressing room trying to think of as many jokes as we could and I wrote them down. One of my main impressions was David Frost so I put the new script on to the clipboard I used for him and clung to it as a prompt during the second spot. Of course, the routine was untested, unrehearsed and understandably went down like a lead balloon. The concert chairman docked £2 from my fee and complained to my agent that I had read my act off the clipboard. Clearly I would need to build up my repertoire.

My mum always encouraged my ambitions and in a way would vicariously live out the dreams of performing she had nurtured as a little girl. I still hadn't passed my driving test, so she would drive me around. It must have been hard for her because she worked such long hours all week, but she loved seeing me improve and had a great belief that I could have a successful career as an entertainer. If I had a hard night, she would get up and belt out a few numbers with the band. Many times she rescued me from a dodgy night.

My dad was far more sceptical. He didn't believe that a career in show business was achievable for a working-class lad from Liverpool. Whenever my mum would buy me a new prop or help me perfect a routine, he would mutter, 'You're wasting your time. You should be thinking about getting a proper bloody job.' Slowly, though, as I seemed to be having some success, he came round and without actually admitting it would become in his own way as supportive as my mum. I had started buying *The Stage*, the weekly trade paper, and my dad could often be found perusing its pages more than the sports pages of his beloved *Liverpool Echo*.

On 20 February 1971 I auditioned for *Opportunity Knocks* in Manchester. There were hundreds of acts – some good, some bad, some absolutely dreadful. I nervously stood before the panel of judges, producer Len Martin and director Royston Mayoh and did my act. It went well and I particularly impressed Mr Mayoh with my finale, the cab scene from *On the Waterfront*. I did the scene word for word, doing both Rod Steiger and Marlon Brando, as Terry Malone. 'I could have had class, I could have been a contender. I could have been somebody.'

'You're marvellous, love,' he enthused. 'We've got to have you. Hughie will love you. We'll be in touch. Get you on when the series starts in April.'

'I don't break up from school until June, and I've got O-level re-sits.'

'I love him,' he shouted theatrically. 'He's still doing his exams. OK, we're still on air in the summer. We'll call you.'

I was thrilled and told all my mates at school, who were excited for me. The Group, not so. Clive thought I was selling out, that we were artistes and above such low-brow entertainment.

'Clive, I love acting, but I just want to be Mike Yarwood or Dave Allen.' I didn't dare tell him I wanted to be like Jimmy Tarbuck.

He just looked at me with disdain as he read Christopher Marlowe's *The Tragical History of Doctor Faustus*.

On 22 June I got the call from Thames Television giving me the date for my first TV appearance. My diary entry was less than emotive: 'Today I got phone call from *Opportunity Knocks* to appear on 24 July. I'm made up.' Then again, most of my entries were short and to the point, usually relating to a story of a trip to the chippy with my mates.

You had to have a sponsor on the show who would introduce you to the host, Hughie Green. Very often it would be a compère or concert chairman from a club, who would say, 'I saw him at our club and I knew his talent was being wasted.' In my case, my sponsor was our Marg. She was very nervous about appearing on

TV but relished the weekend trip to London. We were staying at the Richmond Hill Hotel. It was the most luxurious place we had ever seen, perched on a hill, overlooking a glorious stretch of the Thames. The show was being taped on the Saturday for transmission the following Monday, 26 July.

We arrived on the Friday and that evening went down to the restaurant for our tea. OK – dinner! The room was enormous – high ceilings, tall, Georgian windows with heavy drapes, tables set with silver and glass. The maître d' (I didn't know that word then, so a posh bloke in a suit) handed us the menus and we panicked. It was all in French. Our Marg and I looked at each other and, when he disappeared into the kitchen, legged it. Not only could we not understand the menu, we had also seen the prices. We didn't know that dinner was included in our expense account, there being no fee for appearing on the show. We just knew we couldn't afford it. We ran down the hill into Richmond, found a fish and chip café and then a bar to have a drink.

Thames Studios are situated on the lock at Teddington, and though I have recorded there many times since, on that first day in a TV studio, I was in awe. My spot was basically a set of impressions, most of them stolen from other acts. Norman Wisdom and Mick Jagger skits were taken from Freddie Starr's barnstorming performance at the previous *Royal Variety Performance*, and Sonny Boy by James Stewart, Cagney and Jerry Lewis (the routine I did in the Butlins talent show) had been lifted from *Sammy Davis Impersonates*. Well, if you're going to steal, make sure it's from the best. The embarrassing thing was that a couple of years later I worked with Freddie on *Who Do You Do?* and he said to me, 'Your name was shit in our house for a long time, but it's OK now. I forgive you.' Sadly, I never did meet Sammy Davis Junior, even though he was a great friend of my mate Lionel Blair.

That afternoon I sat in the studio canteen overlooking Teddington Lock, nervously drinking tea. Two young men with Manchester accents came up to me and asked if I was OK. 'Just a bit nervous,' I said. I explained to them that I was doing my first TV spot on *Opportunity Knocks*. They got themselves cups of tea and sat with me for an hour, laughing and joking to distract me from my fear. They had recently won *Opportunity Knocks* and had started to achieve national success. Sid and Eddie, better known as Little and Large, went out of their way to encourage a young, naïve schoolboy that afternoon and I will be eternally grateful to them for their kindness and help.

Hughie Green didn't turn up for rehearsal, so instead the floor manager stood in, doing a wickedly cruel impression of him. 'OK, friends, Uncle Hughie here. Remember, if you can't spell the name of the next act, just put "Crap" on your postcard and we'll know what you mean.' The famous clapometer, which measured the audience's applause at the bottom of the screen, was just a lever that two props guys moved up and down, depending on how well they thought you'd done. The show began and I still hadn't got to meet Hughie. I was incredibly nervous, and my nerves got the better of my performance. At the end of the show, the clapometer, or rather the two props men, placed me in fourth place. Stuart Gillies, a crooner who later had a hit with the ballad 'Amanda', was in the middle of a ten-week winning streak. It could have been worse: Su Pollard lost to a singing dog.

When it was screened on TV the following Monday evening, Lynne invited the Group round to her house to watch. Her mum and dad were the only ones who had a colour telly. I made my excuses because I couldn't bear to watch as Clive frowned at the 'cheapening of my talent' and went instead to a mate's, Ronnie Corbishley, who wasn't one of the Group but whose parents also had a colour TV. Watching myself for the first time was weird, a bit like the first time you hear your voice on a tape recorder. Ronnie and his family laughed politely, but when it was over, I knew that the props guys had got it right with the clapometer. I made a mental note that night to watch my next telly appearance alone.

CHAPTER 7

The Group

The Group would get together for evenings of play and literature readings, and would take it in turns to hold them at their houses. One day Clive commented that I never offered to have them round to mine. I would make excuses, saying we had people to stay or because my dad didn't get home until late, it was awkward. The truth is, I am ashamed to say, I was embarrassed about my working-class family. I was becoming a little snob. Ken and Mandy had, and indeed still have, lovely thick Scouse accents. I worked hard to soften mine. Because my parents worked so hard, the house wasn't always as tidy as it could be and I didn't want my friends to see it. Lynne's house was lovely, Clive's was, and Phil Rimmer's seemed really posh. So did their parents. I know we all get embarrassed about our parents when we are in our teens, but the way I felt was most definitely wrong. Fuelled by the company I kept, I was developing delusions of grandeur and I didn't want my new arty friends to meet my mum and dad.

I would have to relent and have them over. My eighteenth birthday was coming up, so I suggested to the Group that we should have a literary evening at my house. How fucking pretentious had I become! I asked my mum if that would be OK and she said, 'Yes, of course. You can have a party, invite your mates and we'll get our Pat, Marg and Tony over.'

'No, Mum,' I said, horrified. 'I don't want a party. I just want to have my friends round. In fact, I would like it if you, my dad, our Ken and Mandy could be out that night.'

She was, I think, very hurt, but agreed.

On 12 October 1971, my birthday, I took the day off school, not to enjoy it but to clean the house from top to bottom. Half an hour before they were all due to arrive, I put food on the table and ushered my family out of the house. I knew Clive would arrive first: he was so curious to know where I came from. The second he walked through the door I could see that he was looking for evidence of my background. 'No books,' he said almost immediately. Again, it wasn't a criticism. Clive just always needed to know the facts. He is a writer and was therefore fascinated by the details of his friends' lives. 'Here's a book for you. Happy birthday.' His present was a volume on Greek mythology written by one of his university tutors, and Clive had written in it. There was a beautiful pen and ink drawing of a skull and an inscription from *A Midsummer Night's Dream*: 'This is fairy gold, boy, and 'twill prove so.' How prophetic. If I sold it on eBay, I'm sure I would make a killing, but on an educational level the gift that Clive and the Group brought into my life would prove to be much more important than that. Everyone else arrived and we settled into a fun, if pretentious, evening until half an hour later there was a knock on the door. I opened it and there stood my mum and dad.

'What do you want?' I whispered, as my heart jumped into my mouth.

'Oh, your dad forgot...erm...What did you forget?'

'My glasses.'

'Oh, yeah, his glasses.'

It was obviously a lie – they just wanted to check out my friends.

As they came into the living room, Clive jumped up. 'How lovely to meet you, Mr and Mrs Heseltine. Do join us.'

'No!' I shouted. 'My dad just forgot his glasses, and my brother and sister are in the car.'

Ten minutes later, my dad having spoken in his best telephone voice, they left. They had behaved perfectly well and been charming with my friends. My snobbery, however, would continue and, years later, nearly cost me my relationship with my family.

When my friends had left and my parents returned, Dad said to me, 'That blonde girl's attractive, isn't she? You wanna get in there, kid.'

'Dad, we're all friends. It's a purely platonic group.'

'A what? What's "plutonic" when it's at home?'

Lynne and I continued to get on well, and one night after we'd all been to see *Rosencrantz and Guildenstern Are Dead* at the Playhouse Theatre in Liverpool, we were sat on her sofa, having a platonic hug, when suddenly we were snogging. So began one of the most important relationships of my life.

Lynne and I started seeing each other in May 1972, just before her eighteenth birthday. Although she was younger than me by seven months, she was, as all girls are at that age, much older in spirit and experience. Apart from the Group, her friends were older. She was vaguely on the edge of the Liverpool poet scene and frequently went to parties where Adrian Henri, Roger McGough and Peter Maloney could be spotted.

Liverpool was a thriving bed of culture in the 1970s, and the theatre was particularly vibrant. Under the artistic directorship of a young Terry Hands, and later Alan Dosser, the Everyman was presenting some extraordinary productions. In the early 1970s a who's who of today's theatrical greats worked there. Trevor Eve, Julie Walters Bernard Hill, Alison Steadman, Bill Nighy, Nicholas le Prevost, Matthew Kelly, Antony Sher and Jonathan Pryce were all part of the rep company in those early years. The productions there fired my desire to act. Jonathan Pryce was an extraordinary, exciting young actor, and some of his performances have stayed with me all this time. He was a touching Happy in *Death of a Salesman* and a wonderfully comic and evil Richard, which he played as a white-faced circus clown, in *Richard III*. Bernard Hill and Antony Sher, as Buckingham, were also in that production. Jonathan lives quite near me and I have chatted with him a few times in the high street. I have to restrain myself from quoting lines and scenes from some of his performances for fear of coming across as a celebrity stalker.

After that snog on the sofa, Lynne and I immediately became a committed couple. It was as if that platonic phase within the Group had been our courtship. From day one we discussed my career options with reference to how it would affect our relationship. For a while I toyed with the idea of drama school, but as I had already started to make a more than decent living in the clubs, we decided it was OK for me to continue my quest to become Jimmy Tarbuck. The Gielgud quest would have to wait. I had stayed on at school to do A levels simply because I wanted a part in the school play. John Ayres, who had taken over from Bruce Prince, offered me the role of Azdak in Berthold Brecht's *Caucasian Chalk Circle*. And so, to get the part, I had to enrol to do English literature, history and art. With rehearsals for the play and the clubs at the weekend, the chances of me doing well academically were pretty slim. Essays, particularly history, turned up late, if at all, and I left Quarry with just one A level – art. In my school report of that final year John Shields,

CHAPTER 8

The Clubs - Can I Have Some Order, Please?

The social and working men's clubs in the North were thriving when I left school and began my career. Any act worth their salt could work fifty-two weeks a year and never visit the same club twice. Most had a snooker room, lounge and concert room. At that time archaic working-class attitudes in many clubs meant that women were only allowed in the concert room, and only then if accompanied by men. Live entertainment would usually be held at the weekends – Saturdays and Sundays, occasionally Friday. They would generally have two acts, a couple of sessions of bingo and a raffle. The acts were often a singer, group or guitar vocalist and a comedian. Musical backing was provided by an organist, a drummer and sometimes a bass player as well. The clubs were mainly non-profit-making and run by members through the dreaded committee. These were very often the stereotypical cloth-capped working men of the community portrayed by many comedians on shows like *The Wheeltappers and Shunters Social Club*.

On the committee there would be a social secretary, a concert secretary, a concert chairman and so on. Sometimes job titles were hilariously inventive – Head of Pies. Each man would have a little enamel badge with his job description written on it. These guys wore them like badges of honour and some carried out their duties with overzealous jobsworth fervour. Believe me, Peter Kay's brilliant *Phoenix Nights* is not an exaggeration.

There were many Liverpool comedians who would have great success in their hometown but would never achieve the national success that they deserved. Their humour was maybe too parochial, striking a chord with fellow Merseysiders but not able to travel well. Two of my favourites were Jackie Hamilton and Eddie Flanaghan. They were both naturally funny men who, like Tommy Cooper, would have you laughing before they'd even said anything.

Ricky Tomlinson tells a great story about Jackie, or Hamo, as he calls him. There was a movie being shot on Merseyside called *Jenny's War* and Hamo was one of the extras working on it. On the long, hard days of filming he would keep everyone in stitches between takes and became a favourite with cast and crew alike. The day came when they had to shoot a scene in a prisoner-of-war camp. The director took Hamo to one side and said, 'You've been great, Jackie, but I can't use you in this scene because of your stomach.'

'What d'ya mean?' Jackie asked in his thick Scouse accent.

'Well,' the director explained, 'this is a POW camp and you've quite clearly got a beer belly. You don't look like someone who's been on a starvation diet.'

'But I was only captured yesterday!' Jackie quipped back.

Eddie Flanaghan looked like a comedian, with an ill-fitting jet-black wig, thick-lensed glasses and a crooked-toothed grin. You would laugh the minute he walked into the room. Onstage, he could get an audience by saying, 'It's great here, isn't it –

carpets, curtains, electricity.' I know – you had to be there, but I hope you'll take my word for it. Eddie had some national success on Granada's *The Comedians*, but he would never achieve the fame of other circuit favourites like Tom O'Connor and Freddie Starr.

There were ex-servicemen's clubs, Labour, Conservative and Liberal clubs, miners' and British Legion clubs, Catholic clubs and so on. Comics would be very nervous in Catholic clubs as the priest would stand at the back of the room making sure they didn't do any blue jokes. Usually the priest would leave early on Saturday nights because of early Mass on Sunday, so in their second spot the comics could let rip and the air would be heavy with innuendo. I never worked blue, partly because I didn't want to and also because at the age of seventeen, when I started, I looked barely fifteen and wouldn't have got away with routines about sex, the wife and the mother-in-law.

The look on some concert chairmen's faces when I turned up with my mum, my suit-carrier and props case and announced myself as the comedian was a picture. I had many successful nights, obviously, or I would have given it up. I did, though, also have many when I died a proverbial death. Early on I remember Burscough Football Club, where the secretary told Dorene, my agent, that he had to lock himself in his office because of the complaints he was getting from his members during my act. Another time, while I was mid-routine, I noticed a meeting was taking place at the back of the room. The committee! After much cloth-capped debating, the concert secretary walked solemnly to his booth at the side of the stage and before I could do my best and only sure-fire joke, got on his microphone and said, 'Sorry, ladies and gentlemen, we've had a meeting and we've decided we're not paying ten quid for this shit.' There was a uniform groan of outrage and shouts of 'Ten quid – we don't get that all week.' To make it worse, the secretary said, directly into the microphone, 'Plus VAT.' That was it: there was little short of a riot and I was relieved when from his booth, he hit the button and the heavy red curtains closed slowly in front of me.

If a comic was doing badly, very often they would say, 'Thank you, ladies and gentlemen, I'm obviously not to your taste. Goodnight.' I refused to do this, because it would mean the committee wouldn't have to pay me. No matter how badly I was doing I would stay on and go through my routine to the sound of tumbleweed, with my eyes fixed firmly on the clock at the back of the room. I gained a reputation among the acts on the circuit because they commended my bravery and even gave me the nickname 'Bronco', because I could stay on all night.

On one such night in Sunderland (the comic's graveyard), I was working an all-male audience, which is always difficult, especially when you're doing impressions of Frank Spencer and Louis Armstrong. Within minutes I'd emptied the room. To a sympathetic audience of five, I continued bravely until the secretary came to the side of the stage and shouted from behind the curtain, 'Come off, bonny lad. Don't punish yourself. It's OK, we'll give you your full money.' When he went on to the microphone to complaining noises from the returning audience, he said, 'All right, gentlemen. You can complain but it's like water off a duck's back to me. We've just got to face it – on TV he's all right, but live he is shite.'

The clubs reserved the right to pay you off. This meant that if they didn't like you, they could give you half your fee and ask you not to go on for the second spot. Dustin Gee was working a club once and decided to turn the tables on the committee. Midway through his first spot he said, 'Ladies and gentlemen, I've had a meeting with myself, in my head, and I've decided to pay you off. You're a lousy audience and I've had enough. I'm on twenty quid tonight, so I'll give you ten of it. Have a drink and I won't be back in the second half; instead I'm going home to my house in Cemetery Road. I'll go in through my front door, walk upstairs to my bedroom, look out of the window at the gravestones opposite and say, "You think *you* bastards died!"'

Your heart would sink if you got to a club where you had to enter and exit through the front door. If you did badly, you always wanted to slip away quietly through the stage door. I have known comics squeeze through the tiniest dressing-room window rather than walk through the hostile, usually silent concert room. I did a club in Preston where I thought I was working well but the audience just didn't get it. After my show I had to walk across the stage, while they were playing bingo, with my dad behind me, head bowed, carrying my props case. We were almost out of the room and into the foyer when a man from a nearby table called me over. 'Here,' he said, 'can I have a word?' I leant over to hear him above the bingo caller. He said, 'They were rubbish.'

Yes, I thought. He realises it was the audience and not me. 'Thank you. They were, weren't they.'

'No,' he shouted. 'Not "they" – *thee* were rubbish. *Thee* were rubbish.'

Mick Miller, a very funny comedian from Liverpool, was working a club and had argued with the committee that he was only down to do one long spot rather than two short ones. 'No, lad, you can't. It's never been known here. The bingo has to go on at nine thirty dead on.'

Mick argued in vain and after his first spot went to his dressing room feeling pissed off. He had a brainwave. The bingo machine was in the dressing room with him. It was one of those old-fashioned ones where the balls were pushed one by one up a pipe into a little air pocket, to be plucked out by the bingo caller. While he was alone, Mick opened the machine and took out six or seven balls. When they came to play, the game would never end because the numbers the players were waiting for would never come out. It went on for hours, with the caller saying every five minutes, 'Has nobody won yet?' Mick left quietly through the stage door.

Russ Abbot told me that he was once doing a club with the Black Abbots in a small seaside village that was more or less on the beach. Halfway through their set, the chairman ran to his booth and said, 'OK, ladies and gentlemen, you know the drill – everyone up on chairs.' Without panic, everyone in the club stepped up on to their chair as the tide flooded in through the front doors, filled the room and went out again. Then they all got off their chairs and sat down again.

Apart from the committee, the other thorn in the side of comedians in the 1970s – as now – were the hecklers. Every comic has a supply of audience put-downs like 'You are very quick, sir. Your wife tells me that is your trouble!' You could find yourself in bother, though, when you got the dreaded heckler who was funnier than you. Dustin was working the Wookey Hollow Club in Liverpool and every time he got to the punch line a Scouser on the front row would shout, 'Get 'em off.' Eventually Dustin put the spotlight on the bloke and said, 'Look, mate, you are ruining my act. I thought you Liverpool people were funny. Can't you say something constructive?'

Quick as a flash the bloke said, 'Meccano!' When that happens, you're stuffed.

Hughie Green, who I never did meet on the day of *Opportunity Knocks*, came to Liverpool to open a bingo hall. When his act was failing, he made the mistake of going down among the audience and sitting on a little old lady's knee. He said, 'Come on, sweetheart, give old Hughie a kiss.' Straight into the microphone she said, 'Piss off, Hughie, it's taking me all me time to keep me hands from round your throat.' Stuffed!

It doesn't just happen to comedians. Rumour has it that when U2 were playing a huge arena in Ireland, as 'I Still Haven't

Found What I'm Looking For' finished, thirty thousand people were screaming and Bono, with his amazing charisma and power, simply put his finger to his lips and instantly silenced the crowd. Bono clapped his hands once, and then every three seconds he would clap again. 'Every time I clap my hands,' he said – clap – 'like this' – clap – 'someone in Africa' – clap – 'dies.'

The utter silence was broken by a little bloke on the front row who said, 'Well, stop fucking clapping, then.' Double stuffed!

My favourite heckler story, which may well be apocryphal, but I so hope it isn't, happened to Eric Douglas, Michael Douglas's lesser-known and troubled brother, who decided to have a stab at stand-up and unwisely chose to debut at the Comedy Store in London, where the crowd was difficult and indifferent to his material. In desperation, he committed the cardinal sin of asking the audience, 'Don't you know who I am? I am Kirk Douglas's son.'

A bloke on the front row, seeing the comedy gift, stood up, thumped his fist on his chest and shouted, 'No, I'm Kirk Douglas's son.' The rest of the crowd saw what he was doing and all, à la *Spartacus*, stood and shouted, 'No, I'm Kirk Douglas's son.' Comedy cul de sac.

CHAPTER 9

Getting Married - Just Like That!

The club circuit was providing me with invaluable experience and I was clearly doing well enough to consider going professional full time. I had, however, outgrown my agents and needed to think about a change. Dorene and her husband, Stuart, had limited contacts and agreed that I had to move on. When they couldn't find me work, they would farm me out to other local agents like Billy 'Uke' Scott and Ernie Mac or Don 'Izzy' Navarro, who would later make a name for himself as the cult character Shake Hands in Alan Bleasdale's brilliant drama series *Boys From the Black Stuff*.

Without a doubt the biggest agent in Liverpool was Mike Hughes. He had an almost mythical reputation for making household names of his clients within a very short time. *The Comedians* was the new hit show on ITV and a lot of the acts were from Mike's stable. Ken Goodwin, George Roper, Johnny Ball, Freddie Starr and Russ Abbot (then with the Black Abbots) were all managed by him. There were also lots of solid, workaday acts who were on his books, and whenever you asked about him, they would say, 'I've never met him. Worked for him for years and haven't even spoken to him on the phone. Mike Hughes – more like Howard Hughes.'

Just after I'd left school, I auditioned for his agency and Tony Birmingham, Mike's more approachable right-hand man, took me on in a casual, non-contractual way. Immediately I started to get better-class bookings and my fees more or less doubled. I was booked for a week's engagement at the Shakespeare Theatre Club in Liverpool. The Shakey, as it was known, was a beautiful Victorian music-hall theatre that had been turned into a cabaret club. I was the opening comic for the American soul singer Tommy Hunt and my act was a hit with the audience. It was such a different world from the working men's clubs I had been grafting in. No bingo, no committee. The audience had come to have dinner, watch a show and dance into the small hours. There was a full stage crew, lighting, sound and, best of all, a fabulous trio that could read music. So often in the clubs you would hand your dots over to the duo only to be told, 'Sorry, lad, we don't read, but we know most songs. As long as you don't mind us playing in the key of C.' My opening was an impression of Joel Grey's master of ceremonies from *Cabaret*, singing '*Willkommen*'. So, key of C or not, they mostly didn't have a clue.

I loved going to work that week and didn't want Saturday, my last night, to come. On the Saturday morning I got a call from Tony asking if I would come into the office to meet Mike Hughes. Lynne and I were really excited, thinking he might take me on on an official basis. All those stories from acts that had been with him for years without a clue who he was and here I was, going in to meet him, after only six days. Mike's office was on the eighth floor of the beautiful Royal Liver Building on Liverpool's waterfront. I was expecting a plush, elegant office but was surprised to be ushered into a tiny outer corridor with one chair and a floor that was covered in carpet samples with the words 'Mike Hughes Entertainments' imprinted on them. Mike's former job was as a carpet salesman.

'Mike's going through some paperwork,' I was told. 'He won't be long.' Forty minutes later I was called through into a slightly larger office and was suddenly shaking hands with a tall, long-faced man with a head of thick black hair. I remember thinking he looked a bit like Bryan Ferry, although his dress sense was not quite so chic. Red jeans, red shoes and a red sweater. Trinny and Susannah would have had a field day. With a soft Liverpool accent and a curt, abrupt manner, he was very scary and I began to think that the image of a Scouse Howard Hughes was more than appropriate.

'Colin at the Shakespeare tells me you're very funny. You don't look funny. Go on, make me laugh.'

'Err, oh, err,' I stumbled. 'I'm not very good without an audience.'

'Not much good to me, then, are you.'

This is going nowhere, I thought, but after a couple of minutes of awkward chat he said, 'Right, I'll take you on, but not as an agent. I'll be your manager. You'll do exactly what I say and you'll pay me on a sliding scale, up to twenty-five per cent of everything you earn. You'll have to sign a five-year contract and I reserve the right to drop you if things don't work out. Yes or no?'

I was nineteen years old and didn't have the experience or the courage to suggest that I would think about it and call him on Monday. 'Yes,' I said, partly excited but mostly scared by his autocratic, bombastic attitude.

The contract I signed was, of course, not as one-sided as he made it sound that day. Our working relationship would last more than twenty-five years and prove to be a great success for both of us. Although he no longer represents me, Mike remains a good and valued friend.

I came out of the meeting reeling and worried that Lynne would think that I had jumped into something too quickly. She approved, though, and suggested later that evening, as we were driving to the Shakey, that we should detour past his house. We were young and excited and thought we might catch a glimpse of this powerful impresario who was going to shape my future. The curtains of his huge home were open and we did indeed see him, in his well-lit living room, playing with his little boy, Christopher. A couple of years ago Lynne said something to me that made me glad that we don't know what the future holds for us. 'Imagine,' she said, 'if someone had said to us that night, "You two will marry, but it won't last. You, Les, will marry a younger woman and that marriage won't last either. The woman you marry will end up having a child with the little boy who is being picked up by the man you are watching through the window."' Yes, my second wife, Amanda Holden, is now engaged to Mike Hughes's son, Chris.

Mike worked hard to get me some TV work and got me a spot on the new talent show *New Faces*. I didn't win with the panel but did with the viewers. This meant that I came back for a viewers' winners show. The same thing happened: I won again with the viewers and was invited back for a third time when at last, I scored with the panel. I even got good marks from Tony Hatch, who, in those days, made Simon Cowell seem like Mother Teresa. I came back for a fourth time and lost to an even younger impressionist, Tony Maiden. I was in good company, though. Victoria Wood was on the same show.

I started to get more work on the cabaret circuit, which meant that I was away more and more, and this put pressure on my relationship with Lynne. She was studying law at Liverpool Polytechnic, but one evening suggested that she should give it up so that she could travel with me. I felt uncomfortable about her quitting her degree, as she was doing very well, but we agreed that we should go for it, commit fully and get married. I was spending most of my free time at her house and her parents, Molly and Ron, had even let me have the box room to sleep in. Already I was drifting away from my family. I loved Lynne and wanted to be with her, but I also, if I'm honest, liked the comfort and status of a more middle-class environment. Molly and Ron were very welcoming and treated me like a son. Even after Lynne and I broke up, they showed me understanding and love, and I still have deep feelings for them to this day.

Lynne and I decided we wanted to marry in the spring of 1974. I wasn't scared of asking Ron for her hand, but I was petrified of breaking the news to my agent, Mike. When I called him, he said, 'Don't be ridiculous. You're only twenty. You're too young.' He was fast becoming a force in Britain, not just Liverpool. He was like an old-fashioned Hollywood mogul who believed that wives and girlfriends got in the way of careers. I stood my ground, somewhat shakily, and said we were determined to wed and that I needed some time off in the spring. 'You're booked up, so you'll have to do it, if you must, the week that you're at the Shakespeare.' So I married Lynne Mary Webster on Wednesday 1 May, while I was in the middle of a week at the Shakey, supporting the legendary Tommy Cooper. I even wore the same suit for both. I had bought a brown velvet suit for my appearance on *New Faces* and it was proving to be very versatile.

Our wedding took place nine days before Lynne's twentieth birthday and we looked like kids. There is a photo of me next to Hems de Winter, my best man, and it looks like I'm off to a new school rather than getting married. He is six foot seven and so, for the photo, I stood on a step, not realising that the photographer had, instead of cropping the shot, taken a full-length one. Our wedding reception was held in Molly and Ron's back garden, and then everybody came and watched me work in the evening. How many people can say that they got married and all their wedding guests went to work with them? I think I did better than Tommy that night! Probably not! He was fantastic.

On the previous Monday, when I had gone to rehearsal, I had sat nervously in my dressing room wondering if I would meet the great man. You could support stars and not meet them at all because they didn't go on until about eleven. Suddenly a tall man with shoulder-length blond hair and long Bermuda shorts came in and said, 'Hiya.'

Who the hell is this? I thought.

'I'm Tommy. Nice to meet you. Ha, ha, ha, ha!'

Why he had the wig and shorts on I still have no idea, but I found myself laughing all the same.

That Wednesday night, having changed my wedding shirt for a silk, frilly showbiz one, and wearing more mascara than my bride, I did my spot and we all stayed on to watch Tommy's act. Pete Price, the compère and a dear friend, introduced him and for the first five minutes he didn't come onstage. The audience were in hysterics as his voice echoed throughout the room, 'I can't get out. I'm locked in my dressing room. Hello, can somebody let me out?' On he came, this giant of a man with the biggest feet I've ever seen, fez on head, and that brilliantly vacant look on his face. He had that rare gift of being able to make you laugh without doing much. Between the microphone and his props table he placed a garden gate and every time he went to get a prop or magic trick, he went through it. It was hysterical.

At the end of his act, he agreed to do an auction for a local charity. 'What'll you give me for this toaster?' he asked.

My uncle John shouted, 'Two slices of bread.'

Tommy looked straight at him and said, 'That's funny. That's very funny. I like that.' Even he could fall foul of the funny heckler.

Lynne and I didn't get a honeymoon. We spent one night at the Atlantic Towers Hotel and the next day moved into our first home, 104 Sandhurst Road, Rainhill, a modest three-bedroom terrace with a small garden, front and rear. We couldn't afford it, but Molly and Ron had kindly provided us with a deposit to set us on our feet. I went to work with Tommy that night and came back to find that Lynne had lit candles, chilled the champagne and prepared a lovely supper. Although we had consummated our marriage the previous night, this was our first romantic evening in our new home. One of our wedding presents was a duvet, or, as they were known then, Continental quilt. It may be difficult to imagine now but I'd never seen one before – I was used to sheets, blankets and an eiderdown. Lynne went to the bathroom to prepare herself and I got into our trendy new bed. In the candlelight, in a new sexy negligee, she appeared at the door and the seductive look on her face suddenly turned to tears of laughter.

'What are you laughing at?' I asked, hurt.

'Look at you. What have you done?'

Not knowing that you slept under a duvet, I had opened up the bottom, popper by popper, climbed in and was lying inside it!

I finished the week at the Shakespeare and Lynne and I were invited by Tommy to stay behind and have a drink. His stories were so funny. He had been in the Guards before he became a comic and, one day, while on sentry duty, had started to fall asleep. As he came to, he saw his commanding officer looking him furiously in the face. Thinking on his feet, Tommy simply said, 'Amen.'

At closing time the grilles on the bar went down but Tommy fancied another drink. 'No problem,' said a staff member. 'I won't be a minute.' We thought he had gone to get the keys but instead came back with a long bamboo pole with a hook on the end. What on earth was he going to do? we thought. 'Whisky, wasn't it, Tommy?' he asked, as he counted the grilles. 'That's six along and eight up.' He placed the pole through the grille at that point, until it reached the whisky bottle, squeezed the hook on to the optic and the whisky trickled down the hollow bamboo into a glass held at the other end. Only in Liverpool.

When we finally left Tommy and friends in the bar, he said, 'Good luck, son. Don't get too funny.'

I wouldn't work with him again for another ten years.

CHAPTER 10

'It Could Have Been Better, But So Could The Weather'

Over the next few years I would get on with learning my craft, working hard on the club circuit and making the odd TV appearance. Lynne would travel with me and we spent weeks on end away from home, sometimes driving through the night from Bristol to Glasgow, or from Hull to Exeter. Agents didn't give a damn how you got to a venue, just as long as you did. We couldn't afford hotels, so instead had to stay in pro digs. Across the country there were guesthouses that would cater for touring actors and variety performers as they fulfilled their engagements in the town's theatres and clubs. Lynne and I hated staying in them because they were usually full of acts who had been on the circuit for years and were sometimes bitter and disillusioned. They would come back from their gigs and sit up slagging off the successful performers of the time. Comics would bemoan how unfunny Les Dawson and Jimmy Tarbuck were, and singers would tell you how scandalous it was that they weren't recognised as the stars they so clearly thought that they were.

One night, in the bar of one such guesthouse, a tall, skinny, not very attractive guitar vocalist swayed drunkenly as he stuffed egg sandwiches into his mouth and shouted angrily, 'You tell me,' he said, bits of egg flying out in all directions. 'You tell me what Tom Jones has got that I haven't.'

One morning at digs in the north-east, the landlady was chatting away to us as her old, overweight golden retriever waddled into the room and, unseen by her, licked away at the butter that was sitting on the bottom shelf of the breakfast trolley. 'Right,' she said. 'What would you like for your breakfast?' We made some excuse and ran out to the nearest café.

Lynne and I would stay in such digs week in, week out, until one night when I was doing a charity show in Liverpool with Ken Dodd. 'No, young man, you don't want to stay in digs. You'll end up bitter and twisted. Stay in a decent hotel. You'll have a better attitude and you'll be able to claim it back against tax.' Tax advice from Doddy? Oh, the irony.

As it happened, in 1975 I landed a summer season topping the bill on the Butlins late-night cabaret circuit and started earning the kind of money that meant I could afford to stay in hotels. I was in esteemed company, as other weeks the headliners would be Bob Monkhouse, Ted Rogers or the Rocking Berries. The poor campers must have looked at their programme and thought, Les who? Never heard of him. Despite this, though, the room was always packed to capacity. Not because they were dying to see me but because it was the one night in the week where they could, by paying the extra money for the cabaret show, drink beyond the normal hours until two in the morning. For me, it was a chance to work my act up into an hour's set and prove to a captive audience that I could keep them fully engaged and entertained. All those years ago, watching Tommy Trinder and Peter Cavanagh as the visiting top of the bill and now here I was, fulfilling a dream and becoming that very thing myself.

In 1976, because my career was in such a good place, Lynne and I decided to move from our little terraced house in Rainhill and into a large detached house in Woolton, one of the leafier and more affluent suburbs of the city. The house, Cromer, was a huge leap for us. Our first home had cost £6,800 and here we were, suddenly with a mortgage for £22,000. I was only twenty-two and we were buying a house that was owned by a middle-aged couple with a family. On the day we went to view it, they mistook Molly and Ron, Lynne's parents, for the prospective purchasers and were shocked and sceptical when they realised it was us, the couple who looked like we should still be in school, who were making the offer. Often in the years that we would live there, I would answer the door to some salesman or other who would ask to speak with either my mum or dad.

I had, definitely, inherited my mum's desire to better herself, but sadly I developed something that she did not possess, a snobbery and strongly held belief that I was 'better than' my family and that I should distance myself a little from them. After all, I had a lovely home, a good car and, amazingly, a bank manager and an accountant. I'd been on telly and would even occasionally get recognised as I wandered around the city centre. I started to fool myself that I'd never really been like them. Since joining the Group, I had clearly moved into what I thought were new and more exciting circles. You can choose your friends but not your family, as the saying goes. Oh, what a mistake I was making.

We moved into Cromer at the beginning of that swelteringly hot summer of 1976. My season at Butlins the previous year had been successful enough for me to be asked back, so in order to spend as much time as we could in our new house, we would travel to and from the camps in the same night. The trip to Bognor Regis was the worst. We would leave home mid-afternoon, drive for five hours, have a meal and then rest in the dressing room before I would go onstage at one in the morning. Just over an hour later I would come off, drenched in sweat, sign autographs and be back in the car by about 3 a.m. Being a bad passenger and also being wired from my performance, I would drive back home, making sure Lynne chatted to me to keep me awake, and arrive home at eight o'clock, just as the summer sun began to encroach into the air-conditionless Ford Consul that I had recently bought. A far cry from my mum's little Austin 1100.

After one such exhausting journey during that unforgettable summer, we opened the front door to the sound of the phone ringing. When I answered, it was my dad. 'Hiya, kid. Sorry to call you when you've just got in. It's your mum. She's got cancer.'

For months my mum had been complaining of a lump in her throat. Her GP had told her there was nothing wrong with her and had even accused her of being a hypochondriac. Eventually she had been referred to Broad Green Hospital for tests and they had found a tumour on her lung. This, I found out later, had happened weeks before and my mum and dad had decided not to tell me, Ken or Mandy. Marg had been informed and thought that we should know, but was overruled by my mum. 'Our Les has that summer season to do. It's important that he is focused. Our Ken and Mandy are too young – they won't be able to deal with it.' My dad must have lain awake that night wrestling with his conscience until he decided I should be told. The first thing I did was to call our Marg and ask her how bad it was. She told me she was going to see the consultant the following day and that if I was up to it, I could go with her. The next morning we sat in the office of Mr Edwards at Broad Green to be told in a very straightforward manner, seemingly without compassion, that the tumour was quite large and was in the trunk between the two lungs and could therefore not be operated on. His prognosis was six to ten months, at the most. Marg and I came out of the meeting reeling. To this day, she is angry about the way he dealt with it. My feeling is that when you are in that position, you have to put emotion to one side and concentrate on the facts. Just recently, in an episode of *Holby*, I played a man dying of cancer who prefers the no-tears attitude of one consultant to the other's gentle, compassionate approach. They say that actors draw on their own experiences to convince. For that role, I had more than enough memories.

My first question to Marg was whether my mum should know how bad it was. It was a decision we didn't have to make, as later, when Marg was with her and Mr Edwards was doing his rounds, my mum asked him outright. Again, apparently with eyes of steel, he told her matter of factly, 'I'm sorry, Mrs Heseltine, you have terminal carcinoma of the lung.'

As he left and our Marg burst into tears, my mum asked what the matter was.

'It's just it could have been better,' Marg said.

'What could?'

'Your life.'

'Yes,' said my mum, 'but so could the weather.'

My dad buried his head in the sand, refusing to believe that my mum could soon die. He had never been good at showing his emotions, and, as you've read, my mum would often be frustrated at his lack of willingness to talk. The incident with the blazing newspaper is funny but it serves to point out his lack of communication. There is no doubt, though, that Winnie was the love of his life and he certainly wasn't ready to lose her.

Ken was engaged to a girl called Sue, and Marg and I were both married and so didn't live in the family home. Mandy therefore, who was only eighteen, would grow up fast in the next year. Although we were often there to help, Mandy would be my mum's primary carer. It was a huge burden for one so young, but she did a remarkable job.

For a few months my mum seemed fine. She spent a few weeks at Clatterbridge Hospital on the Wirral, one of the great pioneering cancer institutes of the time. She seemed to be responding well to the radiotherapy, and for a short time we joined my dad in his optimism about her survival. He would say, with eyes that were willing it to be true, 'You know your mother – she's a bloody fighter. She can beat this.'

She came a couple of times to watch me at the Butlins camp and told me again that she was convinced I was going to have a long and successful career in show business. Marg took her for the weekend to London, where they went to see Joel Grey (who had played the master of ceremonies in *Cabaret*, one of her favourites) at the Palladium. As she came out of the theatre, she apparently told our Marg, 'That'll be our Les one day.'

By Christmas, though, she had lost an alarming amount of weight and seemed too weak to enjoy the festivities. Lynne and I had a Cavalier King Charles spaniel, who we had pretentiously called Moët, after the champagne Moët & Chandon. When we were kids, we had had a lovely mongrel, Dusty, who had died a few years earlier. One evening I arrived with Moët and my mum shouted, 'Go on, Dusty. See him off, see him off.' The effects of the drugs, no doubt, but it upset me and woke me up to the fact that time was running out for her.

Her weight dropped below six stone, and one evening as I sat with her, she talked about how she was looking forward to the spring, when the grass and the flowers would grow and she would feel stronger. She, too, was clinging to the idea that new growth would energise her and improve her condition. As she drifted into sleep, I removed her glasses and switched off the light. I remembered how as a boy I had gone into her room every night and done the same. She would always fall asleep clutching either a weathered copy of *From Here to Eternity* or Hemingway's *For Whom the Bell Tolls*.

As the first flowers of spring were pushing through the soil, the inevitable happened. It was 29 March 1977 and Lynne and I had gone to bed early. At about one in the morning the phone in the hall rang. As I woke from a deep sleep and stumbled to answer, I knew what to expect. My dad's defeated voice: 'Hiya, kid. Your mum's gone.' Half dressed, I drove the mile or so to the house and let myself in. The image as I walked up the stairs is burnt into the back of my eyeballs like a familiar film scene. Through the banisters, the light from the small bedside lamp spilt into the hallway and I could make out the figure of my dad holding my mum's tiny, lifeless body in his arms, trying to give her the kiss of life. As I grabbed him and held him, the tears stinging my eyes, I felt love, grief and compassion but also an uncomfortable, overriding sense of anger. I was angry with my dad. Why? It wasn't his fault. Over the years and through countless therapy sessions I have tried to compute that feeling and have reached the conclusion that my anger was derived from my mum's conditioning of me. She loved my dad but she always talked about his incompetence: 'He's hopeless. He can't drive. He can't fix a plug...' In my head, as I held him, I could hear her saying, 'He can't even let me go.'

In the weeks following my mum's death, as we were sorting through the flotsam and jetsam of her life, we found a journal she had been secretly writing, in which she talked about her fears and hopes for her family. She wrote:

> Have you noticed that until now I have not mentioned the word 'cancer'? It's just a word. Oh, they never put that word on my medical certificate, although my GP is aware that I know what it is I am suffering from – as I am aware that it will one day in the not too distant future destroy me. What I want the reader to face is the fact that any one of us can one day come face to face with this disease.

I am fifty years old, married to a very dear man and have five children, four of whom are still alive, and I hope that they benefit from my mistakes. I have lived too conscientiously, working for things that now seem to have no meaning at all. I have made the mistake of too often meeting trouble halfway.

I have sometimes felt psychic in my feelings towards happenings in my life and mostly been later proved right. It seemed uncanny at the time, but the logic of it all has sometimes puzzled me, knowing beforehand what was about to happen and nearly always did.

I want to assure my readers that I have not always helped myself. I was foolish enough to carry on smoking knowing full well that it could impair my failing health. But if in reading this story someone can find help and comfort from my foolishness, then the writing of it cannot have been in vain.

I have a lot to tell my readers, if I am allowed the time to relate it, about my son who is working in the entertainment business, who has appeared on television, and although I am sure I shan't live long enough to see it, I hope he will fulfil my dreams and become an actor, which is what I have always worked to be. However, that is past now and my ambition was never realised, but do you know, I think that eventually this ambition will be fulfilled. I have a theory which some people may never agree with but I think that only a spirit which is strong enough in life can overcome death and carry on in one's children. If this is not so, how can anyone account for theatrical families? Do they not inherit some of the parents' genes? And when this is so, friends who knew you in your youth explain to the other people, 'Oh, she gets that from her mother or father,' whichever the case may be, or on the other side of the coin,

> 'He's just like his granddad, he doesn't give a damn.' But these are just my own theories and I believed, rightly or wrongly, that throughout our existence God, being just and fair to His flock, gives us a chance to make amends for our past mistakes and the hurt we have inflicted knowingly or not on others.
>
> I am still feeling very weak from this last infliction I've suffered – I hope I get a chance to finish this story.

Bless her. Secretly she hoped we would find it and she would be published. Well, Winnie, better late than never.

Clinging conveniently to the show business cliché 'The show must go on', I buried my grief and threw myself into my work. Apart from a shaky couple of months that summer, when Lynne and I sold bleach and disinfectant door to door, generously supplied by her dad, Ron, who had a cleaning supplies business, things were going steadily well. I got the odd guest spot on TV shows like *The Comedians*, *The Golden Shot* and *Who Do You Do?* It was on the set of the latter that I briefly met a tall, charismatic guy called Dustin Gee.

I toured the cabaret circuit supporting big names of the time, like Blue Mink, Roger Whittaker, the Drifters and Tony Christie. One night after my spot at the Circus Tavern in Purfleet, where I was opening for the Three Degrees, a portly, middle-aged Jewish man introduced himself as Peter Sontar from MAM. He asked if I would like to do a summer season in Scarborough with Jimmy Tarbuck. After thanking him and saying, 'Yes, yes, yes,' my impulse was to run to the phone and call my mum. Sadly, I couldn't.

CHAPTER 11

Meeting Tarby

We opened on a short run at the Winter Gardens Theatre in Bournemouth. On the first day of rehearsals I stood at the back of the stalls and watched the man I had seen countless times on *Sunday Night at the London Palladium* walk on to the stage. It seemed odd to see him in casual clothes rather than the sharp three-piece suit that he wore on TV, but although he was older, he still had that mop of dark, Beatles-style hair and, of course, that huge, machine gun of a laugh.

Shielding his eyes to see over the footlights, he said, 'Hello, young man. I believe you are from Liverpool. Welcome. Are you nervous?'

'A bit, Mr Tarbuck.'

'Don't worry, son, we'll look after you. Theatre is a lot easier than the clubs.'

He was right. In a club environment, you had to fight for attention from a noisy audience more interested in the bingo or, if it was a cabaret club, eating their chicken in a basket. The opening comic always went on to the sound of clattering knives and forks as dinner, if you could call it that, was being served. In a theatre, people who came through the door had paid to see a show and be entertained. From the second you walked onstage you had their attention, and if your act was good enough, you would keep it. I only had to do a twelve-minute spot, but my main job was to compère and introduce the other acts. How thrilling – I was doing what Tarby had done at the Palladium.

I had a ball that summer, and Jimmy was true to his word. He taught me theatre craft: how to walk onstage, hold a microphone and take a curtain call. Sounds simple but it isn't. Years of working in clubs with lousy PA systems and sometimes hostile audiences had ingrained in me a bad technique. I learnt a more relaxed and gentle approach, and found that twelve minutes was long enough in theatre. In the clubs, you were doing well if you had managed to get their attention after twelve minutes.

Our main season was at the Floral Hall Theatre in Scarborough. Lynne and I rented a flat on the South Cliff. Danny la Rue, at the peak of his success, was at the Futurist on the seafront, and Ken Dodd was at the Opera House. When Doddy is onstage, it's as if it is his first time. He loves it and doesn't want to come off. Summer shows were twice nightly, usually at 6.10 p.m. and 8.40 p.m., and every night the audience for the second show would still be queuing at 8.45 p.m., as Doddy would be saying to the first house, 'Close the doors. Tell them I'm staying on, missus. What a beautiful day for running up to the vicar's door sticking a cucumber through the letterbox and saying, "The Martians have landed!"' His support acts wouldn't even bother staying for the curtain call on the second-house show, as it could be nearly midnight before he finished. The problem was, there was a hypnotist late-night show on after him and the hypnotist would understandably be furious. Doddy told me, 'Do you know, young man, I've had 'em do everything to get me off in my time.

Closing curtains, the hook, turning the lights off, but I've never before had a bloke in the wings going, "Look into my eyes. Come offstage. Come off the staaage."'

Jimmy was a real practical joker. One night at the curtain call he told the audience, 'Ladies and gentlemen, it's lovely when young love blossoms during a summer season and it is my pleasure to announce that our comic, Les Dennis, has just got engaged to our head dancer, Kathy. Step forward, kids.' Both blushing from head to toe, we had to take a bow as the audience applauded thunderously. All except Lynne, who was sat among them with a puzzled look on her face.

There was a great drama on TV called *Out*, in which Tom Bell played the part of an East End gangster called Frank Ross, who had been released from prison. Every week I would catch it in my dressing room and miss the last five minutes because I had to go onstage and introduce Kenneth McKellar. Those were the days before video so, when I came off, I would run into Jimmy's dressing room and ask him how the episode had ended. He would bring me up to speed so that I knew what to expect the following week. In the twelfth and final episode, I couldn't see how it was going to end and had to prise myself away from the telly to do Kenneth's intro. I came off and ran into Jimmy's room. 'What happened, Jim?'

'He got shot.'

'No.'

'Yeah, that Scottish bloke Brian Cox killed him.'

A year later, while watching a rerun, I discovered that he'd been having me on – Frank Ross lived. Jimmy had waited a whole year for that practical joke to pay off.

Tommy Cannon, of Cannon and Ball, got a phone call once from a man telling him he had won a prestigious new award that recognised the sterling work done by straight men. 'We feel the comic gets all the praise,' said the man, 'and that the straight man is often undervalued.' He went on to say how the voting committee thought Tommy was the best in the business and fully deserved the award they were honouring him with.

Tommy was thrilled and asked, 'What was the name of the award again?'

Jimmy's machine-gun laugh at the end of the phone as he said, 'The Jimmy Tarbuck Got You By the Bollocks Award!'

Jimmy's family – his wife, Pauline, and children, Lisa, aged fourteen, and James, aged twelve – were with him for the season. To this day Lisa talks about that summer with great fondness and I can remember her standing in the wings watching her dad, probably already dreaming of a career in the same business.

Over the years I've worked with lots of dads whose kids have gone on to have great success, such as Maxton G. Beasley, whose son Max Beasley is a great actor and a really lovely bloke, and Pete Conway, Robbie Williams's dad. When I did *Shooting Stars* with Robbie, he asked if he could have a photo with me for his dad and whenever I see him now I always ask how Pete is. 'Good – thanks for asking, sir,' he replies.

I haven't seen Lee Evans since he's become such a huge success but I can remember him as a boy, as he too watched his dad, Dave Evans. Dave is a brilliant entertainer and has quite rightly been Lee's biggest influence. Why he never became a star, I'll never know. When he was in summer season, as the singers would be doing a vocal warm-up of various scales and the dancers would be limbering up, he'd walk up and down the corridor shouting, 'There was this fella. There was this fella.' When asked what he was doing he would reply, 'A comic's warm-up.'

On tour with Tarby, from Scarborough we went back to Bournemouth, where every night there would be a famous face. Geoff Boycott, Tony Jacklin, Peter Alliss, Michael Parkinson and countless others came backstage after the show. One night Jimmy said, 'Pauline and I are going out for a bite to eat with some mates and were wondering if you and Lynne would like to join us.' A couple of hours later we were sitting in an Italian trattoria with Southampton stars Ted MacDougall and the legendary Alan Ball. I had to pinch myself to prove it wasn't a dream. I was sat chatting to one of the key players who, in 1966, had won the World Cup at Wembley. I was even more thrilled when Ted and his wife invited us all back to their house for drinks. While the girls sat in the lounge, Ted took the men down to his garden shed, which he had refurbished as a small pub. As Alan talked about that great game against West Germany, I sat listening in awe and sipped beer, not realising that as fast as I was drinking Ted was filling my glass. I don't remember getting home and the next evening, after introducing Jimmy to a packed audience, ran offstage and threw up in the nearest toilet. Later Jimmy laughed, saying, 'You're not a hardened drinker, son. Leave it to the men!'

In the 1980s Tarby and, in fact all of us old-school variety comedians, would come in for much criticism from the new alternative guys. Ben Elton, in particular, would attack Tarby mercilessly on *Saturday Night Live*. These were the years of Margaret Thatcher's government and Jimmy made no secret of being a supporter. His comedy, though, was never racist, sexist or politically motivated like others of his generation, and in hindsight, Ben's attack seems somewhat harsh and unnecessary, especially when you consider that he is now very much part of the establishment and has supported a government that since the war in Iraq, has proved to be equally as unpopular. I recall being at a Light Entertainment Christmas party at the BBC in the mid-1980s and the first hour or so being quite awkward. At one end of the room were Ben Elton, Lenny Henry, Rik Mayall, Dawn French, Jennifer Saunders, Ade Edmondson and Rowan Atkinson. I was up the other end with, among others, Russ Abbot, Little and Large, Dustin Gee and, thankfully, Barry Cryer.

Barry has managed to straddle both camps and so the new guys would come up and chat to him. As the wine flowed and we all relaxed, we mingled more and realised we had one thing in common – comedy. It ended up being a great night. I wish Jimmy had been there – I would have given anything to see him and Ben Elton laughing together.

For me, Tarby remains one of our best live comedians, and I am very much indebted to him for his help and encouragement. At the end of the 1978 season I felt happy with my progress. I was booked for my second summer season at Blackpool's famous North Pier Theatre, where the Crazy Gang and Morecambe and Wise had headlined. I was tucked at the bottom of the bill, supporting the Black Abbots and the Krankies, but what did I care. I was on my way. My personal life was to change dramatically too. On 1 May 1979, our fifth wedding anniversary, two weeks before opening in Blackpool, Lynne told me she was pregnant.

Lynne went into labour on the morning of 22 December 1979. In true sitcom fashion our car stalled on the way to the Oxford Street Maternity Hospital, but we made it. A nurse came into reception and took Lynne through double doors and, ten minutes later, returned with a baby in her arms. Blimey, I thought, that was quick! Then I realised the baby was for a couple behind me, who were waiting to go home. Lynne's delivery wasn't quite that fast, but remarkably for a first birth, Philip was born four hours later, at just after 4 p.m. There had only been one complication and I clearly remember the surgeon, Mrs Francis, calmly saying, 'Oh, dear, the cord's round his neck. Breathe slowly.' It was only later I discovered how dangerous it could be, increasing the chances of oxygen not reaching the brain. He was also slightly jaundiced and so had to spend his first Christmas in the Oxford Street Women's Hospital with his proud mum. Lynne and I exchanged presents in the ward, but they were eclipsed by the tiny, bald, wrinkly gift we had been given. He had hardly any hair when he was born, but with two very blond parents, it was evident that he wouldn't grow to be tall, dark and handsome. Still, two out of three isn't bad!

That night, after the birth, I did a gig in Wallasey, in the Wirral, at a club called the Great Float. Had the birth taken longer, I probably would have still gone to work and missed the joy of being there, but luckily it didn't interfere with seeing my son born.

Over the next months, as I focused intently on this new family, my relations with my old family became even more strained. The hunger I had for success and self-improvement made me ignore the people who loved me, and things came to a head at Philip's christening. After the church ceremony we had a party in our garden at Cromer. We had the usual mix of family and friends, and I admit I concentrated more on my friends than my family. As I rubbed shoulders with my accountant and bank manager, my family stood awkwardly on their own, feeling left out and unwanted. My sister Mandy had probably had one glass too many and at one point I saw her take a bottle of wine and drink straight from it. I challenged her, saying, 'Mandy, have a drink by all means, but please use a glass. I've got a lot of friends here.'

'You and your posh friends,' she retorted. 'That's all you think about.'

As I tried to stop it from becoming a scene, our Ken came to her defence and I suggested they should behave or leave. Because it was such a sunny day, most people were in the garden and were unaware of the row. While my dad was enjoying himself talking to Liverpool's stars Ian St John and Ron Yeats, the rest of my family left quietly.

We would keep the details from my dad, but we couldn't heal the rift for some years. I feel a huge guilt and responsibility for what happened that day. Our Mandy was behaving badly, but since my mum's death I had clearly distanced myself from them and they felt hurt. My head had been turned by the so-called glamour of show business and I felt I didn't really need them in my life. Nearly three decades on, we are close again, but for a long time we all missed out on a valuable support network.

CHAPTER 12

Russ Abbot's Madhouse

When Russ Abbot left the Black Abbots and went solo, I became his unofficial straight man. We were in summer season in Torquay in 1981, and because Russ was more of a character comedian than a stand-up, he would need someone to bounce off. As well as doing my own solo spot, I would work in sketches with Russ. We played two stupid Teddy Boys, Vince and Les, a kind of British Dumb and Dumber. The jokes were stupid, but audiences loved the characters.

'Did you know, Vince, that if you cut a worm in half, it grows again?'

'Not if you cut it lengthways.'

The following Christmas I joined Russ in panto at the Davenport Theatre, Stockport, where he was playing Wishee Washee in *Aladdin*. Russ had already done one series of *Russ Abbot's Madhouse* for LWT and I hoped there was a chance for me to join the team. I would hint at the suggestion during rehearsals but Russ wouldn't say anything. After the opening night Mike Hughes came into my dressing room and told me I was booked for the second series, which would start the following February. He could have told me over the phone but Mike liked to see your face when he told you good news. I later discovered that it was written in my panto programme biog, so the audience on that first night knew before I did. No matter – I was thrilled. My first TV series and I wasn't yet twenty-nine. I had reached my target of TV success before my thirtieth birthday.

When I'd got the summer season with Jimmy Tarbuck, I had wanted to tell my mum but hadn't been able to – at least this time I could tell my dad. When I called him, he was as excited as I was. Since my mum's death, he had concentrated on my career and had become my road manager. He couldn't drive but he would travel with me up and down the country, as, in between summer seasons and pantos, I was still working the club circuit. The job didn't entail a great deal – he would set up my props, talk the musicians through my dots and, while I was onstage, wait nervously in the dressing room. I could judge how well I was doing not just by the audience reaction but also by my dad's behaviour. If I was getting laughs, he would tentatively stick his head out of the dressing-room door and scuttle to the back of the room and order a pint at the bar. I would be able to see him over the footlights standing proudly, pint in hand, laughing along with the audience. If I started to lose them and the laughter stopped, he would quickly put his pint down and, like a frightened rabbit, scuttle back to the safety of the dressing room. If he didn't leave the dressing room at all, I had died a death. On those nights I would come off annoyed, not so much with the audience, but with my dad for his lack of support. He told me one night that if I was going down badly he would stand backstage with his hands over his ears so that he couldn't hear.

'But why, Dad? Do you think I'm that bad?'

'No, kid. I just hate it so much it's as if it's happening to me.

I think you've got the heart of a bloody lion.'

I would remain cross with him on the long journey home and we would hardly speak – not that my dad talked much anyway and many journeys were conducted in silence. I did an interview for a car magazine a few years ago and one of the questions was, 'If you could have a car journey with anyone, dead or alive, who would it be?' The journalist expected me to say some interesting person from history and was surprised when I said my dad. There are so many things I could have asked him about his life and didn't. I regret that.

I joined the *Russ Abbot's Madhouse* team in 1982. I was thrilled that the previous ten years' work had, at last, paid off. After winning *New Faces* in 1974, I'd had the odd TV spot, but then it had quietened down and I'd got on with learning my trade in the working men's clubs and cabaret circuits up and down the country. Now, I was going to feature in a hugely popular prime-time Saturday-night comedy sketch show. I felt that at last I was making significant progress. We were to tape six programmes in February at London Weekend Studios, and they would be shown on TV over the summer months. Myself and Sherrie Hewson were the new members of the team, joining regulars Dustin Gee, Jeffrey Holland (of *Hi-de-Hi!* fame), Michael Barrymore, Susie Blake, Bella Emberg and of course Russ.

The only problem was where I was going to stay. Pro digs were hard to find in London and I certainly couldn't afford a hotel. Mike Hughes suggested that I call Dustin Gee, who, he believed, rented a flat in the West End during the recordings. Dustin had been in *Russ Abbot's Madhouse* since the previous series and was fast becoming a TV star. He already had a huge reputation on the club circuit, being one of those rare stage performers who could pack a cabaret club for a week even though he had had very little TV exposure. Word of mouth alone had made him into a top-of-the-bill draw, commanding huge fees and audiences.

At a time when other comedy impressionists, myself included, were coming onstage in velvet suits and huge bowties and doing Frank Spencer, James Stewart and Mick Jagger, Dustin would skip on in a white, short-sleeved safari suit and open his set with a slightly camp, avant-garde, Vivien Stanshall-influenced rendition of 'The Stork Has Brought a Son and Daughter to Mr and Mrs Mickey Mouse'. He would then do, with the aid of an array of inventive props and wigs, amazing impressions of David Bowie, Gene Vincent, Roy Orbison, John Cleese and, best of all, Robert Mitchum. He would go to his props table and, with his back to the audience, slick back his hair, put on a battered old cowboy hat, stick a cigarette in his mouth, turn round into the spotlight and, believe me, the charismatic, handsome movie star Robert Mitchum was standing before you. As the audience burst into spontaneous applause and laughter, he would walk, as they had seen Robert Mitchum walk in a hundred westerns, to the microphone and say, in overtly camp tones, 'I can't do the voice.' It would bring the house down.

I was apprehensive about calling Dustin. I had met him once in the 1970s when we were doing *Who Do You Do?* but didn't really know him. In my world, he was a huge star and I was just a rookie comic starting out. I plucked up the courage, though, and called him that very afternoon.

'Oh, hello, love.' Dustin called everybody 'love'. 'Mike said you might call. I'm watching a Bette Davis movie on telly right now, but no problem, love, you can stay with me. I'll come and see you tonight and we can discuss it.' I was still appearing in *Aladdin* with Russ Abbot. 'See you after the show, love.' As I put the phone down, I was struck with, I am ashamed to say, a fear born of the teeniest bit of homophobia. Dustin was openly gay and here I was, possibly about to share a flat with a gay man. I remember thinking, What if he comes on to me? It seems ridiculous now. Why do straight men always assume that every gay man wants to shag them? With hindsight, it was a little arrogant and naïve of me to assume that he would fancy me, and also patronising and foolish to think that, just because he was gay, he would be a sexual predator.

My fears were quickly allayed after the show that evening. There was a knock on my dressing-room door and when I answered it, I was struck by how tall, good-looking and charismatic Dustin was. I remember the image as if it were yesterday. Wearing a tweed jacket and open-necked shirt and clutching a bottle of white wine, he smiled and said, 'Hello, love. I come bearing gifts.' How prophetic those words would turn out to be.

Dustin, a wonderfully dour Scottish writer called Russell Lane and myself shared a flat in Dorset Square and I had the time of my life. I was so excited about being in London that I would wake every morning before six and go running in nearby Regent's Park. I'd come back to the flat, prepare breakfast for Dustin and Russell, who both slept late, and then we'd all dash for the Tube at Baker Street. They were heavy smokers so we would leg it to the smokers' carriage, where we would stand smoking (me passively) for the journey to the rehearsal rooms in Kennington.

The show was a sketch show, or, as it is called now, a broken comedy show. We were a kind of rep team who would be cast in various sketches built around Russ. The sketches were recorded in front of a live audience and then edited into a half-hour show. I learnt so much doing that show and benefited from working with such talented comedy performers. Russ had many popular characters: Basildon Bond (licensed to kill and drive a heavy goods vehicle), Barratt Holmes (Sherlock's idiotic brother), Cooperman (Superman with Tommy Cooper's voice) and C. U. Jimmy (an unintelligible red-wigged Scotsman). In one sketch he played a street vendor called Sid the Spiv, who was selling impressions from the back of a street stall. Dustin, Michael,

Jeffrey and I were crouched behind the stall and Russ would invite the audience to shout out people for us to do. Somebody shouted, 'John Cleese,' and Michael jumped up and did his brilliant Basil Fawlty impression. Someone else shouted, 'Vera Duckworth from *Coronation Street*,' and Dustin jumped up and improvised an impression he had never done before. 'Eh, you all right, kid. I don't know where our Jack is.' The audience roared but Dustin didn't seem to know how to take the character further at that point and so I jumped up and said, 'Hello, Vera. It's me – Mavis.' Mavis Riley was the dithery lady who ran the Kabin with Rita Fairclough.

'Eh, are you all right, Mavis?' asked Dustin.

I said, 'I don't really know.'

The audience loved it and it seemed that a comedy double act was born. Russ generously allowed Vera and Mavis to have their own little slot in the show and it proved to be very successful. Michael Barrymore was also allowed to shine in the show and it was a springboard for his huge career.

Michael has had his troubles, as has been well documented, but in 1982 he was a funny and fun man to be with. One afternoon we were all allowed to leave rehearsals early, and like a bunch of naughty schoolchildren, Dustin, Michael, Sherrie and I headed to the nearest pub and proceeded to get very drunk. At about 5 p.m. we all piled on to the Tube, which was totally packed. Sat in the chair nearest the door was a stereotypical City gent wearing the striped trousers, black jacket and bowler hat. He was doing his best to ignore the drunken rabble in front of him as he worked intently on his *Times* crossword. Michael had the devil in him and just before we arrived at Leicester Square he went into a full-blown John Cleese-like rant. 'That's just about the type of philistine pig ignorance we've come to expect from you non-creative garbage. You sit there on your spotty behinds squeezing your blackheads with your Tony Jacklin golf clubs and your colour TV sets, and you don't give a tinker's cuss for the struggling artiste...' and on he went, as the astonished carriage full of commuters watched. Then, as we pulled into the station, he said, 'Right, matey, this is your stop.' He grabbed the poor bloke by his lapels and chucked him out. I can still see the man, bowler hat askew, hammering on the doors as the train pulled away. Dreadful behaviour but dreadfully funny.

Another time as we walked down Oxford Street he whacked an old lady over the head with a rolled-up newspaper and then, holding the paper like a microphone, said, 'Excuse me, madam, I'm from the BBC. What does it feel like to be hit over the head with a rolled-up newspaper?'

'Oh,' she said into the newspaper-cum-microphone, looking around for a camera, 'is that what it was? Am I really on telly?'

Dustin and I became firm friends before we became a double act. He and Russell loved to eat out and go to the theatre. I did too, but I had a family to think about and couldn't always afford to join them. He lived his life to the full and wanted his friends to share it with him, and it was sometimes hard to say no to him.

My dad came to London for a week's holiday. He'd only passed through twice before, once when he was in the navy and once when I received a letter from a big theatrical agent who had seen me on *Opportunity Knocks* and asked if I would come and see her. I wish I could remember which agent it was. All I remember is that she was a very glamorous older lady and her massive, elegantly furnished office was on Park Lane. We were like Billy Elliot and his dad as we travelled by train from Lime Street Station to London to meet her. We ate Wimpy hamburgers at Euston and got the Tube to swanky Mayfair. We sat and chatted with this lovely woman who said she had seen something in my performance and thought I should seriously consider going to drama school. We listened, thanked her, but on the way home decided that the club circuit was the better route to success. Every time I see that scene in *Billy Elliot* where he and his dad go to the Royal Ballet School, it makes me cry.

So, it was ten years later, he was back in London and our decision had led me to getting into a TV series. My dad came down for the last recording and we gave him a week to remember. While we were rehearsing, Dustin's partner, Tony, would take him round the tourist attractions of the big city. They walked everywhere and at the end of each day my dad would say, 'Had a bloody great time today, kid.' In the evenings we would go to the theatre or for something to eat. 'No foreign food for me. I'd rather have a steak.' He had an aversion to Chinese food, believing that rice couldn't be eaten with meat. 'You can't do that. Rice is a bloody pudding.' So it was steak most nights. He came to watch the recording and was thrilled and proud of me. He didn't have to run to the dressing room once. He got on the train back to Liverpool saying it was the best holiday he had ever had. Little did any of us suspect that it was to be his last.

Since my mum's death, five years earlier, I had become closer to my dad than I had been in my entire life. He was my travelling companion and road manager, and though I never really got to know him, we had achieved a kind of understanding of each other.

After my mum's death, though, my dad had lost interest in most things. He loved his family and was still interested in show business but he had lost the love of his life and he never fully recovered. Christmas and birthday cards were still signed, 'Mum and Dad' – quite a shock the first time one arrived – and he was simply waiting to be reunited with her. He talked passionately about an interview he had seen on TV: 'Parky had that Peter Cushing on the other night. He can't wait to be with his wife – he's just waiting to die.'

'But, Dad,' I would say, 'you've got everything to live for.'

'I know, kid. I love the bones of you all, but I just want to be with her.'

When the *Madhouse* recordings finished, I was home for a week or so before going on a theatre tour with Russ. The night before I left for Bournemouth, I was doing a one-nighter at the Police Club in Liverpool. I called my dad and said I'd pick him up at 7 p.m. Whenever he came with me he would sit in his chair with his coat on fifteen minutes before I arrived. I would beep the horn of the car and he would come out immediately. This time, though, when I called to let him know I was on my way, he sounded tired. 'Got a bit of a cold, kid. Don't think I'll come tonight. Call me next week when you're back.' I could hear in his voice that something was wrong, but I pushed the worry to the back of my mind, did the Police Club and headed off to Bournemouth the next day.

We were opening a nationwide tour at the Winter Gardens, the theatre where I had first worked with Jimmy Tarbuck four years earlier. I was staying with a friend, Tony Hardman, who had been the company manager on that show. On the Sunday morning Tony asked if I wanted to use the phone to call home – this was before the days of mobiles. Something made me say, 'No. I'll go to the theatre and call from there.' I don't know what it was but I felt that I had to make that phone call alone. At about 12.30 p.m. I arrived at the Winter Gardens and walked into the tiny public phonebox near the stage door. I dialled home and immediately got Lynne's voice. 'Les. Thank God you called. We've been trying to get in touch with you since the early hours. I'm sorry, love, I've got some bad news. Your dad died this morning.' I knew. I had avoided that call at Tony's because somehow I knew my dad had gone. But not only that, I hadn't given Lynne a contact number when I had left for Bournemouth. I didn't want to face the possibility of him dying. I had heard something in his voice that Friday that told me it was more serious than a cold and I had run away. He had had a massive heart attack, the first since the one induced by shifting that piano in 1969, and had been rushed to Broad Green Hospital. Our Ken had called Lynne in the early hours and thought she was holding out on him by not telling him where I was. The fact is, she didn't know. Typically, my dad had told them not to bother me. 'He's got that show with Russ Abbot and it's bloody important.' His family were at his bedside when he went. All except me.

After the phone call I came out into the sunshine in a state of shock and confusion. The first person I saw was Peter Sontar, the man who had given me the summer season with Tarby and who was producing the Russ Abbot tour. I told him my news and he, bless him, didn't know what to do other than take me to see Russ, who was staying at the Carlton Hotel on the seafront. Russ's reaction was similar. People very rarely know what to do with the bereaved. He called Mike Hughes, who managed Russ as well as me, and after a chat with Mike I agreed that there was little I could do by going home and my dad would have wanted me to carry on with the show. In the end it was my decision, but it is one I regret bitterly. People use that expression 'The show must go on' and so often work rather than face their grief. In hindsight, I think that going on that night and supposedly doing the show for my dad meant that I was still running away from my emotions and my responsibilities. I didn't learn, though. By hiding away and not allowing myself to grieve, I think I did untold damage to my emotional health. Once again, Les Dennis won over Leslie Heseltine and the result was that I went seriously off the rails. I missed both my parents, but it was my dad's death that would impact and resonate more deeply, probably because it was so sudden and I didn't have time to come to terms with him going.

The funeral was the following Tuesday, and relations with

my family remained polite but strained. They still, I think, thought that Lynne and I had ignored their calls for me to come home. We only stayed at the wake for an hour, as I had to leave to return to the tour, which was now in Wimbledon once again. I had an excuse to run away.

CHAPTER 13

Les and Dustin

Dustin and I were booked as ugly sisters to Russ's Buttons in *Cinderella* at the Bradford Alhambra. Dustin was in his element. He loved working with wigs and make-up and was more inventive than the wardrobe department. I hated dressing up and envied Russ his simple Buttons outfit. There is a scene where the sisters are getting ready to go to the ball and so, instead of trying on numerous comedy frocks, we did a spot where we were deciding who to go as. We threw quick-fire impressions at each other and it went down really well. There had never been an impressionist double act before and it looked like we were on to something. Dustin, though, was a big star and I was still, despite some TV success, an opening comic. Even on the bills it said, in huge letters, 'DUSTIN GEE,' and in tiny letters, 'Les Dennis.' So why on earth would someone as successful as Dustin want to give all that up and start a double act with me?

One day I got a phone call from Mike Hughes asking me to go in and see him. The night before I was due to go, Russ said,

'Oh, you're going to see Mike tomorrow, aren't you? He's got a parcel for me that I've been waiting weeks for. Will you pick it up for me?'

I said I would, and the next day went to see Mike, who told me that Dustin had called him. Because of his status, Dustin was on double my fee for the show but had decided that as he and I were doing the same work we should have parity of pay. He wanted to take a cut and give me a raise. It was such a generous gesture and so typical of his nature. I argued with Mike but he said Dustin had insisted. As I was leaving, I remembered I had to collect the parcel for Russ. Mike carefully handed me a box marked, 'Fragile.' 'Take great care with this. It's worth a lot of money and Russ is very excited about it,' he said.

I promised to guard it with my life and walked carefully to the car with it. I went home to Cromer before travelling to Bradford and, rather than risk it being stolen, took it into the house. Philip was a toddler so I put it on the highest shelf I could find. When I left for the theatre, I drove really slowly, keeping the parcel on the passenger seat and braking very carefully. At the theatre, I took extra care because of ice and snow, and at last delivered it to Russ's dressing room.

'Oh, great,' said Russ with excitement. 'It's here, everybody.'

Suddenly members of the cast and Basil Soper, our company manager, crowded into the room as Russ carefully started to open the box.

'What is it, Russ?' I asked curiously.

'It's a crystal mustard pot from Colman's of Norwich,' Basil said, and added, 'No ordinary mustard pot. It's a special edition, made to commemorate their centenary and was only issued to a handful of people. The Duke of Norfolk has one, as has the Princess of Wales, and Colman's have honoured Russ by sending him one.'

At that moment Russ pulled out of the tissue five or six

chunks of broken glass. I literally had to look away and back again because I couldn't believe my eyes. Russ's face fell and he simply said, 'Oh, dear.'

Dustin looked furious and turned and walked out of the room. I thought he was angry with me for being so irresponsible.

'But I guarded it with my life, Russ. Honestly,' I babbled.

'It's OK,' he said understandingly, and worst of all started to try and piece the pot back together.

I was absolutely mortified, but when I got to our dressing room, Dustin's face was like thunder.

'It's a wind-up,' he said.

'What?' I replied incredulously.

It turned out that Mike had got the parcel in the post and had told Russ it was broken, at which point Russ had decided to have some fun at my expense. Afterwards, I could laugh about it – just about. One thing is certain. Russ has never got me with a wind-up ever again! In my state of shock, I almost forgot to thank Dustin for the wage rise, and when I did, he simply said, 'Of course, love. Partners!'

Dustin was a brilliant partner, but I do remember him being a little bit jealous when I did a solo spot on *Live From Her Majesty's*. He wanted us to commit fully to the double act, but this was a prior booking. It would have been far less frightening to have worked with him. Doing a seven-minute stand-up spot on live telly is totally nerve-racking.

That Sunday afternoon, having finished my rehearsal, I was walking up the stairs to my dressing room (the lower on the bill you are, the further you have to travel) when a handsome, well-dressed, tanned gentleman came towards me. He thrust out an impeccably manicured hand and said, with a dazzlingly white smile, 'Les. Hi. Bob Monkhouse.' I nearly fell over. One of Britain's comedy greats was introducing himself to me as if I wouldn't know who he was. It was such an act of modesty and I was instantly charmed. People often said of Bob that his was a fake charm, that it was an act. Well, I experienced it that day, and many times after, and all I can say is that if it was an act, he's up there with de Niro. He was lovely, and his compliments about my abilities made my nerves disappear. Bob was a walking encyclopaedia of comedy and film, and was blessed with an eidetic memory. He stood there and chronicled my career to date and expounded his own theory of why he thought I would last in the business. 'Twenty years from now you'll still be around. You'll put on a few pounds, maybe lose a little hair, but the one thing you'll always have is charm. You are not the funniest comedian in the business but you've got loads of charm. Mark my words – you're a stayer.' I walked to my dressing room feeling a million dollars and that night, energised by his comments, I worked well and did a good spot. Tarby brought me off with the words 'Les Dennis, the pride of Woolton.'

That was the last solo spot I did for a while. Dustin and I teamed up and continued to support Russ on a huge nationwide theatre tour. It wasn't a traditional double act, with a straight man and a comic. We both got a chance to shine as individuals, but the thing the audiences liked was the sparring of impressions between us. Dustin was a tall man who could make a huge visual impact with the aid of a few props. A pair of teeth, hair flattened and a pair of spectacles on a chain and Larry Grayson would appear. We tried to put odd combinations together: Larry Grayson and Boy George, Billy Connolly and Bobby Ball, Rod Stewart and David Essex. Even Vera and Mavis were an unlikely duo because in *Coronation Street* they hardly ever met. We made them into friends and it worked. The seal of approval came when Thelma Barlow and Liz Dawn came to see us perform. Thelma told me, 'Sometimes I get a script and I think, I can't say that! That's not Mavis, that's Les Dennis!' One time in the show, for devilment, she actually used my catchphrase 'I don't really know.' I was absolutely thrilled.

At first I was uncomfortable about dressing in drag and would get embarrassed standing around in TV studios between takes. I don't know what my dad would have said. Whenever Benny Hill did drag, he would say, 'I don't bloody trust him,' and then, inexplicably, 'or scout masters.' I got used to the skirt, pearls and twin set, though, and one day walked calmly into the gents' at LWT, up to the urinal, hitched up my skirt and started to wee. The bloke next to me was horrified. 'No, you can't come in here. This is for men only,' he shouted. The sight of a woman standing at the urinal made him freak out and I hadn't even given it a thought!

One night after a show with Russ in Oxford, a slim young man with thinning blond hair came backstage and introduced himself. 'Hello. I'm John Bishop from the BBC. We're quite interested in doing a TV show with you two chaps. Perhaps we could get some supper.' Over a Chinese he told us the Beeb wanted to do four shows with us for Saturday-night screening, and if they went well, they would commission a further six. Initially I found John standoffish and brusque, but he would prove to be an excellent director and producer and a good, valued friend. We decided our stage name would be Les Dennis and Dustin Gee. I thought Dustin's name should be first, but again, in true generous spirit, he said it didn't sound as good. We recorded the four shows, which were simply called *The Laughter Show*, and guest-starred Roy Jay, Caroline Dennis and Hale and Pace.

The experiment worked and the BBC commissioned six more, as promised. This time the show was called *The Les and Dustin Laughter Show* and the BBC clearly upped the ante. We had better and more elaborate sets, a team of dancers under choreographer Jeff Thacker, a top musical director, Ken Jones, and a team of established comedy writers that included Neil Shand,

Barry Cryer, Minett and Leveson and one we'd never heard of, Gascoigne Abbey. It would be a couple of years before I would discover this mystery writer's identity. The name was a cryptic crossword clue – a 'coin' for a gas meter was a shilling or a bob, and an 'abbey' was a house where monks lived. Gascoigne Abbey – Bob Monkhouse.

We rehearsed at Acton Rehearsal Rooms, which everyone referred to as the Acton Hilton. It was a tall, ugly, concrete building on an industrial estate, where the BBC rehearsed everything from lavish drama serials to variety shows and sitcoms. Going for lunch in the canteen on the seventh floor was, the food aside, like being in the Ivy. I once sat on the next table to Dirk Bogarde and Lee Remick, who were happily tucking into the Beeb's less than fine cuisine. Another time, Liverpool comedian Greg Rogers, who was guesting on our show, was queuing next to Sir John Gielgud. The great actor tapped Greg on the shoulder and asked, 'Excuse me. Are you a comedian?'

Greg later told us in his broad Scouse accent, 'I thought he must have seen me on *The Comedians* but when I told him I was a comedian he said, "I thought so. All comedians have funny curly hair."' (Greg had a naff 1980s perm at the time!) He continued, 'If you had been an actor playing a Resistance man, you'd have neat short hair. But no, you're obviously a comedian. Do have a lovely lunch.' And with that the legend walked off, tray in hand.

As well as recording *The Laughter Show*, we continued to do live gigs and the odd guest spot on TV variety shows. One Sunday in 1984 we were booked on Tarby's *Live From Her Majesty's*, appearing alongside Howard Keel and Tommy Cooper. It was the first time I had seem Tommy since the week of my wedding to Lynne. At the rehearsals in the afternoon he typically had everyone in fits of laughter with a spot that was as funny as any I'd ever seen him do. David Bell, a brilliant and flamboyant producer who had huge success with the equally brilliant Stanley

Baxter, designed the show to look lavishly expensive – an open, modern set, vari lights and star cloths. For his spot, though, Tommy wanted old-fashioned red drapes because his routine needed it. He wore a huge cloak out of which he would produce various items – first small things, like a kettle, then medium-sized, like a fire hydrant, and finally a full set of ladders. The props guy was clearly feeding them through the curtains but that's what made it so hysterically funny. Apparently American audiences didn't get Tommy's humour. They'd watch and say, 'Oh, my God, he's got the trick wrong.' That was the point! David begrudgingly allowed Tommy to have the curtains, even though it spoilt the glitzy look of the show.

Showtime came and Dustin and I stood in the wings nervously waiting to go on – we had the unenviable job of following Tommy. Those live variety shows were both exciting and nerve-racking. Getting laughs from a packed theatre audience was intoxicating but there was always that fear that they wouldn't laugh or that you'd forget your lines. There was no chance to stop and say, 'Sorry. Can I do that again?' or for them to dub laughs where there weren't any. No problem for Tommy. He was going down an absolute storm. I still laugh when I remember him picking up a small chalkboard from his props table and showing the audience a lousy chalk drawing of a hedgehog and saying proudly, 'See that. I did that.' As they laughed at the rubbish etching, he said, 'No. Honestly, I did.' On a wave of laughter, he came to the cloak routine. We watched from the wings as one of the dancers walked on and placed the cloak round his shoulders. 'Thank you, love,' Tommy said. Before she had walked the few steps offstage, he stumbled and fell to the floor. She turned, surprised, then laughed and continued off. The audience laughed as well and so did we. The laughter was uncomfortable, though. What was Tommy doing? As well as Dustin and me, watching from the prompt corner were producer David Bell,

Tommy's PA, Mary Kay, and his son, Tommy Junior.

David asked, 'Is that a joke?'

'Yes,' said Mary uncertainly.

'No,' overruled Tommy Junior. 'My dad's got a bad back and if he fell like that he wouldn't be able to get up again.'

At that moment Tommy fell over on his side and seemed to be snoring.

David calmly said into the show relay-system, 'Cue music. Cue commercial break.' Alyn Ainsworth's orchestra fired into action and crew members ran on to the stage.

Somebody shouted, 'We've called the paramedics. We shouldn't move him until they arrive.'

Jimmy and David went into quiet conversation onstage as the warm-up man tried to entertain the confused audience. Dustin and I assumed the show would be stopped, the audience asked to leave quietly and the viewers at home shown some replacement programme. We couldn't believe it when David turned to us and said, 'The commercial break's about to end. Are you boys ready to go on?'

Tommy had, for dignity's sake, been moved gently behind the drapes and once again, that phrase 'The show must go on' was in my head. If Tommy hadn't used those heavy curtains, it couldn't have gone on. Seconds later the orchestra struck up the theme tune and a clearly shaken Jimmy Tarbuck walked onstage and said, 'Ladies and gentlemen, please welcome Les Dennis and...' He seemed to forget where he was and I had to shout, 'Dustin Gee.' 'Les Dennis and Dustin Gee,' Jimmy repeated, and on we went.

Our time onstage was a blur, but I do remember Dustin later saying that when he went to get his Robert Mitchum hat, he heard someone behind the curtain say, 'It's OK. He's been sick.' Any nerves we might have had were quickly forgotten. What was happening backstage was far more important and our job was to hold the fort.

That night felt like a huge turning point in our career and maybe in a phoenix-from-the-ashes kind of way, we captured some of the spirit of that great comic force. I don't mean in any way that we could ever be as good as him – he truly was one of the greats – but something did kick in from that point and our brief partnership was to be incredibly successful and meteoric. Tommy died later that evening in St Thomas's Hospital, and as we sat quietly discussing his genius with Lynne and Nina Mischoff, Dustin said something strange: 'That's the way I would like to go. I'd like to die with my boots on.' We should be careful what we wish for.

The success we had after that night was like a whirlwind but short-lived. We had two prime-time TV shows on consecutive nights. *Les and Dustin's Laughter Show* went out on a Saturday and *Go for It*, which also featured other impressionists Aiden J. Harvey, Alan Stewart and my great friend Bobby Davro, went out on a Sunday. When we weren't doing telly, we were doing cabaret and private engagements. We were booked by theatre promoter Derek Block to perform at his son's bar mitzvah at one of the big hotels on Park Lane. When we were backstage, a cool-looking black American guy came up to me and asked for a signed photograph. 'Certainly,' I said. 'Who shall I sign it to?'

'Benny King,' I thought I heard him say.

'OK, Benny. There you go.'

'No,' he said. 'Benny King.'

'That's what I've written.'

'No. Ben E. King.'

'OK. Sorry. Ben E...' Oh, my God, it was starting to dawn on me. 'There.'

'Much appreciated,' he said, and walked away on to the stage.

'Was that...?' I asked Dustin.

'Yes, you twat. That was *the* Ben E. King!'

Well, I didn't know the Drifters were on the bill.

One of the guests that evening was Ernie Wise, who came up to us after the show and said, 'Eric loves you guys. He can't be here but wanted me to let you know and to say keep up the good work.'

It was moments like this that made us realise how well we were doing. We were working so hard that we didn't have time to stop and think. The tabloid press started to refer to us as the 'new Morecambe and Wise', which is something they say about every new double act. We weren't anything like them; we were two impressionists for a start, but it was a great compliment.

We were spending so much time in London, Lynne and I decided to buy a small flat so that she and Philip could come and be with me at weekends rather than me jump on the sleeper train and spend two days at home wiped out. We found a lovely one in a converted Victorian house in St Margaret's, near Richmond. When I told Dustin about it, I mentioned that there was another one-bedroom flat available on the top floor. 'I'll have it,' he said.

'But, Dustin, you haven't even seen it.'

'Doesn't matter. It makes sense. We can travel to work together.' And he bought it.

That sounds flash, I know, but he wasn't. He still drove round in the old Rover he had had for years, and his home in Swinton was a modest two-up, two-down. He was prone to impulsive gestures, though, usually for other people rather than himself. He was right as well. It did make sense to travel together, particularly as getting him to work became my responsibility. He was a great creative force but time-keeping wasn't his strength. That was one of the things I had found hard about being in a double act. For years I had travelled around on my own only having to be responsible for myself. Suddenly I was having to make travel arrangements and work schedules for two, and his 'easy come, easy go' nature could be frustrating at times.

I was always more than happy to talk to people at the stage door and on the street, but Dustin encouraged fans into his personal space. I'd often get to the theatre to find two or three of his admirers in the dressing room. Little old ladies sat in my chair, telling him about their ailments, problems with their families and where they were going on holiday, while he sat there putting on his make-up in the mirror. It would get to the five-minute call and I would suggest to Dustin that perhaps they should leave. 'Oh, they're fine, love. They'll sit here quietly while we're on.'

He had one couple who were from Nottingham and their accents were really strong. When she said 'house' it sounded like 'arse'. She'd say to him, 'Dustin, you've got to come up my "arse".' We'd stifle giggles as she turned to her husband and asked, 'What is my "arse" like? Isn't it lovely and clean?'

'Spotless,' he'd reply.

'Are you going to come up my "arse", Dustin?'

He would reply, 'I might slip in if I am round that way!'

One night I was just going to bed in the flat when the phone rang. It was Dustin asking if I had any booze I could let him have. 'At this time of night? We've got rehearsals in the morning.'

'I know, love, but some people have turned up.'

'It's far too late. Tell them to go.'

'I can't do that – they've come miles.'

I searched out half a bottle of whisky I had in the cupboard and took it up to him. There in his living room was a dwarf, a couple who looked like they belonged on *The Jerry Springer Show*, with a scabby dog. 'You remember Mark from panto,' Dustin said.

'We thought we'd surprise him,' said Mark.

As the bloke from the couple was telling Dustin that he

should get out of the double act because he deserved to be in Hollywood, I bid them goodnight and whispered to Dustin, 'Good luck. Get them out as soon as you can.'

The next morning I called him to tell him we had half an hour before we had to leave and he whispered, 'They're still here.'

'What?' I shouted.

'Sssh. They wouldn't go. I'll see you in half an hour.'

As we left the building, the couple were walking their dog. As it lifted its leg and pissed over the wheel of Dustin's car, the Jerry Springer bloke shouted after him, 'What time will you be home, Dustin?'

'About four o'clock,' he replied. As I threw him a look, he whispered, 'It's OK. Roger'll get rid of them.'

When we had done panto at the Grand Theatre in Wolverhampton (*Snow White and the Seven Dwarfs* obviously), we had assigned a personal assistant, Roger Edwards, to help us. Roger looks incredibly like a smaller version of Robin Williams and proved to be so good and such great company he would continue to work for Dustin and me as our tour manager and PA. Then he worked on every one of the *Family Fortunes* that I did for sixteen years and was associate producer on one of the Christmas shows. He is a very positive person who now does many varied things, from work for the Samaritans to teaching guitar in prisons. His enthusiasm is highly infectious and I consider him to be one of my closest friends. He has been there for me through the good and bad times.

By spring 1985 Dustin and I were at the peak of our success. We had done two high-rating series for the BBC and had signed for another, which was to be recorded in the autumn. We were to headline for twenty weeks at the North Pier Theatre for the summer season, and we had been honoured with a spot on *The Royal Variety Performance*, performing in front of Prince Charles,

Princess Diana and the Queen Mother. When we were rehearsing for that spot, Dustin and I fell out. We had never fallen out before, and would only do so once more in the whole time we knew each other. We were working out the structure of our seven-minute routine and Dustin said, 'I'll do Robert Mitchum of course.'

It was a huge crowd-pleaser when he walked forward, cigarette in mouth, and told the audience he couldn't do the voice. Then he would take the cigarette, throw it up into the flies and, as it spiralled down, catch it in his mouth. It was a brilliant moment – when it worked! At least two out of five times he would miss it and there was an awkward silence as he picked it up and tried again. Fine if you are doing an hour's spot, because you could keep going until you got it right, but my argument was that we should keep the seven minutes as tight as possible and there wasn't room for the trick. He went off in a huff and didn't speak to me for a couple of days. Eventually he called me and said, 'Sorry, love. You're absolutely right. I won't do it.' On the night, when it got to that point, he looked at me mischievously and did it. He missed!

Meeting the Royal Family afterwards was amazing. The Queen Mother said the same thing to everyone: 'Such fun. Didn't we have such fun.' I can't remember what Charles said, but Diana said, 'For one moment I thought one of you was going to do my husband.'

Dustin said, 'No, ma'am, but Suzanne Danielle' – who was standing in the line behind us – 'does a great one of you.' Typical of him to include someone else in his moment and also break protocol by introducing her without being asked.

I remember commenting to Dustin afterwards that Princess Diana was beautiful but had a haunted look in her eyes. Only later would we learn how very unhappy she had been at that time.

Cracks were beginning to show in my own marriage. Since my dad's death I had thrown myself into my work and had put my family life on to the back burner. When Lynne suggested we should have more holidays together, I would argue that Dustin and I needed to establish ourselves properly and that there would be time to enjoy our success in a year or two. Philip's birthday is 22 December, so although I was always there in the morning (I would drive home from anywhere to make sure I was), I would have to be in the theatre for a panto matinée by 1 p.m. and would miss most of his parties. Christmas Day was a day off but there was no chance of really enjoying it as there were two shows on Boxing Day. One year Mike wanted a meeting with Dustin and me to discuss our TV commitments. Our only other day off was New Year's Day, and when I should have been home relaxing with my family, we were instead catching a train from Southampton to sit in a hotel lounge in London with our manager. When you're young, you are often so driven by ambitions that you can lose sight of the reasons you are working so hard to achieve them. I began to lose touch with my wife and son in the same way that I had done with my family. Things were too heady and exciting, though, for me to notice what was happening.

CHAPTER 14

Kiss Me Quick

In early 1985, together with John Bishop, Dustin and I devised a show for Blackpool North Pier and under John's expert direction we opened at the end of May. On the opening night the show couldn't have been going better. We got to our dressing room at the interval feeling excited and eager to do the second half, which featured a quick-change *Coronation Street* routine and involved us doing most of the cast between us. Dustin, though, suddenly looked in pain and complained of breathing problems. The theatre doctor was called immediately and told us he had had a heart attack and must go straight to hospital. Three years earlier, before we had teamed up, Dustin had had a heart scare and been diagnosed with cardiomyopathy, which is an enlarged heart muscle. He had ignored the advice to slow down and had instead pursued the success he had waited his whole career to achieve. That night in Blackpool he did the same again. He looked the doctor squarely in the eye and said, 'No, I am finishing the show first.'

'Dustin,' I said, 'it's your health. You have to go now.'

'No, love. I will go when the curtain falls, not before. This is too important to me.'

Reluctantly the doctor allowed him to go on and arranged for an ambulance to be driven the quarter-mile to the theatre to wait until the show had ended.

He was brilliant in that second half, relishing each laugh that crashed towards us over the footlights, harder than the waves that were crashing against the pier below us. His performance in the *Coronation Street* routine was a tour de force and I did my best to keep up. Flamboyant quick changes from Vera to Bet Lynch would have tested the stamina of a fit man, but here was a man who had just had a heart attack growing in energy simply with the aid of Dr Footlights. As the curtain fell and before the audience of VIPs and dignitaries had had time to leave the theatre, Dustin was whisked away in the ambulance. 'That was fantastic, love. I feel great – the doctors got it wrong. I'll be back tomorrow.'

Roger, our PA, went with him to the hospital and I had to go to the after-show party and pretend nothing was wrong. 'Where's Dustin?' people wanted to know.

'He's feeling a little unwell and sends his apologies.'

As soon as it was decent to leave, Lynne and I headed off to see how he was doing. He was sitting up in bed when we arrived but his face was like thunder. 'It is a heart attack and I'm going to be out for weeks. Looks like we will have to postpone the show.'

'Don't worry,' I said. 'You'll be back fitter and better than ever.' I left the hospital feeling very doubtful.

It was decided by the management that the show couldn't close and that night I went on alone but in the guest-star spot. Vince Hill, who usually filled that spot, did the second half and we did OK. The next night I moved back up to the top of the bill, and for three weeks we carried on while Dustin recovered. The

North Pier is a long season and doesn't really kick in until the schools break up in July, so houses were less than full. One night, about an hour after the show had finished, the pier caught fire and it was only Vince Hill who saved it from being burnt to the ground. He raised the alarm, braved the smoke and ran back into the theatre as the fire brigade arrived. The next day the headlines in the evening gazette labelled him a hero. 'The thing is,' he said to me later, 'I only went back in to save my stage suits!'

Dustin's attack was mild enough for him to rejoin the show. He came back on his birthday, 24 June, although he wasn't quite the force of energy he had been. He was, I think, insecure about the fact that I had been able to carry on alone, and one night implied that the houses were bad because of poor word of mouth. I was really angry because we had worked our arses off to prevent the show from being axed. We fell out for the second and last time. Instead of it being a huge row where we fought and cleared the air, Dustin gave me the silent treatment. It reminded me of the rows I watched my mum and dad having when I was a kid. Well, they do say a double act is like a marriage. Roger became our go-between: 'Dustin says that line isn't getting a laugh, so it should be cut.'

We'd go onstage and make an audience laugh but Dustin wouldn't be looking at me. I couldn't bear it and after a week I decided we would have to sort it out or split at the end of the season. One night before the show I told him how I felt and he broke down and wept. He *had* been jealous of me going it alone but also felt that I wasn't socialising with him after the show. I was living at home and travelling the seventy miles or so to Liverpool every night so that I could be with my family. Once he realised that was the reason and that I wasn't being distant, he was fine. The show improved and by high season we were arriving at the theatre to signs saying, 'House full.'

Dustin's health seemed fine, even though he completely ignored the medics' advice to stop smoking and change his diet. It was suggested to me that I should report back if he wasn't behaving, but I refused to be his nanny. I would sometimes come into the room and he would quickly wave smoke away and hide the cigarette he was smoking. 'Dustin, I'm not your mum. You know the consequences of what you're doing. You should pack it in, but I can't make you.' If it would have done any good, I'd have been harder on him, but he was someone who wouldn't be told. He lived his life to the full and was more interested in a good time than a long time. One of my enduring memories of him is when he was being told to do something and he would hold his hand up flamboyantly and say, with a huge smile on his face, 'Fuck 'em.'

Towards the end of the season, our schedule got tougher rather than easier. For three weeks we would do location filming for *The Laughter Show* and then two shows a night. A typical day would start at 6 a.m. when we were driven to Lancaster to film a medieval mini-series (rather like the mini-films the Two Ronnies did). We would wrap at 4 p.m., be driven by fast car to Blackpool, jump in a golf cart at the end of the pier to be taken to the theatre, arrive with the audience, run in, shower, change and walk onstage for the first show. We finished at 11 p.m. and headed back to the hotel before doing it all again the next day.

Filming was great fun. One day we filmed a sketch in Blackpool town centre and Dustin was dressed as a Salvation Army officer. A little old lady thought he was real and came up and put a coin in his tin. 'I always give,' she said, smiling. 'Usually to the lady on Talbot Street.'

'I know who you mean,' replied Dustin. 'Don't have anything to do with her – she's a right cow.'

That poor old lady's face. It must have put her off the Sally Army for life.

Another time we were across the river from the crew when it started to rain. 'It's just a shower,' John Bishop shouted. 'Shelter under that tree and we'll have tea. We'll be back soon.'

As we sheltered, it began to thunder. 'Shit,' Dustin said, 'it's thundering, we are under a tree, and I've got grips in my hair.'

'You've got grips in,' I said, panic suddenly filling my voice as it dawned on me. 'I've got a suit of armour on!'

He was always great company, but sometimes outrageous. Lynne and I had a party at Cromer that went on into the early hours. As always, there was one couple who would not leave. They were parents of a child at Philip's school and stood there in our kitchen talking education and basically boring the pants off us. Dustin started playing with the fridge magnets and I turned round to see that he had written, from the letters that were available, 'T_ke yo_r hu_band h_me,' on the fridge door. They didn't take the hint, though.

One of Dustin's best impressions was Cilla Black. It was a huge over-the-top parody of her that she loved. Cilla says that she never said 'lorra, lorra laughs' until she got it from him. In a red wig, oversized teeth and a flowing green gown he would warble 'Surprise, Surprise'.

In another of our weird pairings, I would chat to him as Prince Charles and as he did a twirl, the audience would catch sight of his undies because the back of the gown wasn't fastened up. It would get a big laugh but one night it got a huge laugh. Little did I know that he had taken off his underpants so that the audience caught a glimpse of his bare arse. We kept it in!

When you are doing summer season, holidaymakers stop you in the street all the time. You're part of their holiday and they want your autograph and to have their picture taken with you. Although it's lovely to be complimented, it does mean getting down the street can take for ever. Someone will come up to you in a supermarket and say, 'What are you doing here?'

'My shopping, same as you.'

'Don't you have someone to do that for you?' they'll usually ask, taking a glance at your shopping trolley.

That's when you're thankful you've hidden the Odour Eaters at the bottom!

One day Dustin was walking purposefully down the prom (the faster you walk, the later it is before people realise it's you) when a woman whacked him on the head with her umbrella. He turned round and she said to her husband, 'See, told you it was him!'

On another occasion we came out of the theatre and as we got to the top of the pier, two girls asked shyly if they could have a photo. 'Of course,' we replied, and stood either side of them, looking for the camera. 'Who's going to take it?' we asked.

They looked embarrassed and said, 'No, can you take a photo of us?'

Our turn to look embarrassed!

The girls at the box office would always talk to us as we arrived at the pier and tell us some of the comments they had had from the people booking for the show. Two elderly ladies had come in one day and asked for tickets to the Les Dawson and Dustin Hoffman show. Wow, now there's a double act I'd like to see.

The Blackpool illuminations mean that the season goes on into the autumn and it was near enough Bonfire Night when we finished and relocated to London to do the studio shows for the BBC. All those weeks of working together night in, night out had honed and perfected our double act, so working in front of a TV audience had become much more natural for us. We were on a roll that autumn and it didn't seem like work. There were, however, a few telltale signs that Dustin's health was not as good as it should be. One day, while we were rehearsing a sketch, he literally fell asleep in the middle of it. 'Shall we wake him?' Roger

Mum and Dad at the Majestic Club where they dated.

Mum, our Marg and either Roddy or me – no one knows for sure!

A happy childhood. Ken and I are in the blue shirts with our Mandy, the baby, in between cousins Neil and Brian. Obviously matching shirts were a big thing back in the 1950s.

Mandy, Ken and me outside our house in Thornton Road, Childwall, with the mint growing in abundance in the foreground, and then (below) in the same spot over thirty years later.

In the dining hall at Butlins Pwllheli. Dad, Mum, Mandy and my friend Stephen Gardner are sat opposite me and my cousin Irene. Ken was probably still splashing around in the boating lake.

A family of performers: Mum came third in the Glamorous Grandma competition while I won first prize in the *People* National Talent competition for my skit of Jerry Lewis.

My first taste of the fame drug: cast alongside Clive Barker (middle) and Nick Suckley (right) in the school production of *Dry Rot*.

Rex Features

'Ooo Betty': doing Frank Spencer on *New Faces* in 1973.

Me and my best man, Hems de Winter. He is six foot seven so I had to stand on the step, but I didn't realise the photographer would show that!

With Lynne on our wedding night at the Shakey. I was supporting Tommy Cooper, so all our guests came to watch me work!

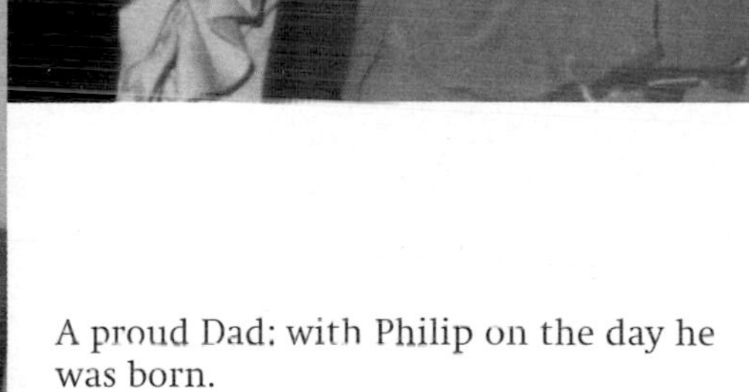

A proud Dad: with Philip on the day he was born.

Thames Television

With the big red book for my appearance on *This Is Your Life* with Philip to my right. It was a very moving experience and there were contributions from Jim Bowen, Ken Dodd, Liz Dawn and Denis Law. I just wish Dustin and my parents could have been there.

Celebrating twenty-one years of *Family Fortunes*. Roger, trying to upstage me, is between the 2 and the 1.

ITV/Carlton

Oh, the irony. Playing the cheated husband Amos Hart in *Chicago*.

Catherine Ashmore

The day we didn't go to San Diego – just check out the body language!

Standing outside the chapel in Vegas after renewing our wedding vows. (From left to right) Andy G, Amanda's mum Judith, me, Amanda, and friends Jess Taylor and Judith Barker.

LA to Vegas: Phil and I driving across the Mojave Desert.

PA Photos

With Barry McGuigan and Bob Mortimer ahead of our boxing match for Sport Relief.

Going into the *Big Brother* house. Not one of my wisest moves.

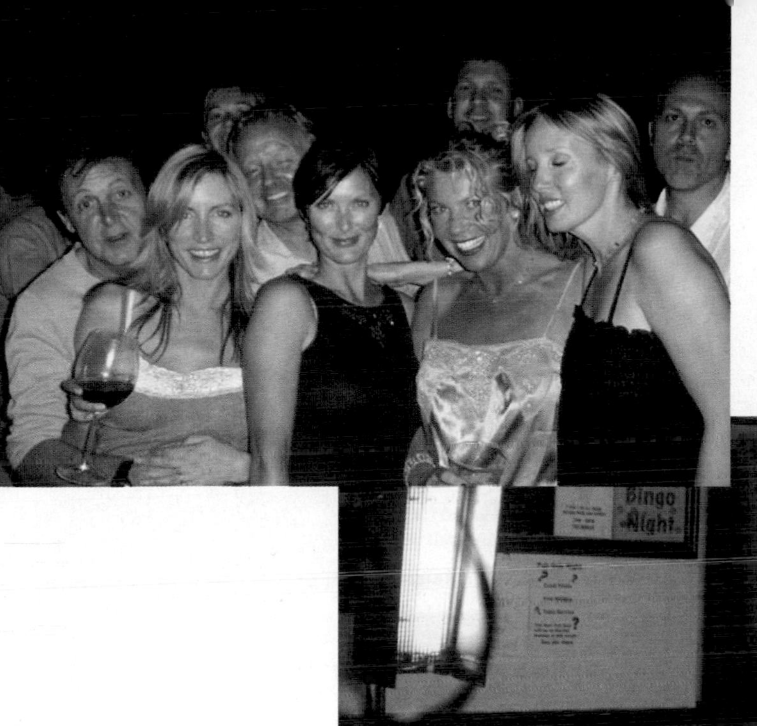

The magical night that Jack Benson (far right) surprised me with at Kenwood, where I met Paul McCartney and Heather Mills.

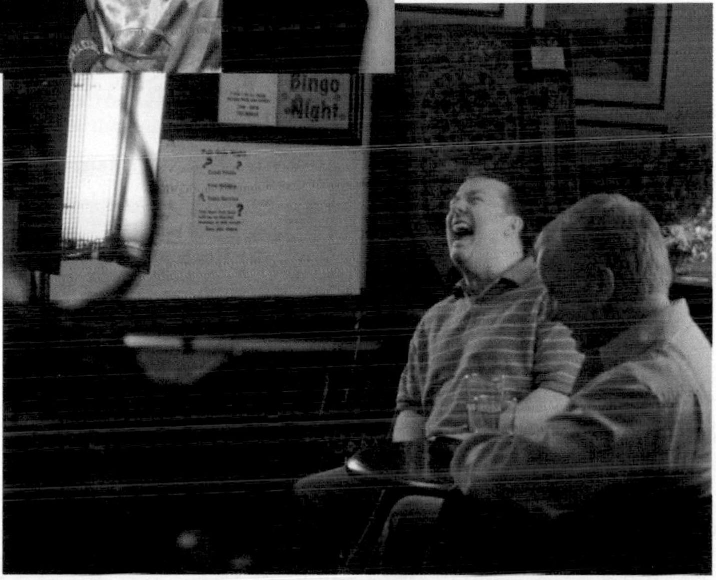

Me and Ricky enjoying a laugh between takes of *Extras.*

Rich Hardcastle © Ricky Gervais and Stephen Merchant 2006

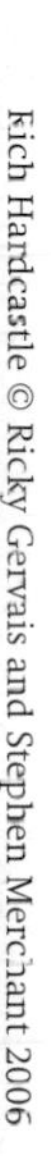

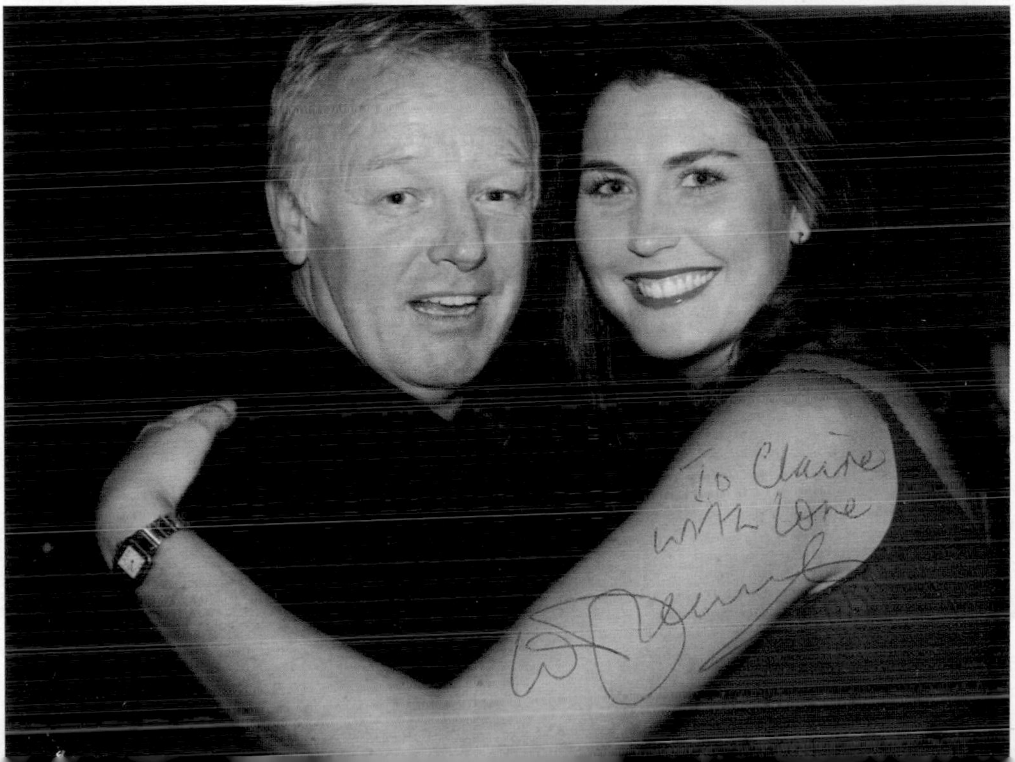

The first photo of me and Claire with my signature scrawled across it. Luckily it didn't put her off!

As Nick Chase, the disillusioned writer, ranting against today's celebrity-obsessed culture, in *Marlon Brando's Corset*.

asked, but John, our director, said, 'No, let him rest.'

One evening Roger had got to Dustin's flat to find he wasn't there and had instinctively driven to Hillingdon Hospital in Richmond, where he found him. He had had a twinge, he said, and had taken himself to A&E. The BBC doctor had been called by the time I got there and had declared him fit but tired. 'Maybe we should postpone the shows,' I suggested, but he was adamant he wanted to continue. 'Well, going straight into panto seems madness,' I said. Again, he fought, but agreed to Mike and John's request for a full and thorough check-up with a Harley Street specialist.

The doctor told him he was fine and fit enough for the gruelling twice-daily schedule of panto in Southport and that he would put it in writing. In hindsight, it was madness for him to continue when his health was at risk, but Dustin had waited a long time for this success. Twenty-odd years of slogging up and down the country doing clubs had led him at last to being on TV weekly and headlining in a double act that was being tipped to reach the same heights as the Two Ronnies and Morecambe and Wise. He wasn't going to let that go easily. I too had waited a long time, but my sacrifice wasn't my health. It was instead the love and affection of my family. Things were still tense between me and my siblings, and I was neglecting my wife and son. Nobody could tell either of us, though, and we continued on our path to success, no matter the price.

We opened in *Cinderella* at the Southport Theatre in early December 1985 to packed houses and good reviews. Typically Dustin had made it even harder for himself and for me. He had suggested to the management that we could play both the ugly sisters and the broker's men. It was a ludicrous idea that meant changing in and out of make-up and costumes on every exit. The uglies have enough changes as it is, so to be wiping off and reapplying make-up all the time was an extra hassle. The promoters of course were thrilled – playing double roles meant they wouldn't have to book another two actors. These days the broker's men are cut from the show to save money.

Dustin equally loved it, though it was as if he knew he was on borrowed time. He wanted to pack as much in as he could, and the same went for his social life. Again I had been asked to be his nanny and again I had refused. I would tell him what I thought but he would accuse me of nagging and trying to spoil his fun.

One night he was in a dilemma. 'I'm on a diet, love, but I really fancy a steak. Roger, would you nip to the chemist for me?' He sent him out to buy some Slendertone pads, those things that pass on mild electric shocks to your stomach muscles. We sat in a restaurant between shows and after every mouthful of his juicy steak he would turn up the current. 'Ow! This steak is delicious. Ow! And I'm losing weight. Ow!'

On another occasion, we were on the next table to Alan Hansen and Kenny Dalglish, who had brought their kids to the matinée. 'Great show, boys,' Kenny said.

Later Dustin said, 'See, love, it's all worth it.'

On the last Saturday of 1985, the first of the third series of *The Laughter Show* went out on BBC1. Dustin was thrilled by the reaction from the public and critics alike. He was particularly pleased with Hilary Kingston's comment, 'Welcome back, boys.'

'I think 1986 is going to be our year, love,' Dustin said.

New Year's Eve arrived, and after the evening show I headed off to spend it with Lynne, Philip, Molly and Ron. Dustin said he was going to have a quiet one with some of the cast. The next day I arrived and as soon as I saw him I knew he had been up for most of the night. He was pale and drawn with eyes that looked like, to quote Michael Caine in *Get Carter*, piss holes in the snow. Our dressing rooms were adjoining and had a screen that could be pulled across for privacy. It was always open, though, and as we both shaved that day, he was telling me about his night. 'You know what I'm like, love, once I start on the champagne. I had a couple of St Rémys as well. I know I shouldn't.' Brandy is a stimulant and the worst thing you can have if you have a heart condition.

I loved him for his honesty, and as I've said, it wasn't my job to be his keeper. As we carried on shaving and he told me more, I was listening but was also concentrating hard on not cutting myself (I hadn't had the earliest of nights either) and so wasn't saying much back to him. Suddenly he popped his head round the screen, face covered in shaving cream and said, 'Oh, for a moment I thought I was all alone there.' Maybe because of what happened later that day, I remember feeling it was a poignant and spooky moment. He had felt for that second that there was nobody there for him.

The moment passed, as did the hangovers, and we got on and did the matinée. We went for tea between shows, and in his typical quirky mode, he was choosing his holiday destination. He had a top hat he had borrowed from wardrobe and was cutting up pieces of paper, writing on them, folding them and throwing them in. 'What are you doing?' I asked, as he gave the top hat a shake.

'Can't decide where to go on holiday, so I've written various destinations from Cleethorpes to Thailand and whichever I pick out is where I'll go.'

'What if you get Cleethorpes?'

'I'll go. Could be worse – I've put Dartford in.' He picked out Bali but sadly he would never see it.

In the evening performance things were going well. We'd done our opening routine, finishing with a gutsy performance of Madonna's 'Material Girl', and had got the appropriate boos when we were unkind to Cinderella. We changed into broker's men, did their opening, then changed back into ugly sisters for the hunt scene. We finished it and walked off into the wings. Dustin was laughing and joking, and was still animated when we reached the dressing room and started to change for the next scene. He removed his wig and costume but still had his ugly sister make-up on as he turned to me, clutched his left arm and simply said, 'I think I'm dying.' He fell to the floor and his face took on a grotesque look, heightened by the make-up, and his eyes rolled back in his head. 'Basil,' I shouted. 'Quick!' Basil Soper, our company manager, ran in and immediately gave him mouth to mouth. Roger ran to call an ambulance as I stood there with tears pricking my eyes.

The paramedics soon arrived and Dustin was taken immediately to the Victoria Hospital. As the audience were being told the show wouldn't continue, I was jumping into my car and following the ambulance. By the time we were allowed to see him he was attached to a cardio machine and drip and, thankfully, the ugly sister make-up had been wiped from his sleeping face. The prognosis was not good. His heart had stopped twenty-one times in the first hour and he was now in a coma. Doctors feared that if he survived he would probably suffer brain damage. Roger and I stood at his bedside willing him to fight. He could definitely hear us and raised a finger in response. It reminded me of his 'fuck 'em' gesture.

The next day the press were constantly on to our agents and management and so a full press conference was arranged. It was my first real experience of the paparazzi. Until then, although we were doing well enough to get media attention, we weren't front-page news. It was only 2 January, so, with little news around, there was a huge turnout and I faced the bank of photographers and journalists assembled at the Victoria Hotel. I have a habit of scratching my nose as I talk and the first time I did it every camera flashed simultaneously. They were, of course, looking for the shot in which I showed signs of emotion.

Very difficult not to when you're asked questions like 'Do you think he's going to die?' and 'How long's he got left – hours, days?' As I left to go back to the hospital, I even got a request from the *Guardian* to write his obituary. I politely declined. There were TV crews and journalists camped outside the hospital, so every time we went to see him we had to go in the back entrance and up and down the fire stairs. A journalist on *Granada Reports* was doing his to-camera piece saying they were waiting for my arrival, while in the background what looked like two burglars scaled a wall of the hospital. The burglars were in fact me and Roger climbing the fire escape. The journalist didn't even notice.

Our friends Cliff and Barb looked after Philip, and Lynne was by my side constantly. When we weren't with Dustin, his mum, Dot, his sister, Marjory and her partner, Mary, were there. On one of those occasions, at 8 a.m. on 3 January, he woke while they were at his bedside and, despite fears of brain damage, sat up, had a cup of tea and asked for some ice cream. Marjory said he was quite chatty but kept apologising for not having his watch on. Maybe he was worried that he was running out of time. He slipped back into a deep sleep before we got there and died at 12.45 p.m. It was sweet that the last people he spoke to were his family.

I couldn't cry at first, though deep down I was of course devastated by his death. I think I was in denial and refused to believe he had gone. That night his death was reported on the nine o'clock news and the floodgates opened. The short time we had been together had been heady and exciting but we were working so hard we hadn't had time to realise how big we were becoming. He would have been chuffed that he had made the national news, and just as he had requested, when he had witnessed Tommy Cooper's death less than two years before, he had died with his boots on! At just forty-three years old, it was, though, far too early to achieve his curious wish.

The nine o'clock news had barely finished when the phone rang. It was Mike and I had never heard him so emotional. He was upset that Dustin had died but also bothered about comments he had heard implying that he had worked him to death. I assured him that Dustin only did what he wanted to do and that he wouldn't have been able to stop him. Before he hung up, through the tears he said he wouldn't be at the theatre for the performance the next day. I came off the phone shell-shocked. I knew that at some point we would have to reopen, but I thought that as a mark of respect for Dustin and compassion for the grieving cast, we would at least have the weekend. But no, the management had decided that *Cinderella* would reopen the next day. Southport Theatre is council-run and relies heavily on panto receipts for its annual revenue. Also, a large cast would have found themselves unexpectedly out of work and members of the public who had bought tickets for the next month or so would be left disappointed. While I had been at Dustin's bedside, a search had been conducted to find a replacement for him. Jim Bowen, thinking he would be standing in for Dustin while he recovered, found himself in the unenviable position of stepping into a dead man's shoes.

Once again I had to decide whether or not to continue in a show at a time when I was still grieving. Dustin was not just a business partner. He was one of the finest men I had ever met and one of my best friends. I made, I think, the wrong decision for my emotional health. At nine o'clock on that Saturday morning I was back in the theatre rehearsing scenes with Jim that I had done only days before with Dustin. Watching him walk on and offstage in the same costumes was eerie and difficult. Only Jim's compassion and humour got us through that day. I know the show had to go on: that was a fact of life. The thing is, though, *my* show didn't have to go on. I should have dug my heels in and insisted that they also found a replacement for me.

Instead, I once again buried my grief and went onstage to make people laugh at a time when I was dying inside. Mike Hughes stayed home that day, choosing to send Tony Birmingham as his representative. It is only in writing this that I realise that I'm still disappointed in him for not being there to support us. There was a sign outside the theatre saying, 'The show continues as a tribute to Dustin Gee.' No, the show continued because of cold, hard economic reality.

Dustin's funeral was held at St Oswald's Church, Fulford, York, on 9 January and there was an extraordinarily large turnout. From Sir John Birt to the Krankies, people came from everywhere to pay their respects to this gentle, loving and supremely talented man. Liz Dawn's flower tribute read, in true Vera style, 'Eh, kid...miss you. God bless.' Dustin's family showed great dignity as press photographers clambered to get shots of them in their grief.

After the cremation there was a drinks reception, but we couldn't even stay and celebrate his life with his family. We had to return for the evening show. The theatre wouldn't even cancel that. I realise that I am writing with a great deal of resentment and anger, but the person I am most angry with is myself. All I had to do was say, 'No, I refuse to go on.' But if I hadn't done it on the nights my mum and dad had died, why would I have done it this time? One thing is certain: I won't ever do it again. I have learnt my lesson, though it was a hard one to learn.

We got through the next few weeks, largely thanks to Jim Bowen's energy, and on the last night Roger and I packed Dustin's large yellow props case for the last time. I drove away from Southport with mixed emotions, glad to leave the show but desperately sad to leave behind the memories of a truly lovely and deeply funny man.

CHAPTER 15

Family Fortunes

Despite press speculation that I might suffer professionally and fade from view, my career went from strength to strength. The BBC commissioned *The Les Dennis Laughter Show*, I continued to guest on *The Russ Abbot Show*, and Tony Wolfe at ITV offered me *Family Fortunes*. When Mike first suggested it, I wasn't too keen on the idea. The show had been a huge success for Bob Monkhouse but had not really suited its second host, Max Bygraves. I had no experience of working directly with the public and was unsure that I had the makings of a game show host. I almost turned it down. Thank God I didn't! I would end up hosting the show for sixteen years and it would prove to be my biggest success.

It is, I think, one of the best games ever devised. The landscape has since changed considerably, with shows like *Who Wants to Be a Millionaire?* and *Deal or No Deal* using drama and tension, expertly delivered by Chris Tarrant and Noel Edmonds, and offering huge cash prizes to hook audiences. Even in 2002, my last year, *Family Fortunes* gave away no more than £5,000 and a car or a holiday. The success of the show was based on that silly little survey, 'We asked a hundred people...'

I am constantly asked, 'Did you really survey a hundred people?' and the answer is, yes, we did! In a manner of speaking, we did it by recycling: when contestants came in to play, we would give them question forms to fill in. We would then save their answers for the next series the following year. That way, we were sure of getting a good cross-section from around Britain. If we had only gone out in London, for instance, and asked, 'Name a famous river,' most people would have said, 'The Thames.' Of course, it could be argued that our contestants were more likely to give obscure and random answers. Indeed, that is the other question I am most asked: 'Where did you get those families from?' and the answer is, we auditioned them. More than six thousand families applied and Roger and contestant researcher, Denise Kelly, would travel all over Britain and play the game with them. The best were re-auditioned and would come to the studios in Birmingham, and later Nottingham, to record the show. Like most game shows, we recorded the whole series in about two to three weeks, doing two or three shows a day in front of the same studio audience. That's why Bruce Forsyth would always get a huge laugh on *Play Your Cards Right* when he said, 'You're so much nicer than the audience we had last week!'

Sometimes it seemed like Groundhog Day. Breakfast at the hotel with Roger and writers Colin Edmonds and Mike Coleman would be followed by a production meeting with the show's producer, Denis Liddington. Next we'd meet the families, rehearse in the afternoon and tape the shows in the evening. Then it was back to the hotel, sleep and do it all over again. It was a great show to do, and although at first I tried too hard to be funny, I quickly realised that the humour should and, indeed did, come organically from the silly answers the contestants gave. When it was announced that I was to be the new host, I got a call from Bob Monkhouse congratulating me. 'Be yourself,' he said, 'and if you get a random ludicrous answer, just smile and look into camera. Sometimes it's worth a thousand quips.' It was great advice and I really appreciated the call. When Vernon Kay hosted a new series of *All Star Family Fortunes* in 2006, I took Bob's lead and called to wish him luck. It felt like passing on the baton.

Some of the answers we got over the years were hilarious. 'Name a popular way of cooking fish,' I asked one bloke.

'Cod,' he said.

'Good answer. I often have my fish "codded". Large plaice, please, and could you cod it for me?'

Then there was 'Name somewhere you might stand in a queue.'

'At the front.'

'Good answer.'

'Name a job requiring a torch,' I asked a bloke from Liverpool.

'A burglar,' was his reply.

I said to his wife, 'Name something, other than doors, that you open.'

'Your bowels, Les.'

The hardest job for me was not to laugh. Denis, our producer, told me to encourage them, tell them it was a good answer.

'Name a popular TV soap.' I expected '*Coronation Street*' or '*EastEnders*' but got 'Dove'.

'Name a number you have to memorise.' Easy, I thought. He'll say, 'Phone,' or, 'Pin number.' He didn't. He said, 'Seven.'

Sometimes the answers were clever. 'Name a bird with a long neck.'

'Naomi Campbell!'

And sometimes they were just plain mad. In the Big Money Game I asked a guy to name a kind of ache. 'Headache' would have won him the car but he said, 'Fillet of Fish'! Was he thinking 'hake' instead of 'ache'?

'Name a famous Arthur.' The guy said, 'Shakespeare.' To be fair, I think he thought I said 'author'.

The weirdest answer I ever got, though, was to the question 'Name something you associate with Dracula.' The young lad who was first to answer, should have said, 'Garlic,' 'Teeth,' or, 'Vampire,' but instead confidently hit his buzzer and said, 'Bob Monkhouse.' To this day I have no idea why.

I remember some of the bizarre answers that Max Bygraves got when he hosted the show. He asked a sweet old lady to give a slang name for money. 'Oh, yes,' she said innocently. 'Bitch.'

'Sorry,' Max said, looking puzzled. 'Bitch – a slang name for money?'

She laughed her genteel laugh and said, 'Oh, I so beg your pardon. I thought you said, "Mummy."'

I dread to think what was going on in her little middle England family.

Then there was the family who, going into the second round of Big Money, only needed thirty-four points to win. Playing last was the dad. He came to the microphone, and Max reminded him of the rules and told him that thirty-four points would secure the Big Money. The first question was 'Name something you take to the beach.'

The bloke looked at Max and said confidently, 'Turkey.'

Max looked confused but like a true pro went on to question two. 'Name a kitchen utensil.'

Again, the same answer: 'Turkey.'

This time Max couldn't hide his laughter. Question three was 'Name a bird you cook at Christmas.'

'Turkey,' he answered again, and the audience burst into spontaneous applause. He had screwed up the game, though, and failed to win the money. The evil looks his family gave him as Max, hardly hiding his laughter, commiserated with him, were priceless. Mind you, they'd all been as bad. In an earlier question 'Name a famous Irishman', the first contestant had answered 'Disraeli'. The next said 'Tom O'Connor', the next 'Des O'Connor' and the next came up with 'Shuey McFee'. To huge roars of laughter from the audience, the next answer was 'Trevor Macdonald' and when it was then thrown over to the other team, one of them at last said 'Terry Wogan'. Top answer!

We got some odd family names as well. On one show we had the Dick family. Surely you'd change your name if you were called Mr Dick! In the afternoon they asked me if I would try not to take the mickey out of their name. I didn't have to. All I had to do was say it and like a group of naughty schoolboys the audience started giggling. 'That's the Robinsons, so let's go over and meet the Dicks. You're the head of the family, so that makes you...the top man.'

Another time we had a John Thomas who was a policeman. PC John Thomas! Now that's just asking for trouble.

It is very hard to manufacture catchphrases; they usually happen by accident. One night when a contestant gave a spectacularly silly answer I said, 'If it's up there, I'll give you the money myself.' It got a laugh from the audience, so I decided to use it for particularly stupid answers. It did backfire on me a couple of times, though, when a daft answer was actually there! When asked to name a way of toasting someone (such as 'cheers' or 'bottoms up'), a young woman answered, 'Over an open fire.'

'If it's up there, I will definitely give you the money myself.' To both my and the audience's surprise it was there, and after the show I wrote her a cheque as promised! Some of the other answers that prompted my catchphrase were:

- 'Name something you wear on the beach.'
  'A deckchair.'

- 'Name a famous brother and sister.'
  'Bonnie and Clyde.'
- 'Name something in the garden that's green.'
  'The shed.'
- 'Name a sign of the zodiac.'
  'April.'
- 'Name a form of transport you can walk around in.'
  'My foot.'
- 'Name something that makes you scream.'
  'A squirrel.'
- 'Name something people might be allergic to.'
  'Skiing.'

In Big Money I learnt early on that I should literally keep my cards close to my chest or the contestants might see the answers. I didn't even know what they were, except in the end game, when only I would be given the top answers. That enabled me to work out if they could win the car or not and so build up and draw out the tension. One night one of the questions was 'Name a Native American tribe.'

The bloke playing said, 'Sigh Ooks.'

'What?' I asked.

'Sigh Ooks,' he repeated

Then I got it. He'd caught a glimpse of my card and the top answer was 'Sioux.'

Another guy who needed only to find the top answer to win the car failed on the question 'Name a food that can be eaten easily without chewing.' He said, 'Chips,' but the top answer was 'Soup.' 'Damn,' he said, 'That's my job. I'm a soup salesman.'

I am often surprised by the people who watched the show. I was at an awards do and big Ron Atkinson came up to me. 'Hard luck Saturday,' he said.

I thought he was talking about Liverpool, who had lost a cup game. 'I know,' I said, 'and we were one-nil up at half-time.'

'No,' he said, 'I meant the Johnson family. They just missed the car.'

Another time, a few years ago, Amanda and I were travelling to Los Angeles on British Airways. The cabin crew recognised us and kindly upgraded us to first class. It was like flying on Celebrity Airlines. George Michael and Kenny Goss were behind us, and Elton John and David Furnish were in front. About an hour into the flight David got up, stretched and looked around. He saw me, bent down and whispered something to Elton. I kind of knew he was saying, 'That bloke from *Family Fortunes* is behind us.' I could hardly believe it when a minute or two later Elton came down the aisle and had a chat.

'Hi. We love your show in our house,' he said. If anything goes wrong at home, we go, "Eugh-eugh." By the way, where do you get those families?' He was asking all the questions that I was sick of answering, but hell, it was Elton John!

The 'eugh-eugh' noise follows me everywhere. As I walk round a supermarket I hear it on about every aisle. It's as if people develop game show Tourette's whenever they see me. And they all think they're the first ones to do it. 'Les! Eugh-eugh!' Lovely, I've never heard that one before! I'm not complaining, though. The show kept me on prime-time TV for sixteen years and is still being shown daily on satellite TV. It was great to do and I will always be thankful for it.

CHAPTER 16

Family Misfortunes

Whenever the goal posts are shifted in my life, I tend to panic and go into workaholic mode. Dustin and I had achieved a level of success that might have enabled me to relax and soft-pedal for a while. But with his death, the rug had suddenly been pulled from under me and I felt compelled to take every job that came along. Lynne again argued that I needed to rest and enjoy the success I had achieved. My TV commitments were enough to ensure a more than comfortable existence, but I felt I had to prove to the media, the public and, more importantly, to myself that I could make it as a solo performer. There was a lot of speculation that I would suffer the same fate that Ernie Wise suffered after Eric had died. However, the difference between them and us was that Ernie had been with Eric for most of his life. They had been a double act in the true sense of the term. Dustin and I had only been working together for a relatively short time and had both had solo acts for years before that.

Just after Dustin's death many newspapers carried articles

about the great toll the business had taken on many of its top comedians. In the previous couple of years it had claimed Eric Morecambe, Tommy Cooper, Leonard Rossiter, Dick Emery, Richard Beckinsale, Harry H. Corbett and Sid James. In one article, Ernie Wise said, 'The tragedy of Dustin is that he was so young. The danger is that your career takes off like an express train and you can't stop, not even when the red light comes up. Young comedians are under tremendous pressure from managers to keep up their appearances on the stage. The audiences want to see you and it acts like a drug.' Despite having two shows every Saturday night, *Family Fortunes* on ITV and *The Laughter Show* on BBC1, I also felt the need to take guest slots on Russ Abbot's show, plus gruelling summer and panto seasons and even store openings up and down the country. All the signs were there telling me that something would have to give but I didn't see them or listen to anyone who tried to point them out. I was a strong young man so my physical health could take it, but the train was about to crash in a very different way.

Lynne and I had married when we were only twenty and had been virgins on our wedding night. Although there had been constant temptations for me along the way, I had, apart from the odd snog, managed to resist getting involved with anyone. I had a loving and loyal wife and a beautiful young son. Why would I want to jeopardise that?

On the first day of rehearsals for one of the many shows I was doing, I was introduced to the cast. As I looked into the eyes of one particular woman, I knew immediately that something was going to happen. Within six weeks of working together we were having an affair. I felt huge guilt because I was betraying Lynne's trust, but though it sounds like a cliché, I just couldn't seem to resist. The show lasted a couple of months so it shouldn't have been any more than a fling. However, she lived in London, and as I was going to be there recording my TV shows for the next few months, we both knew the affair would continue. I haven't named her because I've been unable to contact her to tell her I'm writing this book. She isn't British and no longer lives in this country. She isn't famous, and the last I heard she had married and moved away. When our affair finished, she maintained a dignified silence and never went to the press to tell her story. I only write about it now to explain why my marriage to Lynne fell apart.

The way I treated Lynne for the following couple of years was unforgivable and, in a warped way, helped me to understand and accept what my second wife did to me almost a decade later. Karma will always come round and bite you on the arse.

Lynne was doing a part-time English degree at Liverpool University so it was scarily easy for me to lead a double life. She would come to London for weekends and I would drive home when I got a rare day off, but with her course and Philip's schooling, she was mostly at home in Liverpool. We had sold the flat in St Margaret's and had bought a beautiful apartment in Hampstead as our London base. We would spend weekends there, but as soon as Lynne had gone home, I would drive over to stay with the woman in Battersea. Roger, who was working as my tour manager and PA, would have our three-bedroom apartment all to himself, while I was staying in a tiny flat above a shop.

I felt tremendous guilt but I couldn't stop myself. Having always been an honest man, what disturbed me the most was how I found it remarkably easy to lie and how inventive I could be in my deceit. It was before the advent of mobile phones and even before '1471' so it was very easy to cover my tracks. I would ring Lynne first thing in the morning, but if she called first, Roger wouldn't answer and would then call me in Battersea. I would then phone Lynne and say, 'Sorry. I was in the shower and I missed your call.' Not only deceitful to Lynne but also deeply unfair to use Roger as an accessory.

Just before Christmas I remember dropping Lynne off at Foyles bookshop, where she needed to get some course books, and then driving over to Battersea. I stayed longer than I should (what am I talking about? I shouldn't have been there at all), missed meeting Lynne for lunch and got back to the flat after she returned home. When she asked where I had been, I said I had been Christmas shopping and that she shouldn't ask, as it would spoil the surprise. I had had a glass of wine and Lynne could smell alchohol on my breath. She looked confused but I sneakily got myself out of a sticky situation by saying, 'Come on, Lynne, don't ask. You know that in the very best shops at this time of year they offer you a glass of champagne to entice you to buy.' Oh, what a tangled web we weave where we practise to deceive.

Eventually something had to give. One Sunday night in January Lynne and I were watching a TV drama starring Dirk Bogarde and Lee Remick. Dirk Bogarde's character was having an affair and felt extremely guilty. I sat through it with my stomach churning, knowing I was hiding the same enormous secret. The story ended with his confession to his wife, and his performance was so truthful and compelling I watched with tears streaming down my face. As it finished, Lynne looked at me and asked if I was OK. Like the character in the drama, I broke down and confessed everything. Lynne was absolutely dumbstruck. She hadn't suspected a thing, even though I had been living a lie for over a year. She had noticed that I had become distant, but figured I was still grieving.

I had had three major losses in less than ten years, and instead of dealing with them, I had thrown myself into an almost impossible work schedule. On top of that, I had been conducting a clandestine liaison with a woman I thought I was in love with, so how could I have been anything other than distant. I undoubtedly had strong feelings for this woman, but I knew I really had to do something to stop the web of deceit. Looking back, I don't know how I managed to do my job properly or find the time and energy to compartmentalise my life so effectively.

Once she had recovered from the shock, Lynne and I sat up talking through the night trying to decide what to do. Her initial reaction was for us to split, but eventually, as the anger subsided, she came to the conclusion that if I ended the affair we could work through it and try to rebuild the trust that had suddenly evaporated from her world. This is when our troubles really began – I said that I was unsure I could give up the other woman.

In the blink of an eye I had turned from a devoted, caring husband into a callous, selfish bastard who only cared about what he wanted. The year before had been difficult and uncomfortable, but the year ahead was to be almost unbearable. Lynne did everything to save our marriage. Against my wishes, we sold the house in Liverpool, and Lynne and Philip moved down to London to be with me permanently. She gave up the degree course that she had almost completed and instead put her energies into rebuilding our life together. The problem was that I wasn't prepared to play happy families and continued my affair. I can remember, on a rare day off, leaving Lynne silently crying in the bath and going to get on a train to Manchester to spend an illicit evening with a woman with whom I believed my future lay. There is a Buddhist phrase regarding being truthful with someone, 'Is it kind, and is it necessary?' I certainly felt it was necessary to have confessed my sins to Lynne, but, undoubtedly, how I behaved afterwards was not kind. It was unspeakably cruel. As I write this now, I am finding it hard to believe that the person I am describing to you was me.

Maybe because the furtive excitement had been taken out of the equation, or maybe simply because it had run its course, the intensity of the affair burnt out. We saw less and less of each other and by the September had, apart from the odd phone call, lost touch. Something that had seemed so important and life-changing just disappeared, as if it had never existed. It had, though, left an enormous casualty behind – my marriage. Lynne could no longer trust me. Worse still, I could no longer trust myself.

Later that year I performed in *Cinderella* at the New Theatre in Hull and, true to the showbiz cliché I was fast becoming, fell for my leading lady. With typical female intuition Lynne came into my dressing room one night and said, 'You start an affair with this one and we're finished.' With typical male stubbornness I ignored the warning and did exactly that. The faithful, loving husband had morphed, over the last two years, into a serial adulterer.

The male ego and old-fashioned lust played a huge part in leading me into my second affair. I had met Sophie Aldred on the first day of rehearsals for *Cinderella* and we had hit it off immediately. To most people, she was best known as assistant Ace to Sylvester McCoy's Dr Who. 'My doctor' had always been the original, William Hartnell, and although I had watched during the Patrick Troughton and Tom Baker years, I wasn't a big fan of the show and had no idea who Sophie was. I remember I had a bad cold and a high temperature and that during her lunch break she went and bought me some medicine. She was sweet but I never expected to end up in bed with her. She had just come out of a relationship with actor Daniel Peacock and kept telling everyone, 'No men in my life for six months!'

Before my first affair I had resisted temptation for years, but having given in once, it became easy to do it again. Only weeks into our run in Hull we were sleeping together. My marriage to Lynne had never recovered after the first affair, and even though that had ended, here I was betraying her again. My feelings for Sophie grew deeper and I decided very early on that there was no way I could lead a double life again. It is often said that men don't leave unless they have somewhere or someone to go to. Sophie and I were not yet close enough to know whether we were going to be together long term, but the fact that I was being unfaithful again led me to make the decision to leave Lynne. Enough was enough, and one Sunday in January, after a stormy row, I packed a bag and left our marital home. I had married so young and my life had changed dramatically over those years. I'd always felt I had to play the 'good boy' for my mum and then the 'good husband' for Lynne. I had very little sense of who I was and needed to break free. I just chose the wrong way to do it. The man I am now would have stayed and worked out what the problem was, but I had lost touch with myself and needed to get away. Lynne pleaded with me to see a counsellor, but I refused. I was too caught up in the heady, self-obsessed, false world of the entertainment business and thought that I was invincible. Countless therapy sessions later in my life have enabled me to see that I was, to a large extent, denying my grief, but it is too convenient to blame everything on loss and grief. The problem was that, for a while, I took Lynne and Philip down with me.

After leaving Lynne, I walked down Fitzjohn's Avenue in Hampstead in a daze. I called Mike Hughes from a phonebox and went over to see him at his house in Kensington. I didn't know what to do. All I knew was that it was unfair to carry on being awful to Lynne. Philip, of course, didn't know what was happening other than his mum and dad weren't getting on. He was used to me being away, so for now he didn't have to be told much, although, like most children, he probably sensed something was wrong. I called Sophie and told her I had left and was checking into a hotel. She was shocked. We hadn't talked about being together long term and I think she was worried that I had left Lynne to be with her. I hadn't – I just felt that Lynne and I had reached the end of the road.

After one night in a hotel I went to stay for a while with my friend and flatmate from the *Madhouse* days, Russell Lane. Sophie and I saw each other when we could, but I was paranoid about the press finding out. After a couple of weeks Lynne called and suggested that we should meet and decide what to do. We arranged to have a drink at the Grosvenor House in Park Lane, and as I had a few hours to kill between rehearsals and our meeting, I went to the cinema. Of all the films I could have watched I chose *Parenthood*. Why the fuck it didn't make me see sense and realise that my responsibility was to put Philip first, I really don't know. I wept my way through it but still went to meet Lynne determined that ending our relationship was the right thing to do. Over a couple of drinks in a swanky cocktail bar, our marriage unofficially ended. Lynne gave me the ultimatum that I would have to come home and commit if we had any chance of survival. I said I wasn't sure I could do that and, in another ego-fuelled moment that I shudder to recall, suggested that perhaps we should have an open marriage. Lynne looked at me with deep sadness in her eyes, quietly asked the barman to get her a cab, finished her drink and left. I sat alone in that bar feeling completely numb but believing that what I was doing was right. I had lost my mum, dad, Dustin and was estranged from my brother and sisters. There, over a martini, I ruthlessly added my marriage to the bonfire and struck the match.

The next day I got a call from my press agent, Clifford Elson, saying the tabloids had been asking if there were any problems with my marriage. People at work were puzzled by my behaviour and it was only a matter of time before it would hit the headlines. Lynne called and said that we had to tell Philip before he found out from someone else. That was the worst day of my life. I got to the flat an hour before he got home from school and waited to change his world.

He arrived and looked thrilled to see me. He sat there in his school uniform as we said, 'Phil, we have got something we need to talk to you about.' How do you tell a ten-year-old kid you're leaving? I blurted out something about his mum and dad deciding to live apart but always being there for him and how it would be fun having two houses. The usual shit! At first he didn't seem to react. I said, 'So what do you think? Is that OK with you?'

He looked at me and said, 'Yeah, it's fine,' and then, almost in slow motion, a single tear trickled down his cheek. Just one tear. It broke my heart and does to this day. Still, I didn't pick him up and say, 'No, Daddy's only joking. Everything is going to be fine.' Is that what I should have done? Would Lynne and I have limped on in a broken marriage, or would we have ridden the storm and ended up stronger? I don't know and I certainly didn't then.

A couple of months later I was watching a movie called *Glory*, the true story of a regiment of African slaves in the American Civil War. In one scene, Denzel Washington's shirt is stripped off and he is beaten by his sadistic commanding officer in front of his fellow slaves. He shows no emotion, except for a single tear. The scene ended and I fell to the floor of my trendy new bachelor pad and wept.

The entertainment industry is such a false world. The guys in suits refer to you as 'the talent', so it is easy to believe your own hype and publicity. Journalists want to talk to you, and photographers want to take pictures of you. People in the street want to stop you and tell you how great you are. It's flattering and you think you're special, but you're not. You're just a normal guy who got lucky. And there is definitely a tax on fame. As my friend Andy Grainger once said, 'You have to pay the ferryman,' and I had just made my first instalment.

CHAPTER 17

Weekend Dad

Days later the papers reported that my marriage was over, and the following Sunday the *News of the World* ran with 'Les Falls for *Dr Who* Girl'. In those days, though, today's news was tomorrow's fish and chip paper, and once the initial fuss died down, I was able to pick up the pieces and get on with my life. I bought a lovely house, a converted railway workshop in a mews in Archway, close to my friend Lisa Maxwell. Lisa was my co-star in *The Laughter Show* and became my confidante throughout these troubled times. She is very funny, warm and extremely talented. She got her own show with the BBC and is now excellent as DI Sam Nixon in *The Bill*. I recently guested in an episode playing a man who killed his father and then stuck him in the freezer. It was bizarre doing straight scenes together, and the director, Di Patrick, was very patient when we ruined a few takes by laughing. Lisa and I only have to look at each other to end up in fits of giggles.

Philip would come and stay with me for weekends, and

Lynne and I managed to have a friendly and civilised relationship for his sake. It wasn't easy, though, as I was still continuing my relationship with Sophie. We remained together for three years, though it was always volatile and God knows how many times we split up. Philip was reluctant to get to know her, and I found myself once again living a kind of double life. Photos would be taken down when he came to stay and put back up when Sophie came over. I would continue to have family meals with Lynne and Philip, and felt unsure where my loyalties lay. The first time Philip came to my new home, I nervously showed him round. As we sat together on the roof terrace overlooking the railway, he looked at me and said, 'Nice for you.'

My heart sank and I quickly said, 'It's nice for you too.'

'No, I didn't say that, Dad,' he laughed. 'I said, "Nice view."' Interesting that I heard it so negatively.

For the first time in years I was not doing panto miles away from home and I could have spent the entire holiday and his birthday with him. But I wasn't living with him any more, and as I saw Christmas trees in cosy front-room windows all over London, I felt enormous grief. I decided to start therapy.

In Britain we are still extremely scared of discussing our feelings, believing that if anything is wrong, the answer is to pull yourself together and have a cup of tea. 'Your life's falling apart, dear. I'll put the kettle on.' We've become obsessed with fixing things on the outside. We think nothing of having Botox in our lunch hour, but the idea of talking to a qualified practitioner about one's problems is something we view with suspicion. In America they are much more open to analysis. Woody Allen has built his entire career on it. One of my favourite jokes of his is in the movie *Sleeper*. After being cryogenically frozen for 200 years, he wakes and says, 'Two hundred years. All that therapy I missed. I would have been cured by now.'

Maybe being such a fan of Woody made me more interested

and curious about examining my own emotional health and so, in the autumn of 1991, I started weekly sessions with a woman in Hampstead. I was at an enormous crossroads in my life. Although my career was going well, I was still reeling from three hugely significant deaths and had separated from the woman I had been with since I was eighteen. As I fast approached forty, I was showing all the signs of a classic midlife crisis. I had a new home, a convertible BMW and a new relationship. Like many men before, and I'm sure since, I thought I could solve my problems by starting all over again. I found it fascinating and liberating to rake through my formative years with an objective and impartial professional. Talking to family and friends can help enormously, but sometimes they are too close and too biased to really deal with the problem. And of course I was still very much alienated from my family.

My guilt over leaving Philip has been constant over the years, but therapy helped me to understand that just because I wasn't there, I didn't have to be an absent father. It spurred me on to work hard to forge a strong and loving relationship with him in the best way that I could. It is interesting that where I sought therapy to help me with my issues, Lynne took a different path and instead chose psychotherapy as a career.

Workwise, I was still incredibly busy. In February 1992 I landed my dream job playing the lead role of Bill Snibson in *Me and My Girl* at the Adelphi Theatre. I had seen the show when it opened with Robert Lindsay and Emma Thompson and had loved it. I sat in the audience watching them tap-dance on a huge dining table and thought, I want that part. Every night when I did that scene, I would look out into the audience and remember myself wishing for it. In the whole year of doing the show, I never got bored. How could I when there were so many new skills to learn? The part is all-singing, all-dancing with scenes of extremely complicated comic business and I never stopped learning. It was a toe-tapping, feel-good show, and at the end the audience leaves on such a high you can't help but be infected by it.

My sister Marg and her husband, Tony, came to see it one night. Since the collapse of my marriage she had been extremely worried and we had begun to get close again. Sophie would encourage that closeness, and later my second wife, Amanda, would insist that we healed our rift. There is a scene in the show, in which Bill leads the company in 'The Lambeth Walk'. As the audience clap along, he and Sally, played by Louise English, dance up and down the aisles of the theatre. As I walked past our Marg, I could see she had tears streaming down her face. Afterwards, she reminded me that my mum, weeks before her death, had predicted that I would one day headline at the Palladium. She was close – the Adelphi isn't far away.

I did that show for a year and absolutely loved it. The cast were a delight – Roy Macready, Angela Moran, Louise and, best of all, the brilliant Alfred Marks. Well into his eighties, he was the most professional and conscientious performer I had ever worked with. He always gave 100 per cent, and even when he had to have time off for a cataract operation he was back within a few days. It seemed he too believed 'The show must go on.' When he died a few years ago, his wife, Paddy O'Neill, asked me to unveil a Comic Heritage plaque at the BBC Radio Theatre. I was teamed up with, of all people, Peter O'Toole. What an honour. When asked who would say a few words, Peter said, 'I'll leave all the talking to Les.' When it came to the speech, however, I mumbled some niceties and then Peter said, in that wonderful rich voice of his, 'Alfred was a marvellous comic performer. When Edmund Kean, the great Victorian actor, was asked on his death bed, "What's it like to die?" he replied, "Dying is easy – comedy is hard."' Follow that!

Louise had been one of Benny Hill's Angels and one afternoon the great man came to see the show. Afterwards he came backstage and politely posed for photos with the cast. He was a true gentleman and left to take Louise for tea at the Savoy. It was his last public appearance. Three days later he was discovered dead in his flat. At Benny's memorial service, the church of St Martin-in-the-Fields rang with laughter as the great and good of the comedy world packed it to the rafters in celebration of his life and work. Anthony Burgess read a moving eulogy suggesting that the critics had been wrong about Benny. He said, 'He didn't chase the girls. They chased him, in a harmless McGill-postcard kind of way.' Traditional entertainers had a hard time in the 1990s, as they were often subjected to a McCarthy-like witch-hunt from the PC brigade, and so frequently it was only after death that they were recognised as the comic greats they truly were. I remember huge laughter, though, as we filed out of the church trying to keep in step with Benny's theme tune, 'Yakety Sax'.

A couple of days after Benny's death, Frankie Howerd died suddenly, perpetuating the belief that comics were prone to early death. In the late 1970s I had done a spot on *The Frankie Howerd Show*, produced by Richard Wilcocks, whom I had worked for on Radio 2's *The Impressionists*. Frankie had a reputation for being difficult, a reputation I realised was well founded when I arrived for rehearsals at the Paris Studio on Regent Street early on the afternoon of recording. Richard seemed agitated, and when I asked if he was OK, he said, 'It's working with this bastard. He's driving me mad.' As he talked, his arm involuntarily flew into the air and it was clear he was unwell. Mr Howerd, it seemed, had brought on some kind of nervous reaction, and within the hour Richard had to be taken to hospital and replaced for the show by Danny Greenstone. I grew more and more nervous of meeting this comedy legend, who, as yet, had not ventured out of his dressing room. The writers, who included a young Griff Rhys Jones, then handed me a sketch saying, 'Frankie'll be out in a minute to rehearse this with you.'

The door to the dressing room opened and out he stepped looking every inch the comedy god I had watched as I grew up. Tall, with that ill-fitting ginger wig plonked on his head and wearing a crumpled suit, he bellowed at me, 'Now, then, young man. There's a sketch here. We'll go to the green room and read it. If you're a good enough actor, you can do it. If not, I'll get somebody else.'

'Yes, Mr Howerd,' I said timidly, and followed him into the green room. I must have read OK because he agreed to me doing it with him in the show. It was a sketch about a taxman visiting Frankie at home and I decided to use a southern RP (received pronunciation) accent for the character. All of Frankie's 'ooh's and 'ah's were literally scripted and he read them off the page. I did my first line, 'Good afternoon. I'm from the Inland Revenue,' and, then to huge laughter, he replied, 'Ooh, yes, now, then, really.'

As the laughter subsided, I said, 'May I come in?' The problem was that on the word 'come', my accent slipped and it came out sounding extremely Northern.

Frankie pounced, and shouted, '*Cum* in. Can I *cum* in. Where are you from?' It was comic genius. What had been a reasonably funny sketch became a brilliant comic rant, totally ad lib, from one of our funniest comedians.

After *Me and My Girl* I moved on to do a tour and summer season of French farce *Don't Dress for Dinner*. It had been an unexpected hit in the West End and I was cast alongside Lionel Blair, Vicki Michelle, Mandy Perriment, Les Mills and the wonderful Su Pollard. From day one we all had the most marvellous time. Su gives the impression of being quite a ditzy eccentric but she is a very sharp cookie. Her comic timing and skills are breathtaking and she would steal the show every night with her fine performance. Being in her company is like being a kid again. One lunchtime as Lionel, Su, Vicki and I were walking back to rehearsals, she walked up to the door of a house, knocked loudly and shouted, 'Quick. Run!'

As four middle-aged variety artists took to their heels, I shouted back, 'What are you doing?'

'Knock down, ginger,' she said, as we started to run.

As the homeowner opened his door, I found myself regressing to the age of ten and shouting back, 'Sorry, mister. It wasn't me, it was her!'

In the second half of the play, while Lionel and Mandy were onstage, Su and I would sit in the wings chatting quietly. Then I would make my entrance and a few minutes later she would join us. One matinée afternoon in Woking I went on, did my scene with Lionel, and when Su should have come on, she didn't. Lionel and I improvised in character and she still didn't appear. At this point Lionel gave up, came out of character totally and started entertaining the audience. I was going through my 'wanting to be treated seriously as an actor' phase and refused to join in as Lionel did two choruses of 'Lily of Laguna' with a perfect soft-shoe shuffle. 'Come on, Les,' he laughed.

'Robert,' I murmured, still in character. 'My name is Robert.'

By the time Su came on, looking breathless and anxious, all semblance of the plot and characters had been totally destroyed. We got through somehow, and as the curtain fell, I turned to Su and asked, 'Where the fuck were you?'

'Oh, darling, I had a nightmare of a time. After you went on, I thought, I've got a few minutes – I'll see what's through this door. I went through and it slammed behind me. Worse still, I am suddenly in the middle of the fucking shopping centre in full slap and costume.' She pointed at her micro miniskirt. Woking Theatre is situated slap-bang in the middle of a huge mall and she had to try to find her way back to the stage door. She continued, '"Excuse me, please, I'm locked out," I said to people, but they just laughed at me. Eventually I found the stage door but it was locked and had a sign saying, "Back in five minutes." I'm in fucking bits!'

By the time the show settled in Bournemouth for the summer, my relationship with Sophie was on the rocks. We had split up countless times. Philip had reluctantly agreed to meet her at Easter but things just weren't right. He had met her briefly when we were doing panto together and, understandably, believed she was the reason Lynne and I had split up. She wasn't, of course. The responsibility was entirely mine, but it is difficult for a young boy to see this. My relationship with Sophie never stood a chance. I wanted to keep it secret so that Philip wouldn't have to read about it in the press, and even after three years together, I was unhappy about holding hands in public in case we were photographed. Or was it perhaps my fear of intimacy that had been instilled in me that night as a child when I caught my mum and dad having sex? Either way, I remained reluctant to commit, and when Sophie suggested that we live together, I agreed at first but when it actually came to it, I refused point blank. Sophie had been my lifeboat to take me away from the wreck of my marriage and once again I was about to jump ship, thinking that my future lay elsewhere.

CHAPTER 18

Summer 1993

Don't Dress for Dinner opened at the Pier Theatre in Bournemouth at the end of June, and a week later *The Sound of Music* came to the Pavilion. At their opening-night party Lionel, Les Mills and I were talking with Emma Cooper, who was playing one of the nuns, when a strikingly pretty girl with long blonde hair and the darkest brown eyes confidently walked over, held out her hand and said, 'Hello. I'm Amanda Holden.' I was bowled over not just by her looks but also by her supreme confidence. She launched into a story about doing a photocall for the town's evening paper, the *Echo*, which wanted to a do a 'local girl made good' feature. Amanda's family had always been involved in amateur dramatics and she had gone on to drama school. After she graduated, her first job was the plum role of Liesel in *The Sound of Music*. Earlier that day she had posed in the fountain outside the foyer of the Pavilion and now, without any embarrassment, said, 'As soon as the sun went in it got cold and my nipples took on a life of their own.' Lionel and Les laughed, but

I simply excused myself and went home. Philip and his friend Sam had not wanted to come to the party and were back at the flat, so I was anxious to get home and check that they were OK. Later, in interviews, Amanda said that she thought I was a miserable sod that night because I hadn't laughed at her story. The truth was that I had been instantly attracted to this gorgeous young woman. She looked no older than twenty or twenty-one and I was a bit flustered by that. I was a thirty-nine-year-old game show host, so what would she see in me? And anyway, she was dating the drummer in the show.

For my stay in Bournemouth I had rented a lovely garden flat in a leafy road in Alum Chine, which quickly became the hub of the social scene. Two friends Andy Grainger and Steve Johnson came to stay and the summer became a three-month-long episode of *Men Behaving Badly*! How ironic!

Sophie and I were in trouble. At the time, she was doing a lot of self-development courses and had become engrossed in a particular one that suggested that you made personal agreements that would sometimes shut me out. She was trying hard to find herself, and looking back, I admire her for the work she did, but I wasn't in the right place to see that at the time. I met up with her last summer in Edinburgh, where she goes every year for the Fringe Festival. She is now married to a lovely man, Vince, who is a talented street performer, and has two lovely sons. But that summer, although I had attended some of the courses at her request, I was in no mood for self-improvement. I just wanted to have a good time. I had never been to university, had married young and lived the rather lonely life of a solo performer. I relished that carefree summer with Andy and Steve.

As the weeks went on, the show companies would meet after performances for drinks in the bar at the Bournemouth International Centre and Amanda would come up and chat. Despite that moment of initial attraction, I found that she began to irritate me. I thought she looked down on me, Lionel and the others, as she would ask questions like 'How is your little show at the end of the pier going?' I decided I didn't like her, that she was fresh out of drama school and thought she knew it all. However, that didn't stop me from developing a crush. Every Thursday the companies would go bowling and I would do my utmost to make sure I was on the same team as Emma and Amanda. She has a sharp, caustic sense of humour that takes quite a bit of getting used to. I was also oversensitive about any suggestion that my style or grounding was naff or cheesy. Once I got it, though, I began to understand that her 'end of the pier' jokes were simply her way of teasing and slowly we began to laugh together.

At one of the parties at my flat, I asked Amanda to see if she could spot anything tasteful. The furnishings were rather tacky and I suppose I was trying to let her know that they didn't reflect my own taste. She looked at a pseudo pre-Raphaelite print of an embracing couple on the wall and said, 'That isn't bad.'

'Yes, it is,' I said. 'It is badly painted and simply dreadful.'

'The passion is there, though,' she replied.

I then shocked myself by asking, 'When are we going to get to that stage?'

'In about three weeks,' she answered very coolly. I later found out that she had ended her relationship with the drummer and had told Emma that she was beginning to like me.

One Saturday in August our 'little show at the end of the pier' hit the front pages of most of the daily newspapers. The IRA had strapped a huge bomb to the iron and wooden structure. The bomb contained enough Semtex to blow the theatre apart and throw the dead and injured into the sea. It had been there the night before as we played our farce to a packed house. Why they targeted us I don't know. Perhaps they were theatre lovers! Overnight there were four or five bombs that went off in shops across the town, including one that was hidden under a deckchair on the pier, so that Saturday the show couldn't go on. In true Dunkirk spirit, we joined the cast of the Bournemouth International Centre for a one-off variety show that starred Jimmy Tarbuck and Kenny Lynch. Michael Barrymore, who was headlining there that summer, had been off for a few nights, so Tarby and Lynchy had filled in.

Michael was strange and distant that season, not at all the man we had had such fun with during the *Madhouse* years. He was now a massive star, perhaps the biggest in the country. The press, though, had started to dig into his personal life and he and his wife, Cheryl, were clearly feeling the strain. One night all the show people in town got together for a meal at a local fish restaurant, Chez Fred's, where Michael and Cheryl sat on their own in the corner, he with his back to everybody. 'Is Michael OK?' Su shouted across to Cheryl.

'Fine,' she replied. 'He just doesn't like being bothered when he's out eating.'

He was out with fellow pros and friends, so why did he feel the need to isolate himself? Su wasn't having any of it and shouted across, 'Come on, Michael, stop fucking about. It's only us.'

Looking uncomfortable, Michael said, 'Hello, Su. I see you've been for your loony lesson today.' He didn't join us and left soon after. That was the only social event we saw him at that summer.

After the show with Tarby and Lynchy we all went off to Emma's karaoke birthday party. I sang 'A Little Help From My Friends' and sat with Amanda, telling her, over a bottle of wine, about our adventurous brush with death. 'Imagine the favour they'd have done the light entertainment industry if it had gone off!' she joked. This time I knew she was teasing and could laugh. It had only been my own insecurity about being 'end of the pier' that had stopped me before. That night we kissed and began what, I believed, would be no more than a holiday romance.

On the Bank Holiday there was a benefit show at the Winter Gardens, which had been closed for the season. It was the first time I had been back there since the fateful Sunday in 1982 when Lynne had told me the news that my father had died. I forced myself to go into the phone booth that I had heard the news from, and the grief I had bottled up for more than ten years suddenly poured out. A week before, I had opened a garden fête and Tony Hardman, who had put me up that night in the 1980s, went with me. As we wandered around a few stalls, a fit-looking man in his late seventies strode up and beamed at me. 'Hello, Les. I've wanted to meet you for ages. I played football with your dad. He was a brilliant inside left. A bit lazy, but when he tried, magnificent.' I thanked him and walked around the other stalls in a daze. Here was a man who was the same age as my dad would have been, showing such spark and vitality. I left, went back to my flat and sobbed my heart out.

Noel Edmonds did perhaps his best ever Gotcha! on Lionel that summer. It worked so well, I think, because it was done in front of a live audience, in the middle of the play. Lionel's character, Bernard, was trying to get his wife, played by Vicki Michelle, to go away for the weekend so that he could have his mistress over. As he tells her that he is looking forward to a few days with his old friend, Robert (me), a little man with a flat cap, glasses and huge beard shouted from the audience, 'Don't believe you, Lionel.' It was, of course, Noel Edmonds. Su, Vicki and I knew, but Lionel didn't. We had microphones tucked under our costumes and there were hidden cameras in the wings. Lionel was fazed for a second, but being the trouper he is, carried on. His excuses for wanting Vicki to leave became more elaborate and once again the shout came from the audience, only this time, much louder: 'No, Lionel. You're not telling the truth.' By now the audience was getting uncomfortable and Lionel was furious. He gave the man a vicious stare but still stayed in character.

A few seconds later he came offstage to get a tray of drinks. Su and I played dumb. 'What's going on, Lionel?' we asked, positioning him in front of the hidden camera. (Probably the only time anyone has ever had to place Lionel in front of a camera!)

'Some fucking idiot keeps shouting out, ruining the play,' he said, and went back onstage with the drinks.

'Eh up, Lionel's back,' said Noel.

This time Lionel had had enough and stepped forward, totally out of character, and said angrily, 'You're ruining this for everyone.' Huge applause. You could feel the audience's disgust with the little man in the aisle seat.

The man left and the play continued, but less than five minutes later a diver, in full mask, wet suit, flippers and oxygen tank, entered from stage left. Still Lionel didn't get it. When I asked him later why it took him so long, he said he had had a play interrupted at the same theatre by students a few years before. He thought it was a rag-week stunt. When Noel pulled off his mask and produced the Gotcha! Lionel collapsed into fits of laughter and so did the audience. Noel presented Lionel with his Gotcha! which Lionel carried everywhere that summer, as if it was an Oscar. Noel and the crew then left and we had to start the play from the top again.

Noel got me with a Gotcha! a few years later. I didn't quite fall hook, line and sinker, like Lionel, though. When a helicopter that was taking me from Blackpool for an interview at Pebble Mill was forced to land on a hill outside Birmingham, there was a fun run taking place. The guy who was running the water station suddenly collapsed and the pilot said he would have to take him to hospital and asked if I would stay and check in the runners, who were all in fancy dress, and make sure they didn't cheat. It was incredibly far-fetched and I kind of guessed it was a Gotcha! I played along and dutifully checked in Lady Godiva,

Charlie Chaplin, Spider Man et al. When Noel came out from hiding, I feigned surprise and delight but Noel knew I'd sussed it. 'When did you guess?' he asked.

'Napoleon on a motorbike was a stunt too far,' I laughed.

But back to that summer. As I had with Lynne, I confessed all to Sophie one weekend. She was starring in a musical version of *The Country Wife* called *Lust* with Denis Lawson at the Haymarket Theatre. It was not the most appropriate or sensitive time to make my confession. Sophie sat in tears as we dined out at the Ivy, telling me how irresponsible I was and that I should 'sort my shit out'. I remember feeling embarrassed that she was making such a show in public. What a fucking bastard I had become. I felt I had let Sophie down and decided that the best thing to do was end my affair with Amanda, so one afternoon, as we walked along the seafront, I suggested that as the season came to an end, so should our fling. 'It's impossible to carry on,' I said. 'I'm thirty-nine. You're twenty-two. There's no future for us.'

Amanda became angry and upset, and called me a coward. I dropped her off at Chase Lodge, her parents' guesthouse, and thought that would be the end of it. Amanda later told me she went in and cried to her mum, saying, 'I know it's not over. I know we'll carry on.' She was right.

We invited *The Sound of Music* lot to our end-of-season party, and many drinks later Amanda and I ended up back at my flat. When the season was over, I was going to LA for meetings with agents to see if there was a chance of 'breaking into America'. Then, I thought, this mutual crush would definitely come to an end. I headed off to America, which, in the end, was a fruitless exercise. I saw an interview with Tim Roth a few years later in which he said that you shouldn't go to LA without being invited. Although I got to meet with a lot of studio executives, I found the whole experience quite soul-destroying. They all 'love your work', even though they haven't seen it, and the minute you leave the meeting you know they've forgotten your name.

I stayed at the Universal Sheraton and, when I wasn't having pointless meetings, spent my days doing the Universal tours and going to watch movies. I was on my own so hardly ventured out to any of the other tourist spots. I heard that Sophie had started seeing someone else. I felt sick to my stomach – that ridiculous male-pride thing where you know you no longer want to be with somebody but don't want anyone else to have them. Amanda and I, however, spoke constantly and ran up a huge bill. She met me at the airport when I returned and by January we were living together in my mews house in Archway. We bought a Cairn terrier puppy, which we named Nobbie, and settled into a very happy time together.

CHAPTER 19

Engaged in Hamburg

Amanda was always very ambitious. She told me that she had rehearsed her Oscar speech from the age of eight. I was not disturbed by her desire for success. I admired it and encouraged her to achieve. When she got a role in *EastEnders*, as stallholder Carmen, I was thrilled for her, although she became frustrated when the character didn't become a regular. She was soon back in work, though, when she was offered the part of Cecily in *The Importance of Being Ernest*, which was to play a season at the English Theatre in Hamburg. When she called home, she seemed unhappy and said she wasn't enjoying Hamburg. She was staying in a dreadful run-down flat and was unsure about the production. Lady Bracknell was being played by a man in drag! She had made a friend, though, in fellow actor, Philip Goodhew, who would later direct us both, supporting Julie Walters and Rupert Graves, in a feature film, *Intimate Relations*.

During her time in Hamburg, I was working on a P&O cruise ship, *The Sea Princess*. Why, when I had a top-rating, high-earning game show, was I doing the kind of gig that entertainers usually did when TV work dried up? I still found it difficult to switch off and have a private life. I would get restless on holidays, so a cruise was a perfect way of combining the two. I could visit interesting places but still get the love and validation from an audience that I needed. There was always this nagging doubt that I didn't deserve the success I had achieved and that – as had happened to Dustin – it would be snatched away from me.

It was just a short trip round the Med, so, as Amanda was away, I took my mate Andy Grainger. We had a really good laugh together and he was fast becoming my best friend. Ship-to-shore calls were hideously expensive, which meant I couldn't be in touch with Amanda as much as I wanted. We would talk briefly when the ship was in port, but, as she was rehearsing, it wasn't always possible.

Our last port of call was Gibraltar. We docked one misty morning, walked around the town and were soon bored. Gibraltar is an army town so it's sort of like Aldershot with monkeys. It was too misty to go and see the baboons, so instead Andy and I decided to have a boozy lunch. Over several bottles of wine, I talked incessantly about Amanda, and Andy eventually said, 'Oh, for God's sake, marry her, then.'

'Brilliant idea!' I slurred. 'I will. Let's find a phonebox.' We had been living together for more than six months so it seemed like the right time to make a commitment.

From an old-fashioned red phonebox in the square, I dialled the number of the theatre in Hamburg and eventually got through to the company manager. God knows what he thought as my drunken voice bellowed, 'Hello, mate. It's Les. I must speak to Amanda.'

'Sorry, Les, she's busy right now rehearsing the engagement scene.'

'Ha, ha,' I shouted. 'That's just what I need to talk to her about.' I must have been very drunk because otherwise I wouldn't have been so unprofessional as to drag her out of a rehearsal.

'OK,' he said. 'I know you wouldn't call unless it was important. I'll go and get her.'

A couple of minutes later Amanda's worried voice asked, 'Hello, darling, is everything all right?'

'Couldn't be better,' I said. 'How's 24 August for you?'

'What?' she asked, confused.

'How's 24 August? Would you like to get married?'

'Les, you've clearly been drinking, but are you serious?'

'Absolutely.'

'Well, yes. Can I tell everyone?'

'Of course you can.'

That's when she knew I meant it, because I was happy to make it public news. Where I had been reticent about making my relationship with Sophie known, I wanted to shout my love for Amanda from the rooftops and this, in the years to come, would prove to be my undoing.

As Amanda went off to tell the cast she was getting married, I stumbled out into the square to meet Andy.

'What did she say, mate?'

'She agreed, though she thinks August is a crap idea – too early. We're going for next year.'

'Great,' he said. 'Shall we have another drink?'

'No,' I replied. 'I feel strangely drawn to that church.' There was a huge church across the way and I wanted a quiet, reflective moment. We weren't allowed in, though – we were clearly too drunk – so had a noisy, reflective moment or two over another beer (or two) in the less than holy surroundings of the nearest pub. When the ship docked in Southampton, Andy and I travelled back to London, and later that evening I caught a flight to Hamburg.

Amanda met me outside a restaurant where she and the cast

were eating and we held each other tightly. 'Sure you haven't changed your mind now you are sober?' she asked.

'Definitely not,' I said, clear for the first time in a long while that this was what I wanted.

The next day, while Amanda was having coffee, I found a jeweller's and bought a ring. Nothing too flashy or expensive – just a simple solitaire diamond. We had a lovely couple of days and moved from her dingy flat to a room at the nearby Atlantic Hotel. I left her to finish the run and caught a flight home. The next evening was Lynne's fortieth birthday and I had arranged a small surprise gathering for her, her mum and dad, Philip and some friends at the restaurant Christopher's in Covent Garden. I decided this was not the occasion to give her the news that I was engaged to be married – that could wait until the following week.

When I did tell Lynne, she reacted with great dignity. We cried together, reflecting on lost love, and she wished us happiness for the future. She even suggested that I ask Philip to be my best man. He was coming up to fifteen and was maturing into a lovely young man. He and I had developed a closeness when we went away on a skiing trip and had managed to maintain it. I couldn't ski at all, but one day he had coaxed me out of the nursery lesson I was in and made me join him on a blue run. What he didn't know was that I hadn't yet learnt how to stop and for days afterwards he would burst out laughing at the memory of me hurtling down the slope, zooming past him, poles flying everywhere, screaming, 'Philip, help me!' When he met Amanda, they got on instantly.

Amanda and I found and fell in love with a house on Hampstead Lane in Highgate. It was owned by Martin and Shirley Kemp, and when we had finished viewing it, I chatted with Martin in the garden. He had, of course, had amazing success with Spandau Ballet and had proved to be an excellent actor in the film *The Krays*. When I asked him what he was working on now, he seemed vague and a little evasive, but as he'd just returned from LA, I put it down to jet lag. We went straight from the house to the agent's office and put in an offer, only to be told that the house was no longer on the market. We later found out he had discovered, that very morning, that he had an enormous brain tumour. No wonder he was distracted. When he learnt that the tumour was benign, he put the house back on the market and we were first in the queue. They are a lovely couple, and buying a house from them was a simple and happy experience and I still have an elegant over-mantle mirror that they generously left when they moved out.

Amanda and I did our first job together, a panto in Glasgow. We worked with Gerard Kelly, who I later worked with on *Extras*, when he played the hilariously camp director of the show, Bunny. Then, on 14 May 1995, we were married at the United Reformed Church, Bournemouth. Amanda was forty minutes late in arriving at the church, and with lots of press photographers around I was beginning to get a bit jittery. Apparently, Sven Arnstein, who was photographing the wedding for *Hello!*, wanted extra shots of the preparations and Amanda's dad, Les, had booked a horse-drawn carriage as a surprise. Very nice of him, but the church was quite some way from their house! She got there at last and the service went through without a hitch. Amanda looked stunning in a simple ivory gown, and when we walked out of the church into glorious sunshine, I felt like the luckiest man in the world.

The reception was at the Rhinefield House Hotel in the New Forest. The guest list was hardly glittering: apart from Lionel, Su, Vicki and Roy Walker, the 120 guests were family and friends from all walks of life. *Hello!* had put pressure on us to invite more stars but we wanted to keep it simple. We weren't paid a huge fee by the magazine. They just gave us the photos, which took ages to do. The meal was delayed, the chef was extremely upset, and the guests were starving when we eventually sat down at about 5 p.m. The evening guests started to arrive as the speeches were being given.

In his speech, Les was very touching about Amanda. He is her stepfather but has been very supportive of her, her sister, Debbie, and mum, Judith. Philip did a great job as my best man and was very funny making jokes about my lousy DIY attempts. I was proud of him and I think he enjoyed the laughter. We danced into the evening, and as the party got into full swing, Amanda and I sneaked away to our room to reflect quietly on the day over a glass of champagne. Two days later we flew off to Jumby Bay, near Antigua, for our honeymoon.

Our first year of marriage was filled with happy times but also some highly explosive rows. When things are going well, I have a tendency to want to bomb my own ship and, at the first sign of any difficulty, would suggest that we weren't going to make it so we should just split up: 'I always said the age difference was too big. You'll get fed up with me sooner or later, so best that it ends now.' But as quickly as I had started a row, I would be apologising and saying we would be OK. Somewhere deep inside, I feel unworthy of happiness and want to sabotage the good things I have – a kind of self-fulfilling prophecy that wore Amanda down.

However, there were the funny moments that highlighted our age difference. One spring morning a plumber arrived to fix our washing machine, and while I was chatting to him in the kitchen, Amanda came in and said, 'It's Grand National Day. We've got to have a bet.'

'OK,' I said, and handed her a ten-pound note.

'Oh, we need to bet more than that. I feel lucky!' she replied.

I handed over another twenty pounds and the plumber looked at me, tutted and said, 'Kids, eh!'

We both appeared in Philip Goodhew's movie *Intimate Relations*, which was filmed in Abergavenny. I was working in summer season alongside Su Pollard and Roy Walker at the North Pier, Blackpool. Philip offered me the role of Maurice Guppy, half-brother to Rupert Graves's character, in a blackly comic take on a true-life murder. Julie Walters starred, and Laura Sadler, who would later star in *Holby City* before dying in a horrific accident, made her screen debut. However, there seemed to be a clash in the schedule and it seemed, at one stage, that I would be unable to do the film because of my commitments in Blackpool. I had two meaty scenes with Rupert that had to be filmed on a Monday and Tuesday in July. Monday was my day off, but on the Tuesday we would be filming in Wales until 5 p.m. and I had two shows in the evening, the first of which started at 6.10 p.m., back in Blackpool. So determined was I to achieve my ambition of appearing in my first feature film that I hired a helicopter and paid for it out of my own pocket. It was hilarious. One minute I was dressed in a 1930s tanktop and flannels, crying on Liz McKechnie's shoulder (she played my wife), having just discovered that my brother had killed his landlady and her teenage daughter. The next I was running across a field full of cows, jumping into a two-man helicopter and racing back to Blackpool. With minutes to spare we landed and I ran in through the stage door, changed into a full tuxedo and tap-danced my way through 'Anything Goes' with Su Pollard. Talk about from one end of the scale to the other.

After a slow start Amanda's career began to take off. She was picked by Channel 5 to be a member of their new flagship comedy show *We Know Where You Live*, which also starred the then unknown Simon Pegg, Sanjeev Bhaskar and Fiona Allen. Then came *Kiss Me, Kate*, a BBC sitcom with Caroline Quentin and Chris Langham. She was showing a talent for comedy and I was very proud of her. Despite her success, she seemed rooted in strong family values. She had a deep love for her grandparents, Jim and Ethel, and made huge efforts to see her parents when she wasn't working. She also helped me to regain the bond with my family.

For years we had neglected my mum and dad's grave. I think none of us could deal with the loss and didn't want to visit and be reminded of it. We hadn't even updated the headstone for them. It still only said that it was the resting place of my brother Roddy. Amanda tackled me on it. 'Come on, Les, you've got to get a new stone. You have to have somewhere you can go and pay your respects.' Like an ostrich, I had buried my head, preferring to remember my parents as they were, not wanting to believe they were in the ground. However, galvanised by her energy, we arranged for a new stone to be made. But what would we say on it? After much discussion, we decided on the phrase my dad always said about each of us: 'We love the bones of you.' It may appear shocking to any passerby, considering what's lying six feet under, but to us, it was funny, moving and appropriate. We decided to leave the 'bloody' out for decency's sake!

One cold November afternoon in 1996 we arranged a family visit to the grave, which was in the vast Allerton Cemetery. The problem was, we didn't know exactly where in the cemetery it was. So for about an hour and a half we split up and wandered around checking out all the graves in the area. It was farcical. The light was fading and it looked as if we were going to have to abandon the task when our Ken suddenly shouted, 'Over here.' Marg, Tony, Mandy, Amanda and I scuttled over from the four corners of the cemetery and gathered round the beautiful new stone.

'Right,' I said. 'I'll just say a few words.' As I began recounting some fond memories of our childhood, an electronic pinging sound came from our Ken's pocket. 'What's that?' I asked.

'I've got a message,' he said, pulling out his mobile phone.

'Ken, switch it off. This is important.'

'Yeah,' he answered, 'so could this be. It's a new phone and somebody might need me.'

'You're a bloody taxi driver – sorry, Mum. Nobody needs you right now. Switch it off.'

Reluctantly, he switched it off and I carried on with the speech. As soon as I'd finished, I heard the Nokia theme and our Ken looked sheepishly at us. It was hilarious, and we all burst into laughter.

'Has anybody noticed,' asked our Mandy, 'the date of my mum's death?'

On closer inspection it revealed that she died not on 30 March 1977, but on 30 March 1997, which technically meant she was still alive. A stonemason's mistake had given Winnie the last laugh, and I swear that at that very moment the sun broke through the darkening clouds for the briefest of seconds. It reminded me of that old joke about the Yorkshireman who goes to a stonemason and asks him to make a stone for his departed wife.

'What do you want on it?' the stonemason asked.

'Lord, she was thine,' he replied.

The next week he went to see it, but it said, 'Lord, she was thin.'

'You've missed the "e" off,' he said.

'Don't worry,' said the stonemason. 'Come back tomorrow and I'll have it right.'

The next day he returned and upon reading the stone saw, 'Ee, Lord, she was thin.'

That year Amanda and I did a panto in Sheffield with Danny la Rue. Danny is a true old pro who has had enormous success throughout his career. His club was a popular haunt for the 1960s glitterati and it was there that a young Ronnie Corbett played comic feed to Danny. There are hilarious stories about

Dan's grandness. One time he called a theatre and said, 'Hello. Danny here. When I arrive next week, I'll be bringing my dog, Janty.'

'Sorry, Mr la Rue,' the theatre manager replied, 'we don't allow dogs in the theatre.'

Dan put the phone down and two minutes later called back and said, in his rich, showbiz baritone, 'No dog. No Danny.'

Another time, he was in summer season at the Opera House, Blackpool, and Les Dawson was at the nearby Grand Theatre. Dan wasn't doing great business, but Les was, so one evening Les got a call from Dan. 'Les, darling,' he started, 'could you please get your queue to line up the other way. They're blocking my box office.'

That season in Sheffield, I was in my dressing room one Sunday matinée and could hear Dan talking to his dresser, Annie, as he sat carefully applying his make-up. There had been a full feature on him in the *Sunday Telegraph* magazine and he was obviously thrilled. 'Do you know, Annie, that journalist said that I was the last of the great variety performers.'

No reply from Annie.

Then Dan's voice: 'And do you know, he's right.'

Not one for false modesty, our Dan.

Towards the end of the run I began to get anxious about Amanda's behaviour. Whenever I came into a room she would be on the phone and would end the call hurriedly. On a shopping trip to Leeds she bought an expensive trousersuit at Harvey Nichols. I thought it was a ridiculous buy as we were going off on holiday to Barbados in a few weeks. Being a typical man, I wondered when on earth she was going to get any use out of it. We rowed about it on the way back to Sheffield. What I didn't know was that she was secretly planning my appearance on *This Is Your Life*. All those calls were with Jo, the programme researcher, and Roger, who was helping her coordinate the guest list. So, early in February, as I finished recording an evening of *Family Fortunes* shows at Central Studios, the board behind me went mad – large 'X's appeared all over it and that wrong answer noise, 'Eugh-eugh', was repeated over and over. I looked behind me to read, 'Les Dennis, this is your life.' At first I thought it was a surreal wind-up, but then Michael Aspel walked on with the 'big red book' in his hand. Stunned, and touched, I was whisked off to the Commodore Club, where my family, friends and guests were already congregating. There were filmed messages from Thelma Barlow, Liz Dawn, Bill Tarmy and Ken Dodd. Guests included Jim Bowen, Freddie Starr, Bobby Davro and, as already recounted, the football god Denis Law. A particularly touching moment for me was the appearance of Bruce Prince, the English teacher who had cast me in all those school plays. Sadly, they couldn't find Ken Othen, though he watched the show, got in touch, and we met up again in Manchester.

Philip came on and was his usual laidback self, something that Lynda Lee-Potter would comment on in the *Daily Mail* (26 February 1997) the following week. There was a column on her page that was headlined 'Cool Kids With So Much to Hide.' It read:

> Last week's *This Is Your Life* programme featured the comedian and impressionist Les Dennis. Michael Aspel asked Les's teenage son, Philip, if he was aiming to go into the entertainment business. The boy said he might but he wasn't sure. 'You don't seem very enthusiastic about it,' said Michael. 'That's him,' said Les irritably, 'he's never enthusiastic about anything.' It was a painful moment highlighting the perennial gap between adults and offspring. Parents desperately want their children to be bright-eyed, keen and bursting with ambition. Teenagers yearn to appear indifferent, cool and blasé to hide their inward

> uncertainty and embarrassment. I suspect Philip was anguished by his father's involuntary remark, and that Les was anguished that he'd said it. Meanwhile every parent must have identified with Les and every teenager sympathised with Philip.

I'm annoyed with myself, even now, that I said it, but I know that at the time I most certainly was not irritated with Philip. Lynda made a hugely valid point, though, and caused me to reflect on my relationship with my son and see that, perhaps, there were some echoes of the distance from my own dad. Sometimes it is hard for Phil to have a well-known father. When he was asked as a child what it was like to be my son, he said something funny: 'I get my head patted more than that little bloke on *The Benny Hill Show.*' The question he now gets asked is, 'Are you going into the business?' but I think that watching some of the down times I have had may have jaded his interest in the business. He definitely has talent and, at any stage could consider acting as a career option. He now though works hard for a living in the building trade and I am enormously proud of him. He has grown into a very caring, respectful young man who shows amazing compassion for others.

CHAPTER 20

The Beginning of the End

For some stupid reason, in 1998 Amanda and I decided we needed a bigger house. The Hampstead house was easily big enough for two adults and a dog. Although we had discussed having children, Amanda's career was taking off so quickly that we both agreed it would not be the best time to start a family yet. I think my humble, working-class roots make me constantly insecure about my success. I suffer, like many people, from 'impostor syndrome' and always expect someone to tap me on the shoulder and say, 'Sorry, mate, you don't belong here. Time to give it all back.' While this has made me driven, hard-working and has contributed to my success over the years, the self-doubt and angst has fuelled my need for material possessions by which to measure my success. The bigger the house, the better I was doing. We had already bought a cottage near the north Norfolk coast for holidays. Perhaps having a young, attractive wife was another way for me to validate my success and falsely inflate my self-esteem.

My career was ticking along nicely but I had times when I felt artistically unfulfilled. When I started hosting *Family Fortunes* in 1987, I thought it would last for a few years, but eleven years later I was still doing it. Despite the first few years, when people associated it with Bob Monkhouse, I managed to make the show my own and the ratings were regularly 10 to 12 million and sometimes higher. Many current producers would like to achieve such high figures now, but with many more channels and wider entertainment choices, those days seem to have gone. As the show would only take two or three weeks to record, I was free for the rest of the year to do other things. It was an enviable position to be in and gave me the chance to flex the acting muscles I hadn't really used since the Everyman days with Clive Barker, Jude Kelly and the Group. I set about looking for some dramatic acting roles. At the same time, Amanda and I found a house in St Mark's Square, in trendy Primrose Hill, and, together with the building's developers, set about renovating it. It was a ludicrously large, sprawling house for two people. Set over six floors, just walking to the top of the house was utterly exhausting. As an investment, it would prove to be very wise, but as our home, it would provide more unhappy memories than good ones.

In the summer of 1998, before we moved into 9 St Mark's Square, Amanda got her first lead role in ITV's 1970s sitcom *The Grimleys*, playing opposite Brian Conley and rock legend Noddy Holder. At the same time I landed my first dramatic stage role, playing the bullying, grief-stricken restaurateur Tom Sargent in David Hare's *Skylight*, directed by Euan Smith at the Watermill Theatre in Newbury. It was brave casting on Euan's part, and was insanely ambitious for me to attempt such a huge and complex role, which had been created by the brilliant actor Michael Gambon, and was later played by the equally accomplished Bill Nighy. I took the role of Tom in the three-hander alongside more experienced actors Teresa Gallagher, as Kyra, and Richard Hanson, as Tom's eighteen-year-old son, Edward. Thanks to Euan's excellent direction and support, I managed to pull it off and even got some half-decent reviews.

The biggest compliment, though, was when people said that at first it was odd watching Les Dennis in such a role but minutes into the production, they forgot and believed in Tom. In the closing moments Tom angrily throws Kyra's schoolbooks around the flat and rants about 'these fucking children'. The audience at the Watermill are very close to the stage and one night I heard a woman whisper to her friend, 'Ooh, he doesn't use language like that in *Family Fortunes*!' I was much prouder on another evening when a lady's reaction to the same scene was, 'It's two o'clock in the morning. What are the neighbours going to think?' She was so engrossed that she believed Kyra's neighbours would be disturbed by the noise! At the end of the run I was hooked and determined to use the financial security that *Family Fortunes* provided to continue taking risks in the less well-paid provincial repertory theatres around the country.

In November 1998 Amanda, Nobbie, our dog, and I moved into the house in Primrose Hill. Christmas came and went and 1999 began well. I became the host of ITV's new prime-time talent show *Give Your Mate a Break*, did a new play, *Mr Wonderful*, at the Chester Gateway opposite Helen Atkinson-Wood and Judith Barker, and *Family Fortunes* continued. Amanda did a second series of *The Grimleys* and landed a starring role in a two-part comedy drama, *Happy Birthday, Shakespeare*. Photos of us together began to appear in newspapers and magazines, and we were fast becoming a celebrity couple – something I baulked at to begin with but decided to accept. The press were obsessed by the age difference between us and seemed to be waiting, with pencils sharpened, for what they felt sure would be the inevitable split. We'd been married for nearly four years now, though, and for a while the media attention had been reasonably positive. Amanda enjoyed a happy relationship with Fleet Street and clearly loved the fuss. She did countless interviews and would always talk of her happy home life. Sometimes she would give away some outrageous snippets of information, which would embarrass me, and I suggested she didn't have to tell journalists everything about her private life. 'Oh, don't make a fuss, darling. It's all a harmless bit of fun.' What she didn't realise was that she was slowly building a file that would be referred to constantly when we hit the rockier waters that were to come.

If I was uncomfortable with some of the interviews she did, then I was very unhappy when she agreed to do raunchy, scantily dressed photo shoots for men's magazines like *FHM* and *Loaded*. I respected that it was her decision but felt that she was endangering the chances she was building to be taken seriously as an actress. I began to notice that Amanda was listening less and less to any advice I gave her. Just like I had in the 1980s, she became impatient if anyone suggested that she should take stock and plan her career path more carefully. I felt that if she wasn't careful, she was going to be destined for a future as 'telly totty'.

Having said all that, I was genuinely proud of her success and thrilled that she was getting invited to functions in her own right and not just as Mrs Les Dennis. I even joked that I was becoming Mr Amanda Holden. I have often been asked if I felt threatened by Amanda's flourishing career, and although I didn't want to admit it at the time, to some extent I was. The scales were tipping and my ego was taking a battering. I remember joking with Bob Monkhouse at Ronnie Barker's garden party that I was becoming Norman Maine, the character played by James Mason in the movie *A Star Is Born*. The film is the story of a successful movie star who falls in love with a talented starlet. They marry and slowly her career begins to eclipse his. He turns to drink, becomes washed up in Hollywood and in the end walks out to sea and is drowned. In the closing scene, Judy Garland as Vicky Lester, picks up her Oscar and tearfully tells the applauding audience, 'I am Mrs Norman Maine.' Heady and dramatic stuff, but the fact that I made the joke to Bob meant that deep down that was how I was starting to feel. I was certainly aware that Amanda was being hailed as a talent to watch and that to some extent I had become 'telly wallpaper' with *Family Fortunes* having been on TV for so long. So, yes, there was a part of me that was envious, but I always remained supportive and was thrilled when she got the part of Alice in *Happy Birthday, Shakespeare*. In fact, the so-called nepotism that we had been accused of worked in my favour this time when I was given a cameo role in the production as the grown-up Milky Bar Kid.

Happy Birthday, Shakespeare was the story of a hapless coach driver, Will, played by Neil Morrissey, who is unhappy in his marriage to Kate, played by Dervla Kirwan. Will, on a trip to Shakespeare's birthplace in Stratford, falls for the charms of a glamorous tour guide, Alice. In a press article in early 2000, Amanda admitted having some sympathy with her character. 'She had a job, her children and an unemployed husband, so she was the main breadwinner. Her means of escape from reality was the excitement of having an affair. It made her feel very powerful and attractive – the exact opposite to the drudgery of her real life. But the affair was based on a total lack of honesty.' Well, no children and no unemployed husband, but perhaps Amanda was subconsciously drawing parallels with how she felt about her own life. If I'd read the article at the time, warning bells might have begun to ring.

From the moment Amanda started the job something in her manner began to change. Where before if she had a few days off, she would make the effort to come home or we would go to the cottage we had on the north Norfolk coast, she became more keen to stay at the unit hotel. I noticed very quickly that she couldn't stop praising Neil, saying how funny and what a brilliant actor he was. It was a real case of mentionitis and I began to feel pangs of jealousy and anxiety. Usually if an actor has to do love scenes with their co-star, they are sensitive to their partner's insecurities. Amanda, though, seemed to delight in telling me how well they were getting on. 'Neil was so funny today – he did make me laugh.' Her face would light up and it was as if she was talking to a girlfriend about a crush she had, rather than to her husband. I, like an idiot, would smile and listen intently, wanting to be supportive but inside feeling a mixture of fear, anger and jealousy. We were presenting an award at a fundraiser at the Dorchester on the evening that Neil and Amanda were filming a bath scene together. Matthew Kelly was hosting, and we had been given our own room to change in. I wasn't working that day, so I got there early and waited anxiously for Amanda to arrive. She waltzed into the room and, while quickly changing into her evening dress, took me excitedly through her day at work. It was a bizarre 'honey, I'm home' moment.

'Oh, Les, it was so funny. We had to be naked in a bathtub in front of the whole crew. Well, not naked. We had knickers on, of course. The bath was full of bubbles, so I could have worn a bra, but I said to everyone, "Oh, it's nothing you haven't seen before."'

'What?' I asked incredulously.

'Oh, you know what I mean. All the girls go topless on beaches these days. So I just jumped in and got on with it. The crew gave me a round of applause.'

I'll bet they fucking did, I thought.

'Bit scared when we started to snog, but I've got to tell you, he is a fabulous kisser.'

'Amanda, enough, I don't want to know.'

Looking in the mirror as she fixed her make-up, she added, 'You see, like me he's got big lips. It makes kissing so much nicer.'

I was in shock, but before I could answer, there was a knock on the door telling us they were ready for us. As we stood together presenting the award at the glitzy ceremony, I was dying inside and wanted to flee from the stage. I suppose, though, like most people whose partners cheat, I was in denial. Even later when, at her mum Judy's fiftieth-birthday party, Amanda had placed a photo of her and Neil (albeit a continuity polaroid of them in character but looking every inch the happy couple) on the mantelpiece in the bedroom, I pushed the fear away.

I was becoming aware that Amanda was beginning to show that she was embarrassed by what I did. We were invited along to *An Audience With Cliff Richard* and Bobby Davro and I did a routine with him. We sang 'The Young Ones' with Cliff and gently took the piss. At one point I was behind Cliff intently studying the back of his ears and Davro asked, 'What are you doing?'

'Looking for the scars,' I said. It went down really well, but when I rejoined Amanda, she was bright scarlet and refused to clap along with the rest of the audience to Cliff's medley of hits. 'Neil and everyone at work may be watching and they'll take the piss out of me.' For the first time I felt like a parent who had embarrassed their teenager by doing some awful, dad dancing.

When I did my scenes with Neil, even though he was perfectly friendly I felt uncomfortable. I had lunch with him and the producer, Gareth Neame, and during breaks in filming he welcomed me into his winnebago. He, like Amanda, had mentionitis and couldn't stop talking about her. 'Holden's great to work with,' he must have said a dozen times.

Hello, I thought. 'Holden', that's my nickname for my wife – not yours. She got more name-checks in our brief conversation than Rachel Weisz, his girlfriend at the time. I nodded along and pretended to listen, but in my head I was thinking, You fucker, you've had a bath with my wife.

One weekend when Amanda was filming the scenes in

Stratford, I went to visit her and we went out with some of the cast and crew for a meal. The lovely Nick Hurran, the director, was there and so was his wife, Michelle Buck. Michelle is a very successful drama producer and knows the business inside out. Over dinner she said an odd but interesting thing. 'Come to check out the chemistry?' she asked.

'No,' I said defensively. 'Just here to support Amanda.'

'Right,' she said. 'Don't worry – everyone does it. It's difficult for spouses. I think you are OK, though. There's a spark but I doubt anything's going on.'

I decided my fears were in my head. It was something I'd never really experienced before. In my job as a host there was never any love interest – the only snogs I got were from excited grannies who jumped all over me if they won a food mixer. I had played opposite attractive women in the plays I'd done, but there hadn't been any raunchy scenes, so Amanda had shown no concern. That conversation with Michelle put my mind at rest for a while.

As the new millennium approached, though, Amanda still seemed distant. We went to her mum and dad's in Devon for Christmas and had a dreadful row on Christmas Day. It was over something seemingly trivial. Every year, as well as main gifts, Amanda and her family would give each other silly ones from under the tree. Amanda would buy hers and, as most couples do, would give them from the two of us. This year, however, she gave them out with tags on that said, 'From Amanda.' I was shocked and confused. I felt so angry and humiliated that I hadn't even known and now had nothing to give them from me. As soon as everyone was out of the room, I tackled her on it.

'Don't ruin the day. You know how much I love Christmas,' she retorted.

I should have left it but continued to push and we had a huge row. At one point Amanda cried to her mum, 'I don't want this any more. I want out.'

We managed to patch things up and didn't allow it to spoil the day for her grandparents, but it was a significant moment in the breakdown of our relationship. New Year's Eve 1999 was spent at our house with both families and many of our friends, but things remained strained between us. As we all gathered to watch the fireworks on the Embankment from the top of Primrose Hill, I felt a huge emptiness inside as I wondered anxiously what the new millennium would bring.

CHAPTER 21

Mr Cellophane

The New Year brought new jobs for both of us. Amanda got a meaty role in a new BBC drama series, *Hearts and Bones*, about a group of twenty-something friends in south London. It also starred Hugo Speer, Damien Lewis and Sarah Parish. I joined the cast of *Chicago* at the Adelphi Theatre, playing the cuckolded Amos, husband of Roxy Hart. Amos's big number in the show was 'Mr Cellophane', in which he sang about the wife he had been married to for seven years who no longer noticed him. Talk about art imitating life! I opened in the show on Valentine's night and then two days later, on 16 February, it was Amanda's twenty-ninth birthday. We had supper after the show with some friends and then met up with the *Hearts and Bones* cast at Soho House, a members club in London. They were all very welcoming and friendly towards me – it was only Amanda who seemed distant. For months I had become increasingly anxious that our seemingly happy marriage had taken a huge turn for the worse. Neil's name came up constantly, and one Sunday morning towards the end of March Amanda had gone out to get the papers but took an hour. Odd, I thought, as the newsagent was round the corner. She came into the house and plonked down the tabloids, which all had the same front-page story, 'Neil Morrissey and Rachel Weisz Split'.

'He'll be devastated,' Amanda stated.

I wanted to say, 'Well, you should know. You've just been on the phone to him for the past hour,' but I held back. I knew in my heart that something was going on but I was too afraid to bring it to a head for fear that it might actually be true.

Instead, I did the thing that most people will do when they suspect their partner is cheating – I went through her phone bills and found the same number came up again and again. One morning, while Amanda lay sleeping, I took her phone, sneaked into the bathroom and texted Neil. I knew, again from Amanda's urge to talk about him all the time, that he was abroad filming and so, with the time difference, it would be OK to contact him. 'Good morning,' I wrote and pressed send.

Almost immediately the phone beeped, indicating there was a new message. I panicked, worrying that Amanda would wake up as the noise echoed around the bathroom. 'Hello,' I read. 'You're up early.'

'Yes,' I wrote, wondering what the hell Amanda would say back. 'Can't sleep. Thinking about you.'

'Call you later,' came the immediate reply.

Later that day I decided to call him, but this time from my phone. I felt like Meryl Streep in *Heartburn* as I dialled the number and got Neil's voice.

'Hi...' Long pause. '...Who's this?'

'It's Les...' I left an even longer pause '...Dennis.'

'Hi, mate. How you doing?'

'OK, considering.'

Massive pause.

'Considering what?'

'Considering you phone my wife so much and she phones you.'

'Right...' Pause that Harold Pinter would be embarrassed by '...mate.'

'Look, she is a married woman. I'd like you to respect that.'

No pause. 'Cool.'

'By the way,' I said, 'it was me who texted you this morning. Couldn't sleep. Thinking about you.' I hung up.

I couldn't eat or sleep and began to lose a lot of weight very quickly. One night, after doing a corporate gig at the Hilton Hotel and drowning my sorrows with my friend Justin and some of the clients, I made the mistake of deciding we should all go to the Met Bar. Under normal circumstances, it is the last place that I would go – hip, trendy bars are not my scene – but I felt like I was going through a midlife and marriage crisis and wasn't thinking straight. I remember standing on the steps outside and stroking a dog while negotiating with the doorman to let all my 'friends' in. As I did so, a cluster of flashbulbs popped, but it wasn't until the next day, when I woke blearily to the sound of my phone, that the impact of my stupid escapade hit me. It was my press agent, Pat Lake-Smith, asking, 'Have you seen the papers?' All the tabloids were full of my 'don't you know who I am?' debacle. Matthew Wright in the *Daily Mirror* (30 March 2000) was the kindest of all. To the accompaniment of photos of me looking tired and emotional and a headline saying, 'Please Les Me In,' he wrote:

> Fortune wasn't shining on Les Dennis when the quiz show host was barred from entering an exclusive London bar. The *Family Fortunes* star turned up at trendy members-only Met Bar in the early hours of Wednesday with a gang of friends. The group, all clutching half-full glasses of champagne,

were obviously determined to continue their celebrations. Les, 46, who is married to beauty Amanda Holden, 29, bowled up to the doorman first and asked to be let in. 'I'm Les Dennis from *Family Fortunes* – can you let me in?' the quiz show host, currently starring in the West End musical *Chicago*, asked the doorman.

'Who?' the bouncer replied politely, before refusing Les's request.

'Look, I must be famous – the paparazzi are taking my photo,' insisted Dennis as flashbulbs exploded, only heightening his embarrassment.

Thankfully for the tired and emotional star, another doorman did recognise Les and agreed to let him in. But his friends, who were waiting on the pavement on Park Lane, were left out in the cold. After disappearing for a couple of minutes, Les returned to try to get his pals in for last orders. 'Please let my friends in,' he begged, but to no avail. A manageress came out to adjudicate but wasn't any more sympathetic to his plight. The star and his friends were far too drunk, and besides, the bar would be closing at 3 a.m., she told them.

After arguing for twenty minutes, Les and his friends eventually gave up the ghost. They were last seen ambling down the road in the direction of the nearby Hilton Hotel.

Needless to say, I haven't dared darken the door of the Met Bar since!

When Amanda finished filming *Hearts and Bones* at the beginning of April, she booked a holiday with her friend Jane Wall, whom she had known since drama school. Jane was appearing in *The Bill*, and they both needed a break. When Amanda and Jane returned from Cuba, she suggested that it might be a good idea if she bought a flat of her own. She argued that it would make a good investment and then tentatively suggested that she might need 'some space'. I should have told her to go, as she had clearly fallen out of love with me and all my instincts told me she was interested in somebody else. Why I didn't tell her to sling her hook I don't know, any more than I know why I did what I did next. Like an idiot, I chose to support her in her decision to have some space and even went viewing flats in Belsize Park with her.

It got worse. Shortly afterwards, Amanda was away filming a lavish two-part drama, *The Hunt* for ITV, in which she played a young woman whose marriage to her husband, played by Philip Glenister, was in trouble. I remember waking one morning and switching on *GMTV*. I sleepily watched Lorraine Kelly introduce in her inimitable way, 'two lovely, hunky men. Oh, I'm so lucky! Here with me now are the gorgeous Hugo Speer and Neil Morrissey.' Imagine, then, my confusion when Lorraine announced, 'Boys, I've got a wee surprise for you. On the line right now, on location in Devon, is the lovely Amanda Holden.' I would love to watch that footage again because Neil's face was suddenly struck with horror and I am sure the blush that crossed his face was well off the red scale and bordering on purple. I was suddenly wide awake as I heard Lorraine, in all innocence, ask, 'So, Amanda, just a bit of fun, but who is the better kisser, Hugo or Neil?'

Shit, I thought, am I still dreaming?

Hugo looked embarrassed, while Neil looked like he was desperately searching for a shovel to tunnel his way out of the studio, as Amanda giggled, 'Oh, they are both great, but if I had to make a choice, it would be Neil,' and added, possibly for my benefit, 'I'm talking onscreen, strictly professional, of course.'

Lots of giggles and Lorraine signed off with, 'Great to talk to you, Amanda, it really is.'

I stared blankly at the screen as Neil and Hugo swiftly moved on to the subject of Warchild, the charity that they were on the programme to promote. Those alarm bells should have been deafening me. No, I convinced myself, it's just actors' banter. Amanda needs to promote her new drama. That's why she did it.

Soon after, while Amanda and I were in our house sleeping, somebody broke in without forced entry (Amanda's bag had been stolen from her dressing room earlier that week) and took my wallet, watch and Amanda's diamond engagement and eternity rings. It seemed to be an omen. The insurance company came through and gave us the money to replace the stolen goods. One day in Harrods we found a new engagement ring and incredibly Amanda suggested I go down on bended knee in public to place it on her finger, but really this was an elaborate pretence of a romantic moment between a happily married couple.

When the story of Amanda's affair broke a few weeks later, some papers would report that I was brave and honourable to fight for my marriage, while others would label me a lily-livered cuckold. The latter were clearly right, and it's true that love is blind. Only my love was clinically insane as well! Thinking about it now, the only explanation I can come up with for my spineless behaviour was that karma had come round and on some level, I was getting what I deserved. When I had first achieved my success, in the 1980s, I had treated Lynne appallingly and had felt invincible. I could see parallels in what was happening to Amanda, and as Lynne had, in vain, all those years before, perhaps I too hoped that Amanda would come to her senses and realise what she had. What do they say? There's no fool like an old fool.

CHAPTER 22

'Les, You'd Better Sit Down'

It was a hot Sunday morning at the beginning of May 2000, the first really warm day of the year. I was a few months into my run as Amos Hart in the hit West End show *Chicago*. After eight shows a week, a day off was to be savoured and spent wisely. Amanda was still filming *The Hunt* for ITV, so as it was such a lovely day, I decided to invite some friends over for a barbecue. Karen and Justin arrived first to help me with the preparations. Karen and the kids settled happily in the garden, while Justin and I hit Sainsbury's on Finchley Road and bought enough food to feed a small country for a month. We got back to the house and dumped the bags on the kitchen table. While Justin was parking the car, the phone rang. It will be Amanda, I thought. The last time we had spoken had been the day before as I left for the matinée and the conversation had been strained.

'Les,' she said. Immediately I knew this was something serious. 'I think you'd better sit down.' I was in the hall, so I fell rather than sat on to the bottom stair, my stomach doing a thousand somersaults, as she said, 'The *Daily Mirror* have got photos of Neil and me leaving a pub after lunch together.'

I didn't have to ask, 'Neil who?' There was no Neil in the cast of *The Hunt* and I was certain it wouldn't be a member of the crew – not her style. 'Morrissey,' I said, almost to myself.

'Yes,' she replied. 'You were right.'

I sat on the stairs that Sunday morning and knew, at last, that all my suspicions and fears had been well founded. Amanda was crying softly on the other end of the phone as I kicked instinctively into survival mode. 'Right. It's all over between us. I hope you two will be really happy together – you deserve each other,' I shouted, and slammed the phone down.

My friends hardly had time to ask what was wrong before the phone rang again. It wasn't Amanda ringing back, but Pat, my press agent, making the difficult call to tell me the devastating news that I already knew. Well, so I thought. It turned out that there were also photos of them on a romantic country walk and returning to the holiday cottage they had rented for the weekend. It was now clear to me, as it had been subconsciously for some time, that their affair was not something new. Since New Year Amanda's feelings towards me had seriously cooled. She had talked about how she thought perhaps she had married too young and that she might need a break. I had tried to be understanding and had gone along with everything she wanted, including supporting her to get her own place, but now I knew for sure that her distance had been due to her feelings for Neil and wanting to spend time with him.

When I came off the phone to Pat, I calmly told Justin and Karen what was going on and ignored their suggestions that we should cancel the barbecue. 'But Gary and Jane are coming round,' they said.

'That's OK,' I replied. 'We'll tell them the facts, eat and get totally shit-faced.'

And that's what we did. I suppose I knew that all hell was about to break loose and so chose to anaesthetise myself for a few hours rather than deal with it. We sat at the bottom of the garden, ate burgers and salad (well, they did, while I pushed mine around my plate), drank copious amounts of red wine and slagged off Neil Morrissey's performance in *Men Behaving Badly*. Amanda had told me once that Neil's favourite wine (mentionitis again) was Alex Corton, a red burgundy. 'I've got a magnum in the cellar,' I remember telling my friends. 'Let's destroy the fucker!'

As I was about to head towards the cellar, my mobile rang and 'Amanda Mob' came up on the display. Fully intending to disconnect, I heard myself say, 'Hello. Are you OK?'

'No,' she said, breaking down in tears.

'Do you want me to come down and see you?' I asked.

'Would you?' she asked incredulously.

'I'm on my way.'

Despite protests from my friends, who implored me to retain my dignity, I listened to my heart and decided instead to do everything I could to save my marriage. An hour later I was in the back of a car heading for a village near the one in which the film crew for *The Hunt* were staying. I didn't want to turn up at Amanda's hotel in case the paparazzi were already camped out there, so instead I arranged to meet Amanda in a café the next morning, went to an anonymous hotel, checked in and collapsed on my bed in a wine- and grief-fuelled coma.

As dawn broke, well before the alarm went off, I woke from a fitful sleep. I remember dreaming that I was in a celebrity football match and going in for a hard tackle against Neil Morrissey. I kicked out to beat him to the ball, but suddenly realised that I had in fact kicked the duvet off the bed and halfway across the room. My waking thought was, Oh, shit! It's all in the *Mirror*. I hadn't dared to order a copy at hotel reception, so instead had to wait and watch breakfast TV to see what the reaction was. Weirdly, I saw the front-page headline of the *Mirror*, 'Amanda and Neil's Romantic Weekend Trip', and photos of them walking down a country lane on *The Big Breakfast* as Johnny Vaughan and Lisa Tarbuck discussed the morning papers. I remember them both looking into the camera and berating Neil for having an affair with a married woman. Their support felt good, if a little surreal.

I checked out of the hotel and got a cab to the café where Amanda had asked me to meet her. No photographers had managed to get down from London yet, so we were able to talk with a degree of privacy. She looked drawn and upset as I heard myself asking, 'Good weekend?' There is, I think, something morbid in human nature that makes you want to know all the intimate details of a partner's infidelity.

Amanda again talked to me as if she was having coffee with one of her girlfriends. 'Apart from that one visit to the pub, we ate in mostly. Neil's a brilliant cook. Makes his own scones and everything.' She even admitted to buying new underwear for the weekend.

It wasn't only the sexual details (which I'm sure she'd have shared, had I asked) that hurt, but the thought of intimacies like breakfast, a dinner in front of a roaring fire or a walk along a country lane. In the photos the *Mirror* had taken, Amanda was wearing a jacket I had bought her and, devastatingly, a Tiffany love bangle. The idea of the bangle is that your partner locks it on to your wrist and keeps the key, as a token of love and fidelity. Amanda had actually asked for one the previous Christmas.

To be betrayed by a partner is an awful experience; to have that experience examined by the nation, on TV and in the media, is horrific. I was cuckolded and it wasn't just the people in my village whispering behind my back; it was the great British public, who were discussing it openly over breakfast, at dinner parties and on radio phone-ins. That day on Radio 1, Sara Cox actually played a song for 'poor Les'. Still I clung to the belief that we could survive the affair. 'What do we do now?' I asked.

'I can't give him up,' she answered.

'Right, so why have I wasted my time coming here?'

Her phone rang and I could tell from her tone of voice that it was him. There was a warmth and concern that I hadn't had directed towards me in a very long time. 'I'm going home,' I interrupted.

She put the phone down and said, 'Please, Les, come with me to the set. I'll get one of our drivers to take you back.'

I should have accepted that it was over then, walked out of that café and kept my pride intact. Instead, like an idiot, I went with her to the set, knowing that everyone was thinking I was mad. Her co-stars, Adrian Lukis and Samantha Bond, were polite, but behind their eyes were unmistakable signs of pity and embarrassment.

Filming was taking place at a huge stately home. As we walked around the grounds discussing the future, Amanda mentioned something about wanting to live in the country with a big family and lots of animals. I knew, although she didn't say it, that she wasn't including me in this idyllic fantasy. That's when I decided to jump into a unit car and head back to London. Her driver took me home. I sat in the back of the luxurious Mercedes feeling numb and unsure of what life had in store for me. I rang Nigel West, the director of *Chicago*, to say that I would be returning to the show the following evening. The tabloids would later report that I had deserted the show for a whole week. In fact, I only missed one night. The other call I remember making was to the producers of *Stars in Their Eyes* to cancel a performance that Amanda and I were due to make the following week. Thank God we hadn't already recorded it. I don't think I could have coped with the embarrassment of watching us walk through those doors and saying, 'Tonight, Matthew, we are going to be Elton John and Kiki Dee singing "Don't Go Breaking My Heart".' That would certainly have made the list for *The Fifty Most Embarrassing Moments of the Year*!

That night I stayed with Justin, Karen and family, and the next morning I returned home to find six cars parked outside the house. As I raced to get through the front door, flashbulbs popped and shouts of 'Les, can you give us a quick quote?' and, 'Les, where is Amanda right now?' echoed throughout the street. I ran into the house and slammed the door behind me. The doorbell rang repeatedly all day. Some tried to deliver flowers as a way of getting me to answer; others put notes through the letterbox, assuring me that I could tell my side of the story sensitively and with dignity. I felt like a prisoner in my own home. At 6 p.m. Justin arrived to take me to work. For the hundredth time or so, I would play Amos, the cuckolded, faithful husband who stood by his wife when she murdered her lover and is eventually let down by her,

My performance this time would require no acting. I ran out to Justin's car and jumped in as a dozen or so photographers ran towards us. They literally threw themselves at the bonnet trying to get that front-page photo. The madness had begun.

CHAPTER 23

Breaking Up Is Hard to Do

When I returned to *Chicago* so quickly, the press seemed a little disappointed. I think they expected me to do a Stephen Fry and go AWOL for a while. Where I hadn't had reviewers when I'd opened, suddenly the tabloids had a renewed interest in my dramatic performance. It was a red-top gift: let's face it, the parallels between the character I was playing and my own situation were glaringly obvious. As I left the stage door that evening, a newshound from the *Daily Star* shouted, 'Les, are you surprised that it took this long?'

The media attention that the whole sorry mess generated was extraordinary. I remember the company manager at the theatre saying that it would all die down in a day or two, but three weeks later I still had a line of cars parked outside my house from 7 a.m. until I left for the theatre at 6 p.m. For a few days I was reluctant to leave the house but soon decided that the only thing to do was face the music. I didn't have a garage so the walk to my car meant that I was accompanied by a crowd of paparazzi all looking for me to drop the false smile and show the anguish I was feeling inside. My house was very near a bus-stop, so I would walk out to shouts from the waiting passengers of 'Leave him alone' or 'Leave her, Les – she doesn't deserve you.' It didn't end when I got to the car, as the more persistent freelance snappers would jump into their cars and follow me to wherever I was going. Sometimes I would drive for hours with a line of cars content to chase. I eventually got experienced at shaking them off, and if I was ever to fall on hard times, I think I would have great credentials to be a getaway driver.

Luckily, because I had healed the rift with my family, I was able to lean on them at this point in my life. Marg was my rock. I just wish I had been there for her. Recently I was talking to Marg about Dustin and asked her if she remembered him doing a particular funny thing. 'No, love,' Marg replied, without bitterness. 'We never met Dustin.' How awful that during one of my most successful times they weren't around and they missed out on knowing one of the loveliest human beings I ever met. My mum would have been very angry with me if she had been alive.

On hearing of my troubles, our Marg immediately came down to London and stayed with me until I persuaded her I could cope and that her family needed her at home. Phil was also a great support, as were Justin, Andy Grainger, Andy Davies and all my close friends. Amongst the anguish there were funny incidents too. Some of the journalists and photographers were embarrassed about invading my privacy though they were, obviously, only doing their job. One afternoon I looked out of the window to see them all in brightly coloured fright wigs and sunglasses standing in a line. They were letting me know that they hated the situation as much as I did. I got Anna, our lovely housekeeper, to take them tea and biscuits, which they raised in salute. It was a welcome show of compassion.

Amanda's friend, Jane Wall, who had been staying at the

house for a few months, left one day and a few photographers chased after her and followed her as she drove off. The next day it was reported in the *Sun* that Les Dennis was being consoled by pop diva Diana Ross. Jane was none too pleased, being some thirty years Ms Ross's junior! Diana Ross was then quoted as saying, 'I've never met the man but wish him well in his troubled times.' The funniest moment came when, in the *Sun* again, a headline read, 'Did smirking Les set hordes of gays on Morrissey? Riddle of ad.' Someone had placed an advert in *Loot* saying, 'Crouch End, N4, beautiful clean double room and en suite bathroom in large flat, share with gay guy, 34, £70 pw, inc.' and put Neil's mobile number! According to the *Sun*, he got 'bombarded with pleas from hundreds of gay men to shack up with him'. He told the paper, 'I've had hundreds of calls because some prat put my number in *Loot*. I suppose I will have to change my number. Loads of people have it but none of them would do this to me.' Well, I had it – the question is, would I have done it to him? At the time, absolutely, if I'd thought of it! But did I? No. Whoever did, if you're reading this, it was an inspired idea. Thanks!

Amanda moved temporarily into a flat in Hampstead. And who moved her in – her famous new lover? No. Supportive friends and family? No. Her idiotic, pathetic, jilted husband. I have no idea why I continued to cling to the chance of reconciliation, except that when you are in that situation, and you love someone, you will do anything to make it right. The difference is, most people do it in privacy, not under the full glare of a media spotlight. Leslie Heseltine, like his father, would have shrivelled up at the fuss, but Les Dennis had become addicted to it and seemed to revel in public attention even in the throes of heartbreak. In writing this book, I have looked back at some of the cuttings from that day, and although they tell a slightly different story from the one I remember, they make for grim and embarrassing reading.

What I remember is that Amanda came home that morning to pack a bag. We were in our bedroom and there were a couple of photographers outside. 'Let's show them we're OK,' she said, and flung open the window. I, in my grievous state, thought she meant that we would be OK and that we were getting back together. So there were photos of us leaning out of the window smiling, looking happily at each other, and I am holding her hand. What she really meant was that we were OK in the sense that we were dealing with the situation in a friendly, civilised manner. Why, then, did I agree after she had filled the biggest bag in Big Bag Land to struggle out with it, like a flustered hotel porter, as if she was off on holiday? Sean French believed there could only be two explanations for our behaviour, which he expounded in the *Guardian*:

> One is that...Les Dennis and other celebrities are producing a postmodern comedy show for Channel 4 as some surreal revenge on the media. The other is that there is a category of people for whom the idea of 'off camera' and the concept of embarrassment no longer exist.

Sobering stuff. In my defence, emotions were working overtime, and logic and reason were replaced by feelings of hurt pride, disbelief, rejection and anger.

From the day our wedding photos appeared in *Hello!* it was as if I'd had a taste of a new and exciting drug. Since our break-up I've been like someone who's been in celeb rehab. I moved away from Primrose Hill, where there is a photographer on every other street corner and I rarely accept invitations to go to movie premières. When the whole affair thing happened, I think I enjoyed the public sympathy and attention. It was like a modern-day version of a Victorian melodrama. Neil was the evil villain, Amanda the not-so-innocent damsel in distress, and I was the sad but likeable victim. However, the sympathy soon turned to pity as I continued to allow myself to be taken for a fool. In a few short weeks I lost my self-respect and dignity, and I became as desperate to regain them as I was to save my marriage.

In an article in the *Mirror*, Tony Parsons wrote advising me that nobody can steal your wife. They can steal your TV or car radio but not your partner. He was absolutely right, but I never actually said that Neil had stolen Amanda. 'It takes two to tango' is a cliché, but it's true. Amanda had run into Neil's arms because something was clearly missing from her relationship with me. I wasn't giving her something she needed. When we talked about it, she said that Neil was a free spirit who took risks in life and who lived very much for the day. I am, by nature, a worrier who sticks to the rulebook. I also, as I have already said, have a tendency to bomb my own ship and can be gloomy and negative. Like my mum said of herself, I will meet trouble halfway. These character traits have infiltrated all of my personal relationships, particularly the intimate ones, and it is something I have been working hard in therapy to explore, understand and overcome. When somebody reaches out to hug you or show you love and you pull away from them because you fear someone may be looking and judging you, it can be frustrating and upsetting for them. That's not to say that I condone the fact that Amanda had an affair, but I can understand some of the reasons why and take responsibility for my role in it.

Although Amanda moved out into a rented flat in Hampstead, she would call frequently saying how confused she was about what she wanted. I suppose that gave me some hope that she would tire of Neil's attention and return to me. I was due to take time out from *Chicago* to record the next series of *Family Fortunes*. My heart sank when the producers told me that in the very next studio Amanda would be taping the new series of *Kiss Me, Kate*. When I should have been trying to focus on my job and having a bit of a break from London, my estranged wife would only be a few corridors away in a nearby dressing room.

Amanda had decided to carry on her tryst with Neil, visiting his flat and having him over to hers. At the same time, though, she suggested that we spend our wedding anniversary, 4 June, together. In my desperation, I agreed, against the advice of all my friends and family. To placate them, I decided that we would invite some of them for moral support. We met Justin, Karen and family in the Wrestlers pub in Highgate for Sunday lunch. The paparazzi rarely strayed up there and so we felt we would be able to spend time together without it getting into the papers. Had there been photographers around, they would have captured me leaving angrily and storming off down the high street. Amanda had mentioned casually over the roast beef that the previous night she had had dinner in Hampstead with Neil. 'By the way, Les, I hope you don't mind but I used the Amex card. Don't worry, I'll pay you back when the bill comes through.' I walked away from the pub outraged and determined that we would remain apart. She had bought him dinner with my credit card the night before our wedding anniversary, which she'd said she wanted us to spend together, then had casually dropped this snippet into the conversation as if it was nothing unusual. That, for me, felt like the last straw.

The next day she went off to Majorca for a short holiday with her friend Jess and I drove up to begin taping the new series of *Family Fortunes*. Despite the deep hurt and rejection I was feeling, I still missed her terribly and wanted her back. At those times of intense pain, your emotions are all over the place. One minute you resolve to split up, and the very next you are doing everything you can, against rational thought and advice, to salvage your damaged relationship. By the end of the week Amanda was in Nottingham to record *Kiss Me, Kate* and I realised how close she was when our two dogs, Nobbie and Fudge, came running down the corridor to greet me. As I returned to the studio to rehearse with the families, Amanda wandered in to watch, as if nothing had happened. The contestants and the entire crew seemed embarrassed, as I was, and a runner from our crew had to ask her to leave the studio as her presence was affecting the show. Slightly miffed, and seemingly unaware of her own insensitivity, she got up and left quietly.

From then on the producers of both shows undertook a logistical exercise to keep us apart. If I'm honest, though, every time I walked round a corner, into the canteen or make-up, I would be aching to bump into her. When her filming finished and I had a two-day break from *Fortunes*, she suggested that we should go off quietly together to our cottage in Norfolk so that we could talk things through. It was a reasonably remote, unpretentious sanctuary where we could escape the madness of London life. Our friends Jeanne and Paul Whittome own a lovely sixteenth-century inn called the Hoste Arms in Burnham Market, and even now when I visit them, I feel a sense of clarity and calm. It seemed like a good idea for us to go there and discuss what was happening to us away from the watchful eyes of the press. So, having told no one what we were doing, I picked up Amanda and the dogs from her hotel and we drove across Lincolnshire and into the Norfolk countryside.

As we approached the cottage, we became anxious that there might be a press welcoming committee. Although we had kept the trip from even our closest friends, there was always a chance I had been seen at her hotel or that we had been followed. There were times during those weeks when it felt like I was in a *Bourne Identity*-type thriller, always looking in the rear-view mirror to check if I was being followed, and always scared to tell anyone anything in case it appeared in the tabloids the next day with the tag 'a close friend says'. My poor friends would always ring and begin conversations with 'It wasn't me.'

No press were around as we pulled up outside our gate – just Bob and Pat, our lovely next-door neighbours. They have lived in the farm workers' cottage most of their lives and are genuine, warm Norfolk people. Although Pat was an avid fan of TV soaps and celebrity magazines, they made no mention of our situation but, instead, welcomed us with fresh eggs from their chickens and potatoes from their plot. Immediately we felt we could relax and take time to talk things through. On a long walk along the Peddar's Way, Amanda told me that, although she still had strong feelings for Neil, she loved me and wanted to come home. I held her tightly and told her that was what I was hoping to hear but that when she returned to her flat in London she should think it through carefully to make sure it was definitely what she wanted. When we got back to the cottage, she said she would have to call Neil.

'Why?' I asked. 'Probably best not to tell him until you're sure.'

'No, it's not that,' she said. 'He doesn't know where I am. I'll just call him and say I've gone to see a friend.'

It was a weird moment. Suddenly I felt as if I was the one she was having an affair with and she had to lie to her husband about where she was. It made me aware, I think, that it wasn't just because I loved her that I wanted us to get back together. It was also pure old-fashioned male pride and I wanted to win over him. I felt a certain sense of satisfaction that she was lying to him and that she was, in fact, with me behind his back. With hindsight, it would have been better for all concerned if that trip hadn't happened. We would most likely have split for good and I would have got over it sooner rather than later.

I went back to Nottingham to finish the series and Amanda went back to London. I kept getting texts from her saying that she had told Neil and was excited about coming home. On the last night of filming I returned home to find her back in the house. Because we'd been away, the press vigil had dispersed and so for a few days our reunion remained undetected. It didn't take long, however, before we were seen in public and were being followed again. Now, though, I was happier to be photographed and to show the world that I had won and had reclaimed what I had lost. How pathetic.

Ironically, it was now Amanda who was less comfortable about being photographed and resented it. She had encouraged it for years and enjoyed the attention while she had been building her career and had loved the spotlight being on her. Now she began to complain about the infringement of her privacy. If she spotted a long lens, she would dive grumpily into a newsagent's and come out with a magazine to cover her face. Never *Now* or *Closer*, I noticed – only *Tatler* or *Vanity Fair*. The photos that appeared would always have me looking uncomfortable and miserable because my wife wouldn't have a photo taken that showed both of us looking relaxed and happy to be back together. No wonder I was labelled 'Les Miserables'.

There was actually one time when I lost it and, I'm ashamed to say, hit a photographer. We had been to a preview of our friend Philip Goodhew's new film, *Another Life*, and were besieged by photographers as we left. As we walked through Soho, a young girl protested and shouted, 'Leave them alone,' and stood in front of one of the snappers to stop him from getting a shot. He angrily grabbed the girl's arm and pulled it behind her back, really hurting her. I was upset for her and, in true John Prescott fashion, landed him a right hook on the chin. He knew he had done wrong and apologised, but not before the other photographers had caught the punch on film. Interestingly, none of the photos made the papers the next day. It's my belief that they didn't want that image of me. Noel

Gallagher, Jay Kay and Neil Morrissey could be bad boys, but I had to remain the sad, jilted husband.

During the time that Amanda and I were separated, I had decided that, when I came out of *Chicago* in July, I would rent a house in France for a month and have family and friends to stay. Now that we were back together, Amanda was going to spend some time there with us, but I'm not sure my other houseguests were too thrilled at the prospect. It seemed that I was the only one who was happy that we had got back together. Since her return, our relationship had shifted. I was more insecure in my heart but remained determined to show that I was confident and didn't see Neil as a threat. Who was I kidding? Certainly not the people who cared most for me.

I rented a house in Provence, but Amanda was working when I drove down with Phil, so the first couple of weeks were spent with Marg and Tony, Justin, Karen and the kids, and Andy Grainger and his wife, Ruby. We all had a great time enjoying the relaxed atmosphere of the French Riviera. When Amanda joined us, however, the dynamics changed immediately. My friends didn't know quite how to react, particularly as I was painfully overcompensating, trying to prove to them that we were OK and our 'glitch' was over. She had been there a couple of days when she started pleading with me to fly back to London to attend the film première of *X-Men*.

'Why would you want to leave the beautiful south of France to watch a movie that you can pay to see when you get back?' I asked.

'We need to show the media that we're back on track. You know I've never been to a full-on première before. It will be exciting.'

In my eager-to-please, low-self-esteemed state, Amanda managed to persuade me it was a good idea. When I told our Marg and tried to convince her that it would be good for us to show a united front, she looked at me as if I had gone quite mad. She didn't argue, though, but simply said, 'Yes, love. Whatever. Tony will drop you at the airport.' I asked her recently what she thought at the time and she confirmed that she thought I had lost the plot but had wanted me to realise my mistakes by myself. Through that whole mad time no one could talk any sense into me. I think my belief that we could repair our marriage came from the fact that we had had genuinely loving times in the beginning. When you've had that and it's gone, you want so desperately to recapture it and will sometimes do the most ridiculous and humiliating things to make it happen. I really believe Amanda felt that too, for a while. There were no children, so there was no feeling that we had to stay together. She came back because she wanted to try to make it work. Neither of us wanted to have a failed marriage, certainly not another one for me. Although it was clear to all around us that our relationship was technically over, we couldn't accept it or let it go.

Turning up at a glitzy film première did nothing to confirm we were happy, of course. It just made us look like an attention-seeking celebrity couple again, which I suppose is what we were. There were rumblings on Fleet Street that all was not well in the newly re-formed Dennis-Holden household.

Instead of getting on and living our lives in relative privacy, we tried once more to prove that we were OK. Towards the end of that holiday I agreed to do something that I had never done before, and have, most certainly, not done since. We were advised that the tabloids needed evidence that we were happy and that if we gave them a photo opportunity, they would leave us alone once and for all. I'm ashamed to say we agreed and set up a shoot. Celebrities do it all the time – tell the press that they're going to be shopping in Knightsbridge or holidaying in the Bahamas. I even joke about doing it in *Extras* when I call *Heat*: 'I've just seen Les Dennis in Bond Street and he was spending a fucking shitload of money.' I had never done it for real, though, until then.

We were going to visit friends of mine from Liverpool, Barbara and Cliff Graham, at their home in Port Grimaud. They were then taking us on their boat for lunch near St Tropez. Without them, or anyone else knowing, we tipped off the *News of the World* that we were going to be there and they sent a boat with a guy, armed with the biggest lens I had ever seen, to photograph us being 'naturally loving together' as we splashed about in the beautiful Med. Of course, the photos look staged and it didn't mean that they left us alone in the future. We were playing an extremely dangerous game because by setting up the photos, you relinquish all rights to privacy in the future and have no grounds to bleat about it whenever a lens is stuck in your face. I also deeply regret not being honest with my friends. It was yet another example of how all rational thought and dignity had flown from my body – behaviour that was certainly causing alarm in my family.

In spite of the negative publicity, Amanda's career continued to flourish. *Hearts and Bones* was a critical success, *The Grimleys* was re-commissioned, and *The Hunt* proved to be a popular hit for the ITV drama department.

For me, *Family Fortunes* entered its fourteenth year in production and was, for the second time, nominated for a National Television Award. The ceremony is one of the most glittering in the TV calendar and one of those occasions I really enjoyed turning up for. It's extremely nerve-racking as you sit there in the packed Albert Hall and hear Sir Trevor McDonald say, in his inimitable style, 'And now, to announce the nominations for Best Quiz Show. Please welcome...' You sit there with a camera directed right at your face (something I should have been used to by now) while the final four are read out. '*Who Wants to Be a Millionaire?*, *A Question of Sport*, *Have I Got News For You*, *Family Fortunes*.' You hide the agony with a fixed smile as the envelope is torn open and then you hear the words 'The winner is...Chris

Tarrant for *Who Wants to Be a Millionaire?*' You break out into an even bigger smile and murmur congratulations while inside you're going, Shit. Bastards! Everyone does it, but some hide it better than others.

That evening Amanda and I were also presenting an award in the Best Daytime Programme category. We were both a little nervous because, apart from the *X-Men* fiasco, it was the first thing we had done together since the split in such a public arena. We, inevitably, got more attention walking in on the red carpet than we did because I was nominated. As we went to present the award, there was a little unease from the industry audience and, probably, embarrassment. Amanda looked stunning in a green backless gown and new-look brunette hair. She opened the envelope and read out the winners, who were Richard Madeley and Judy Finnegan for *This Morning*. The next couple of minutes of live TV were absolutely extraordinary. Richard and Judy accepted their award from us and stepped forward to the microphone to make their acceptance speech. Suddenly there was a huge roar of shocked laughter. Richard thought it was for him and said to the audience, 'No, I'm not doing my Ali G. impression.' More laughter. 'No, I'm not doing it!' I glanced at Sir Trevor, who looked at the overhead monitor. I followed his eyes and realised what had happened. Judy's gown had come undone and her bosom and lacy strapless bra were on full view to the audience and the millions of viewers at home. They remained oblivious and continued to thank the viewers for the award.

For a split second I contemplated going to the rescue but thought that if I approached from behind and started making a play for a television legend's breasts she, and the entire nation, would think I had completely lost the plot. Instead, Amanda tried to subtly help Judy, but, again, she remained sublimely unaware. Just in time, John Leslie ran up the steps, covered up Judy and spared her blushes. Considering what had happened, they were great sports and laughed along as we were led to the press room for interviews.

The next morning, when Richard ran the clip on *This Morning*, Judy looked suitably embarrassed but told viewers that she had been inundated with offers from Wonderbra, Marks and Spencer and even the Queen's lingerie expert, Rigby and Peller, to model their bras. Richard and Judy are a lovely couple and I was honoured to do a special edition of *Family Fortunes* on their last ever *This Morning*. Amanda and I would also be their first guests on their new Channel 4 show, *Richard and Judy*.

Amanda and I also did some other work together. We did a spot on *The Royal Variety Performance* that year in front of Prince Charles. In the line-up after the show Charles asked us how we had learnt our lines. Amanda confidently said, 'Not far from you in Norfolk, Your Highness. We did them as we walked the dogs along Holkham Beach.' (Holkham is very near Sandringham.)

'Oh! Marvellous,' he said. 'Did you walk as far as the beach huts at Wells-next-the-Sea?'

Ever since, whenever I am on that glorious stretch of beach, I look out in the hope of seeing him walking the corgies.

We ushered in the New Year – 2001 – and eagerly said goodbye to the old with friends at the cottage in Norfolk. We then went on a short holiday to Las Vegas and Mexico. It was reported that we had gone to renew our wedding vows, but we hadn't. It was a fraught holiday, partly because we had been followed to Vegas. The flight we took to LA was the one that Elton John and David Furnish were on – when Elton told me that he would make the *Family Fortunes* 'eugh-eugh' noise at home – so when they were whisked away through airport security, the photographers saw us and decided to cut their losses and follow us instead. Although they didn't chase us as far as Mexico, we found it hard to relax. Tabloid stories hit the streets again, suggesting Amanda had received texts from Neil on Christmas Day. Trust between Amanda and I was definitely breaking down, and I think we both knew it was only a matter of time before we would split for good.

I had a guest role in *Brookside* for a couple of months and appeared in the stage play *Misery*, based on Stephen King's novel, at the Oldham Coliseum Theatre. I played author Paul Sheldon, who suffers a near-fatal car crash in a Colorado blizzard and is rescued by reclusive Annie Wilkes and taken to her remote farmhouse. She turns out to be not only his number-one fan but also a psychotic ex-nurse who is enraged because he has killed off her favourite character, Misery, in the books she loves. She holds him hostage, and if you've seen the movie with James Caan and Kathy Bates, you'll know that it is a tense, sometimes horrific thriller. Annie was played, in our version, by a lovely actress, and a dear friend, Ann Bryson. We had a great time working on the piece with director Alan Rothwell, and it proved to be a popular hit at the same theatre where Charlie Chaplin and Eric Sykes had begun their careers. In the book, Annie chops off Paul's foot. This was considered too gruesome for the film version, so Annie smashed Paul's ankles instead, but in the play, we kept it in. With the aid of a prosthetic foot, deft lighting and plenty of stage blood, the effect was truly horrific as Annie dropped a dripping foot into a wastepaper basket, while Paul's agonising screams rang round the auditorium.

One night after the show, the front-of-house manager couldn't hide his laughter as he told us about a couple of elderly ladies he'd overheard as they left the theatre. One turned to her friend and said, 'Well, that'll explain why Les Dennis limps, then.' I love stories about audience reactions to plays. My friend Duncan Preston, best known for his work with Victoria Wood, told me a story about when he was performing with the Royal

Shakespeare Company in *Macbeth* with Sir Ian McKellen. When Macbeth got to the speech that begins, 'Tomorrow, and tomorrow, and tomorrow...' a woman on the third row said, quite loudly, 'That'll be Thursday.'

Another time, he and actor John Woodvine had to enter through the auditorium at a vital part of the play and make a commotion. They would listen from behind the doors of the foyer for their cue and then burst in. They heard what they thought was their cue and bustled noisily through the audience shouting, 'Alarums, alarums,' at the tops of their voices. They quickly discovered, to their horror, that they had entered two pages too early and had to creep out quietly. This time, embarrassed, they listened intently until the cue was given and, once again, came running out shouting, 'Alarums, alarums.' The audience looked daggers at them and one woman shouted, 'You're spoiling this for everyone.'

Just before Christmas, Amanda managed to get herself in the papers for all the wrong reasons again. She was invited to the Comedy Awards at the LWT studios. I was doing a gig in Gloucester and couldn't go but watched the show on TV in my dressing room. The next day she drove up to spend Sunday with Jim and Ethel, her grandparents with whom I had been staying the night before.

'How was it?' I asked.

'Great,' she said. 'I spent most of the night with Andy Harries.' Andy was the controller of comedy and drama at Granada and responsible for *The Grimleys* and *Cold Feet*. Most recently he has had Oscar success with *The Queen*, starring Helen Mirren. The following morning, as we drove back to London, Amanda with her grandparents in her car, and me with her mum and dad in mine, she flashed me to stop at the next lay-by. I jumped out and walked over to her.

'What's wrong?' I asked, when I reached her car.

'I've just had a phone call to say those bloody 3 a.m. Girls have gone for me again,' she cried, and babbled on.

'You're making no sense. Slow down. What is it?'

It turned out that the *Mirror*'s gossip columnists, the 3 a.m. Girls, had been at the after-show party and reported that Amanda spent the night openly flirting with Mr Harries. They wrote, 'The pair walked around the LWT studios hand in hand, while Andy kissed Amanda on the cheek.'

'It was totally innocent,' she assured me.

She didn't have to. Andy was her friend, a married man, and I knew nothing was going on. When I saw the picture, though, I thought, What bloody idiots. They were holding hands and Andy was looking deeply into her eyes. Talk about asking for trouble. What did she expect? Did I tell her this? Tell her that I was cross about her behaviour? No. Instead I wrote a letter to Piers Morgan, editor of the *Mirror* at the time, in her defence. He later printed it in the first volume of his autobiography. I wrote:

> Amanda and I are very strong and will not be rocked by such salacious and vindictive gossip. It seems she cannot be seen out in public without your 'girls' suggesting there is something furtive and underhand going on. Andy's a valued friend of ours and it's a sad reflection on our times if a man is chivalrous and offers a woman a lift home and it is reported as something sordid. Finally, I take exception to being given patronising advice from your staff. I am not a victim and can make my own mind up about the future of my marriage. I was not sitting sadly at home, I was working. As it is, we now feel like prisoners in our own home again.

When I later moaned about it in the *Celebrity Big Brother* house, I did myself no favours with the 3 a.m. Girls, but Piers's comment in his book was, 'I rather admire him for writing to me like that.'

*

While on holiday in Tuscany in June 2001 Amanda and I got a call to say topless pictures of Amanda in the grounds of the house we were staying in were on the front page of the *Daily Star*. Under the article were the words 'More stunning photos tomorrow.' How could that be? we wondered. The farmhouse we had rented was totally secluded, nestled in the middle of a private vineyard. A photographer, it seemed, had managed to sneak on to private land, hide among the vines and, with a very long lens, take the shots. Amanda was distraught and I felt very sorry for her. Yes, when you appear at a première you expect, and sometimes want, the photos to hit the papers. Even when you're walking the dogs, or having your car clamped, you accept that the next morning you might see shots in the tabloids. When you are holidaying in a private house, though, you do expect and deserve some kind of privacy. We called our solicitor, Peter Crawford, and he immediately served the newspaper with an injunction preventing them from printing the next day's photos. Taking Peter's advice, we decided not to complain to the Press Complaints Committee but instead to sue under the Human Rights Act for a breach of our right to respect of our private life. At the time there was a stream of complaints from celebrities including Anna Ford, Naomi Campbell, Sara Cox and, of course, Michael Douglas and Catherine Zeta-Jones, in their case against *Hello!*, all of whom had turned to the Human Rights Act to keep the paparazzi at bay.

After a lengthy legal battle we were awarded an out-of-court settlement for damages and the *Daily Star* had to meet all legal costs. It seemed like a victory. The European Convention on Human Rights includes a statutory right to privacy. Where complaints from the Press Complaints Committee had fallen on deaf ears, this route seemed, for a short while, to stop editors from being complacent. Those photos we had set up in St Tropez though were beginning to sit uneasily in my mind. Litigation is a dangerous and sometimes foolhardy game.

CHAPTER 24

La La Land

Cutting It, the story of two rival hairdressers in Manchester whose sex lives were as tangled as their clients' split-ends, was a huge hit for the BBC and starred Amanda, Sarah Parish, Angela Griffin, Ben Daniels and Jason Merrells. Its success encouraged Amanda to take a trip to Los Angeles and try her luck in Hollywood. Every year countless British actors head out for pilot season in the hope that they can strike gold and land a role in a TV series or even a movie. As I remembered from my visit in 1993, though, the odds are short and the competition is fierce. It really is a 'gold-rush town', where every waiter telling you about the daily specials is an out-of-work actor. As Dionne Warwick sang in 'Do You Know the Way to San José?', 'All the stars who never were are parking cars and pumping gas.'

When you go with a calling card, though, you have more chance to be taken seriously and Amanda certainly had a calling card. Her show reel included *Kiss Me, Kate*, *The Grimleys*, *Cutting It* and the more dramatic *Hearts and Bones*. For all the early talk of her getting where she was because she had married me, she had proved that she was a good and bankable actress in the British TV market. I was proud of her and encouraged her to go and chase her dream in America.

Because of the fragility of our relationship, though, neither of us wanted to be apart for a possible three months. The short working schedule for *Family Fortunes* gave me not only the luxury of pursuing my acting career – I did a short tour of Alan Ayckbourn's *Just Between Ourselves* for the Theatre Royal, Bath – but also to take time out whenever I wanted. So I took three months off and accompanied my wife on her quest to crack Hollywood.

Hotels would have been far too expensive and impersonal for such an extended stay, so instead we rented a house just off Mulholland Drive, high in the Hollywood Hills. A Spanish-style villa with enough bedrooms for family and friends to visit, it had a lovely garden with its own lemon tree and pool and was an idyllic place to stay. While Amanda was intent on getting work in the city, I was thrilled at the prospect of exploring the Californian coast. All my life I had worked hard, never taking more than a couple of weeks off for a holiday, so to be away in such a lovely environment for three months was perfect.

Amanda had a manager out there, Melanie Green, who got her countless meetings, including one with Quentin Tarantino, for *Kill Bill*, and David E. Kelley who was producing *Ally McBeal*. Although she came close to a couple of things, that elusive Hollywood contract didn't come her way. It seems that if you are really serious about making it in Hollywood, you have to be prepared to move out there permanently and almost turn your back on your career in the UK. We had fun, though, and even got invited to the odd glitzy Hollywood party. Melanie's husband, Peter Morris, a witty Scot, ran the LA division of BAFTA and invited us to a tribute to George Lucas. In the anteroom, before the dinner, I was within spitting distance of Harrison Ford, Sir Ben Kingsley, Steven Spielberg and Carrie Fisher. It was weirdly like being at Madame Tussaud's as the dummies came to life. I was the only one I didn't know!

While being perfectly civil and affable, the people in the entertainment industry in LA can be seriously ruthless. At one party, a well-known actor was chatting about a producer to Peter and me. 'What do we do,' he asked Peter, 'kill him or suck his dick?' That phrase sums up the attitude out there – to schmooze or not to schmooze. Andy Grainger came out to stay with us for a while. At a drinks do at the house, he was chatting to a camp, flamboyant agent whose eyes were darting all over the room.

'Who's that guy over there?' the agent asked.

'Oh,' said Andy, 'that's John Morton, a very successful comedy writer.'

'Then why the fuck am I talking to you?' said the camp guy, as he moved away to schmooze John. 'Just kidding,' he shouted back, but we both knew he wasn't.

Amanda's mum and our friends Judith and Jess came over and one weekend we all drove off to Las Vegas. On the second night Amanda told me she had arranged for us to have a quiet romantic dinner alone at a secret location. While we were waiting outside the hotel for a cab, a huge white stretch limo turned up and Amanda said, 'This is for us.' I remember thinking it was a bit extravagant for dinner for two but got in and sat with her on the back seat. 'Have you noticed what it says on the window?' she asked. In gold embossed letters it read, 'The Little White Wedding Chapel.'

'What?' I asked, confused.

'I've arranged for us to renew our wedding vows.' She smiled.

I was absolutely stunned. Stunned and thrilled, you might think, considering what we had been through in the past two years. Thrilled, though, was not the emotion I was feeling. I felt strangely cheated. Surely when a couple decide to do something as personal and monumental as renewing their vows, they do it jointly and knowingly. One of the couple does not suddenly spring it on the other as they are in the car driving to the church. We had also been rowing for the previous few days, and Andy later told me that he had received countless phone calls from Amanda saying that it was off and then it was back on. Yes, if Amanda and I had talked about it and planned it together, I would have been thrilled to show that we were committed to getting our marriage back on track, but to be the one on the receiving end of such a surprise made me feel uneasy.

As we approached the chapel where Frank Sinatra had married Mia Farrow, my stomach was churning and my desire to flee was almost overwhelming. Instead, I buried my anxiety and took Amanda's arm as we walked in to face the smiling faces of our family and friends. I remained stunned for the short ceremony, and when we signed the register afterwards and had photos with our friends, I felt that we were simply papering over the cracks. Once again we were running away from the break that we both knew in our hearts was inevitable. What should have been a joyous celebration was, for me, an uncomfortable, false pretence that everything was OK. As we hit the LA freeway, storm clouds were gathering.

Over the next few weeks I became increasingly moody. I had received a call from Mike to say that *Family Fortunes* was possibly going to be moved to the day time. I was worried about its future and also uncomfortable about being in LA simply to support Amanda. Sitting in the sun, picking lemons from the trees for the gin and tonics is fun for a while, but when you are idle in such a work-driven town, you soon become restless.

Of course, when we had free time we would explore the city and beyond. We had a few days in Palm Springs, regularly hiked through the beautiful Runyon Canyon and skated along Venice

'No!' the women had snapped. 'It's his own fault. He behaved badly and deserves to be left alone.'

I found a small inlet in the bay that was full of – guess what? – sea lions! Some playing, some swimming, some sleeping. They were fascinating. I spent the next hour watching them as the others worked their anger off over a leisurely lunch. Then, in a gift shop, I bought Judith a picture book about a bear who was truly sorry. I had totally regressed to the age of ten. As I met the others, and gave Judith the book, I told them about the sea lions. 'It's probably even better than Sea World,' I said feebly.

They smiled politely and came to watch them, probably just to humour me. The journey back was conducted in strained silence, although we did try a half-hearted singalong to a *Best of Frank Sinatra* CD.

'Jess and I have dined out on that story so many times,' Judith told me recently. 'It was so funny!' In a reflective moment, though, they both said that it was a defining moment for them as joint friends of both Amanda and me. 'We realised that we were witnessing the breakdown of a marriage. You weren't right for each other – your personalities were too different. It was sad because we loved you both.' It seemed that everyone could see what was happening except Amanda and me.

Melanie, Amanda's LA manager, wanted us to extend our stay a couple of weeks so that she could carry on with the meetings she had set up. The house was already rented to somebody else, so we moved into the Four Seasons Hotel to finish our stay. Mike Hughes was staying there at the same time as us. Our relationship had shifted significantly over the last few years. He was no longer my manager. I had wanted more control over my career and was keen to do more acting work. Mike is very much a variety agent and so he agreed to let me move on to Jan Kennedy at the Billy Marsh Agency. I stayed with Jan for a couple of years and later joined International Artists, where I was looked after by Mandy Ward. With him at the Four Seasons was his son, Christopher, and Christopher's fiancé. Amanda and I saw quite a lot of them during those two weeks, often going out to dinner together. I hadn't seen Chris since he had come, as a young boy, to do work experience on *Family Fortunes*. Before that, the only time I had seen him was that night when Lynne and I had driven past Mike's house in the 1970s and seen them playing together through the window of his house.

When a relationship is in crisis, you look for ways to mend it before making the inevitable decision that it is truly broken and unfixable. After the affair with Neil, Amanda had come back home because she wanted to and we did try hard to make it work again. The trust had disappeared, though, and I think when we got back to London, we both knew it was a matter of time before we would go our separate ways. In one last-ditch effort to make things work, we decided that a house move might prove to be the answer.

One day while walking in Norfolk, we came across a lovely, newly renovated house overlooking the Wash. Reasoning that relocating to the country would allow us more privacy and time for each other, we put in an offer the next day, which was accepted. Of course, the problem is, you can't escape your situation just by moving. You take your karma with you.

CHAPTER 25

Celebrity Big Brother

I got a call from my agent, Mandy Ward, saying that Mark Wells at Carlton wanted a meeting to talk about the next series of *Family Fortunes*. I went along to Carlton's offices in Portman Square one sunny afternoon and duly met with him. *Fortunes* had been running successfully on prime-time ITV for some sixteen years, but the schedulers felt that it needed a new timeslot. Their suggestion was that, instead of transmitting it weekly on a Saturday or Sunday night, it should be moved to the lively 5 p.m. slot and run daily from Monday to Friday. At first I was interested. The day schedules were proving to be a winner for game shows and I understood that *Family Fortunes* was a long-runner that couldn't sit in prime time for ever. After listening to what Mark was offering, though, we decided that it was time to give up the show. My decision to leave came in for quite a bit of criticism. The papers asked why I would leave such a successful show, particularly when I had no other offers on the table. I released a statement saying that I had had the best years of the show and that it was simply time to go. The prizes were to be reduced, the show was to be recorded without a studio audience, and laughter and reaction would be dubbed on afterwards. I said that I felt that I should leave the show while it was still a quality programme and performing well. All of these reasons are true and, to my mind, legitimate. However, there was one other reason I decided not to reveal at the time, and that was a financial one. When you do a daytime show, you know that the fee will be reduced. That is to be expected. However, to be told that your salary will be cut by a staggering 93 per cent is too insulting to accept. I don't know anyone in the workplace who would be prepared to take that kind of wage cut. We politely thanked Mark Wells and left the meeting knowing that my contract with ITV would finish. I have no bitterness about their decision. Business is business.

The pay cut ITV had offered me was so big it made me reflect on whether I had jumped before I was pushed. The prime-time schedules were being dominated by more and more presenters in their late twenties and early thirties. Just like any industry, men who were approaching their fifties find it hard to adjust to a fast-changing business. If I had been telly wallpaper until now, maybe the executives were thinking it was time for an extreme makeover. My dignity was more important to me, though, than appearing regularly on TV. Or was it? I was prepared to go three rounds in a boxing ring and to quite literally take a punch in the face to keep my face on prime-time TV.

In the spring of 2002 I got a call from a bloke who said, 'Les, I think we should have a fight.'

Who, I thought, is this? It turned out to be Bob Mortimer, one half of the brilliant double act with Vic Reeves.

'Hello, Bob. I didn't realise I'd upset you.' The last time I had seen him was when I'd filmed a spoof documentary called *The Club* for the excellent series *Bang, Bang, It's Reeves and Mortimer*. 'Why do you want to fight me?'

He explained that he was planning a celebrity boxing match for the summer telethon Sport Relief, and at first he'd thought of fighting Paul Whitehouse. He continued, 'Then I thought, No, I'd rather go three rounds with the French Fire Engine.' When I had appeared on their show *Shooting Stars*, Vic had introduced me as *Les Dennis* (French pronunciation), the French Fire Engine. Fans of Vic and Bob will still shout that at me in the street.

Without giving it much thought, I said, 'OK, Bob, I'd love to.' As I put the phone down, I thought, Well, it'll be fun. A little spoof boxing match might be hilarious viewing and would, no doubt, raise money for a good cause.

When I met Bob and the production team at TV Centre the next day, however, the reality of what I'd let myself in for quickly and frighteningly began to sink in. It was not going to be a comedy stunt but, in fact, was a full-scale three-round bout in which the punches would be real and the victor would win the Sports Relief Belt. 'But I've never been in a ring in my life,' I argued.

'Doesn't matter,' replied the producer, Andy Harris. 'We train you over the next five weeks. You'll be fitter than you've ever been in your life.'

'It'll be great, eh, Les?' asked Bob.

'Yes, fantastic,' I answered, smiling feebly. I left the meeting filled with fear and dread. Why he picked me, I don't really know. I imagine Paul Whitehouse was busy or said no, but there is certainly more jeopardy in pitting a trendy alternative comedian with a more traditionally based one.

Over the next five weeks we separately trained our socks off. Bob worked with Barry McGuigan while the former European Featherweight champion Jim McDonnell, who had actually beaten McGuigan and was known in the boxing world as Jimmy Mac, put me through my paces. Day after day I would run, skip, punch the bag and spar with Jim. It was the toughest exercise regime I had ever undertaken, but I knew that when I stepped into that ring in front of a baying celebrity crowd I would have to be prepared. I did a day on the pads with Frank Bruno, who told me – whether he was just trying to encourage me or not, I don't know – that I had a useful right hand. I even went into the ring with three white-collar boxers, young City blokes, who boxed to release the aggression and energy that accumulated from their stressful work lives. I had to do two three-minute rounds with each of them, and although I was wearing head- and mouthguards, when they caught me with a punch, God, did it hurt! I gave a few good right-handers back, though, and when the final bell went and I came out of the ring, with my nose pouring with blood, I felt strangely euphoric. I had always viewed boxing as a slightly barbaric and a needlessly violent pastime, but after my five weeks I came to view it as a noble, honourable sport in which the Queensberry rules were of paramount importance. Everyone I have met in the boxing world has been an absolute gentleman and has shown the utmost respect for anyone who even attempts to enter the ring. I decided that my fighting nickname would be the Blond Bomber, while Bob chose to be the Woodpecker. The fight took place on a Sunday night in June at BBC Television Centre. The studio was transformed into a glittering Madison Square Gardens-like arena, and the seats were filled with famous faces. Supporting Bob, among others, were Paul Whitehouse, Charlie Higson and, of course, Vic Reeves. In my corner were Bobby Davro, the *Cutting It* girls, Harry Enfield, who was filming a new sitcom with Amanda, and, of course, dressed to the nines as a boxer's moll, Amanda herself.

Jim McDonnell and his team relaxed me in my dressing room as the fight approached, and in his motivation speech Jim said in his almost falsetto cockney burr, 'Remember, Les, PMA – positive mental attitude. Oh, and karma – that's with a K.'

Just before we went out into the ring, Bob came in and suggested we take it easy in the first round. 'Remember, we want to go the full three rounds, so let's entertain them in the first round, just dance around a bit and then go for it in the second and third.'

The adrenaline I felt as I walked through the crowd and into the ring was more intense than any first night in the theatre. Steve Collins was the ref and Charlie Magri was one of the judges, so it had the feel of a professional occasion. Steve checked our gloves, made us touch each other's and asked for a clean fight. We went back to our corners, and when the bell went, we came out fighting. Well, I, of course, thought we were coming out dancing, at least for the first round. I came out, moved around Bob a little and within seconds took the biggest right-hand straight to my jaw. As I, literally, saw stars, I remember thinking, You bastard, Mortimer. You set me up. Dancing, my arse. Luckily, I didn't go down. In fact, the anger helped and I went for Bob like a vicious terrier.

I gave as good as I got in that first round and returned to my corner to face a screaming Jim McDonnell. 'What were you doing in those opening seconds?'

'He told me we'd take it easy in the first,' I said.

'You fucking idiot, he scammed you. Get out there and show him what you're made of.'

Although Bob had narrowly taken the first round, I had him in the second, and then in the third he literally turned and ran away from me as I was still punching. Steve Collins stopped us both and said, in his lovely Irish brogue, 'You –' he pointed at Bob – 'stop running away, and you, Les, stop punching him in the arse.'

As the final bell went, my supporters were going wild. They were convinced that I had nicked it. We stood either side of the ref as he held up our hands and the announcer declared a split decision but that the winner was...Bob Mortimer. I was gutted. Even his supporters seemed surprised, but he still danced for joy. Afterwards Charlie Magri and Steve Collins said they thought I had been robbed. It turned out that one of the judges later admitted that he had voted for Bob because he was a big fan and thought he was funnier than me. Story of my life – what has 'funny' got to do with a fight result? A week later Bob called me and said that, having watched it on video, I had definitely won. Small consolation, but it was nice of him to have said it.

There was nobody beating a path to my door to offer me any new and exciting projects, so my agent, Mandy, and I decided that we had to do something to raise my profile. The problem was, the thing we decided to do was *Celebrity Big Brother*. I had never really watched any of the *Big Brother* shows. I was aware of the whole Nasty Nick controversy and thought that Craig the Scouser was quite endearing for confronting him. To me, though, it seemed a pointless idea to sit on a sofa watching people sitting on sofas. Somebody said recently that ordinary people used to sit at home watching talented people on television and now talented people sit at home watching ordinary people. When Comic Relief did the first *Celebrity Big Brother*, however, I got absolutely hooked. The mix of housemates was fascinating. They included Anthea Turner and Vanessa Feltz, who had both had and lost huge TV success. There was Claire Sweeney, an actress who was best known for *Brookside* but little else at that time, and then there was Jack Dee. As a hugely successful stage and TV star, Jack hardly needed to reinvigorate his flourishing career. I think he was probably there as an ambassador for Comic Relief and to encourage other celebs that it was 'safe' to do. He was hilarious, rebelling against the rules, refusing to wear his microphone all the time and even staging the first *Big Brother* breakout. He was a kind of celebrity version of Steve McQueen's character in *The Great Escape*. Claire's career was definitely helped by her appearance in the house, and she has gone on to prove her versatility and charm as an actress, singer and presenter. Much was made of Vanessa's so-called breakdown. When she wrote on the table various ways to describe her feelings of entrapment, the nation became concerned that she might be losing her marbles. I think she was simply a little stir crazy and in subsequent *Big Brothers*, my own included, there has been much more obscure behaviour and far more reason for concern.

For Comic Relief that year, the show proved to be a huge success and Endemol and Channel 4 quite rightly saw the potential for doing another. This time, though, Comic Relief and Richard Curtis would not be sponsoring it and so, of course, the editing and content were under the more commercially driven auspices of Endemol. Nevertheless, when I heard about the one planned for November 2002, I was interested in being one of the housemates.

It was Amanda who first told me that they were doing another celebrity version. She had been to an industry function and had got chatting to two of the producers. 'I suggested that they should approach you,' she said.

'Do you think I should do it?' I asked.

'Certainly, darling. Look what it's done for Claire. Also, I think it would give you a chance to do something on your own that would maybe stop us from simply being viewed as a celebrity couple.'

I called Mandy and asked her what she thought. 'It's a risk, but if you are yourself, you can't help but come across well. Let's have a meeting with them.'

We met with the two producers, Philip Edgar Jones and Sarah Freesby, at a pancake house across the road from my agent's office, and over coffee and waffles they told me what they wanted from the show. 'Look, it's going to be ten days not seventy, and there will only be six contestants, all well known in their fields. It's a pre-Christmas schedule, so we want an entertaining and lively show. You will make an ideal housemate.'

They left and Mandy and I decided to go for it. 'What have you got to lose?' she asked. Hell, the answer to that question would prove to be very interesting.

When I told friends and colleagues, the reactions were mixed. Andy Davies, like Amanda, thought that it would show me as myself and not just as Mr Amanda Holden. Others, though, including Andy Grainger, were more sceptical. 'You're still at a low ebb and I'm not sure you'll react well. Also, you're already a household name, so why would you need to do something so risky?' I explained that I thought I had become telly wallpaper, always there but doing the same show for sixteen years, and that I needed to shake things up a bit. So many of my contemporaries had been left behind by the changing landscape of TV. Instead of grumbling about the domination of reality TV and the death of variety, I was determined not to allow myself to become a dinosaur – after all, if you can't beat them, join them. *Family Fortunes* had ended and I had to take this chance to reinvent myself. It is easy to say, 'Oh, I'm only doing it for charity.' Yes, it is great that you can help a worthwhile cause, but the main reason is self-promotion. These days, of course, if you go into the house or the jungle, you are given a huge personal fee as well. Back then, you did it for charity and self-promotion. I certainly did it to change people's perception of me and, of course, to get an injection of the drug I was now totally addicted to: public affection. Little did I suspect the kind of press attention I was about to attract.

In an article for the *Mail on Sunday*'s *Night and Day* magazine (15 December 2002), Alexei Sayle was frighteningly bang on the money:

> All performers are in effect taking a drug: they are using other people's love and laughter to make them feel better

> about themselves (because deep down in their blackest souls they think they are really worthless). But comedians are the most hopeless addicts, mainlining the purest, most lethal form of that drug, and when their supply of public attention dries up, they suffer the most appalling withdrawal symptoms...Imagine it, you are hitting fifty, your career is declining, but you're well and truly hooked on getting laughs. So, instead of having your own TV series, you submit to freak shows such as *Celebrity Big Brother* that constantly remind you of what you once were.

Ouch! Not, then, the best frame of mind to be in as you agree to be scrutinised twenty-four hours a day by the British public on national TV. Let's face it, going on holiday with five of your best friends can be stressful enough, but at least you can get away for a day. Here, you volunteer to spend ten days with five other celebrities who are also keen to be seen in a new and more interesting light. In the *Big Brother* house, I remember having a heart to heart with Mark Owen, who said that since the Take That split, he got a lot of abuse, which really upset him. 'I just need something to get up for in the morning,' he said.

Looking back, I can see that one of the reasons I went into the *Big Brother* house, and the reason why it was such a disaster, was because I was still being driven by the fear that had always haunted me: that one day I would lose it all and end up unknown and poverty-stricken. Stan Laurel, in my opinion the funniest man to ever live, lived his last days in a tatty motel room, reprising his brilliant routines for anyone who wanted to watch. The audiences who once loved you forget surprisingly easily. If I'm stopped in the street and someone knows me but can't put a name to my face, I feel a sickness in my stomach. It's the five stages of fame: 1) who is Les Dennis? 2) get me Les

Dennis, 3) get me someone like Les Dennis, 4) get me a young Les Dennis, and finally, 5) who is Les Dennis?

I can see now that I did, to some extent, feel competitive towards Amanda. My wife had become more successful than me, and I had always nurtured and supported that success, arguing that I could never be jealous because we were not in competition. It is not as if we would ever be up for the same roles. The competition lay deeper than that, though. It was a competition that struck at the very core of old-fashioned male pride and ego. No matter how much I fought against it, no matter how in touch with feminist thinking I thought I was, I didn't like the idea that I was fast becoming Mr Amanda Holden. I wanted to prove something, to reinvent myself.

Like the creature that bursts out of John Hurt's stomach in *Alien*, Les Dennis couldn't resist the massive stage that was on offer and burst all singing, all dancing out of Leslie Heseltine's stomach. The shy, retiring man, the one I had hoped to show during those ten days, didn't stand a chance.

On the day you enter the *Big Brother* house, you really feel you are being taken to a maximum-security prison and that you won't be experiencing the outside world for a very long time. Endemol provides you with two trendy aluminium suitcases – one large and one small with wheels and a pull handle. You take the smaller suitcase into the house with you. Both are stamped with the iconic *Big Brother* eye and you are told by the producers that after the show they are yours to keep. Yeah. Great! I'm really likely to take them on holiday. Imagine the looks you would get as you wait for them to come off the baggage-claim carousel! As you leave your own home, both cases are shrouded in black cloth bags and hastily put in the boot of the waiting limo. Before you are reunited with them, they will be extensively searched for contraband, such as reading and writing materials, and mobile phones. Once the cases are safely in the boot, you are smuggled out of your house and almost bundled into the back of the car. Even though there is always massive press speculation as to who the celebrity housemates will be, Endemol are keen to keep their identities under wraps until the first live broadcast.

A new *Big Brother* house had been built for our show, and the location was fiercely guarded from the press before we went in. In the car, my driver politely asked if I would mind wearing a blindfold. Even I was not supposed to know where I was going. I got the feeling that if they could get away with hypnosis, they would. I knew that if I refused the blindfold, I would be firmly told that it is an order, not a request, and so agreed to travel to the hideaway hotel, or safe house, in total darkness. I next saw daylight in my hotel room, as I met with the producers for my briefing.

The rest of the day was taken up with photocalls (these are the photos that are used alongside the phone numbers when viewers are asked to call to vote), interviews with Dermot O'Leary for *Big Brother's Little Brother* and the handing over of my entrance homework. We were asked for samples of our handwriting, to hand-paint a mask and to draw a scene showing a train leaving a station carrying the most significant people in our lives. You know, as you fulfil these commitments, that they will be used as fodder for the TV pundits and psychologists. 'Ooh, Les is clearly in trouble. He keeps touching the back of his head – an obvious indication that he wants to return to the womb.'

An hour before the circus began, each housemate was taken to a separate room for a last meeting with friends and family. It is a hugely professional exercise in which the TV production team ensures that no housemates bump into each other. Once I was in my room, my visitors were quickly ushered in to see me. My son, Philip, was there, friends Justin and Karen, my press agent, Pat Lake-Smith, my agent, Mandy Ward, and the two Andys. One of the papers would later comment that I, bizarrely, have a lot of friends called Andy! Two, it seems, constitutes an unhealthy obsession. Amanda's mum was also there and of course Amanda. Despite the fact that she had made the initial suggestion to the show's producers and had encouraged me to go into the house, as the deadline approached, her support seemed less enthusiastic. For weeks now she had been saying, 'This is going to be dreadful for me. It's OK for you. You won't have the press following your every move.' While she was initially keen for me to do something for myself, she could now only see it in terms of how awkward it might be for her.

Our marriage had limped on for two and a half years since the Neil Morrissey affair. We both, I think, knew that it would end eventually, but were loath to unleash the media frenzy that the decision would inevitably cause. When we had got back together, we expected the interest to die down, but it hadn't. They were always watching for the cracks to appear. I think the fact that all the parties involved were well known ensured it was a story that would run and run. I was so tired of being photographed looking unhappy, and even more tired of seeing the headline 'Les Miserables'. I was hoping that my stint in the house would change those perceptions once and for all.

In that room, filled with family and friends, Amanda did her best to put on a brave face. I had resisted her pleas for me not to go ahead and do the show. I had had enough of putting my career on the back burner and being seen as Amanda Holden's has-been, washed-up husband. Whatever the outcome, it was my decision and I was sticking to it. Her attempts at making light of the situation failed to put me at my ease. 'Don't worry, darling,' she announced to the room, 'I'll definitely have your voting number on redial to keep you in. I'll enjoy a bit of freedom.'

Nervous laughter from the others.

'And you know of course that I won't be able to get away from filming to greet you as you come out. The Beeb have got me on an extremely tight schedule. Not even sure I'll be able to watch a lot of the show. Be thinking about you, though, darling.'

More nervous laughter as everyone thought desperately of a way to stop her from carrying on. Mandy, my agent, tried to come to the rescue. 'Oh, Laurie tells me there's a strong rumour that Endemol are putting an extra, secret housemate in at the last minute, possibly tomorrow, once the six of you are settled.'

'Wow,' Amanda interrupted. 'Wouldn't it be amazing if it was Neil. You two in the house. That would be fascinating.'

The poor researcher that came in at that moment to tell me that visiting time was up and I needed to get ready must have wondered what she had walked in on. All of my guests looked like the movie audience from the scene in *The Producers* as the first chorus of 'Springtime for Hitler' echoed through the theatre. Jaws had to be picked up, as I quickly said my goodbyes. When Amanda and I hugged, I whispered, 'Why the fuck did you say that?'

'Oh, darling, it's only a joke. Lighten up.'

'Right,' I said. 'See you when I see you.'

It wasn't long before I was in the *Big Brother* house, live on national TV. The nightmare had begun. Since coming out of the house, I have always been over-defensive in interviews, stating that I never watched the show back or read any of the press cuttings. However, when I decided to write this book, I bit the bullet and looked at the press cuttings from that time. I was so shocked at just how much of it there was and how much suggested that I was a man in emotional meltdown that I asked Endemol for the tapes of the show. One weekend, from further behind the sofa than I had watched *Extras*, I viewed an edited version of that watershed in my life. And you know what? Hands up – I now accept that I was having an emotional crisis on live television. I sang show tunes with Anne Diamond for hours on end, I talked to chickens, I moaned too much about the press, in particular about their treatment of my wife, and most importantly, I forgot that it was only a game. I agonised about having to vote other housemates out. That's the whole point of the show! I complained that the cameras were following me all the time, but they were, of course, following all of us.

The moments I found the most uncomfortable to watch were those immediately after some of the evictions. As Anne leaves and then later Sue Perkins, I can see that I'm listening intently to hear if there's a big crowd outside. I desperately wanted to know that people were watching and that the show was a success. It was also hard to watch one of the show's psychologists describe me as an altercaster – someone who uses a strategy to 'force' others into a particular role that elicits behaviours that meet the needs of the altercaster. At the time I wasn't aware that this was what I was doing, but the occasion the psychologist was referring to was when I left the diary room having nominated Sue and Anne. They knew I had voted for them, as it was broadcast into the living room, and I used my guilt and sorrow to get what he called a 'scrum of sympathy' from the two people I should have been comforting.

I know it seems impossible, but there are times when you forget the cameras are there. These, I think, are the moments that the producers eagerly await, when you let the mask slip and talk about, or confess to, something that perhaps you haven't even told a close friend. They know the buttons to push, and they push them mercilessly. One night they gave us a Trivial Pursuit-like game that had questions specifically tailored to make us talk about our private lives. Anne was asked, 'What is the age difference between Les and his wife, Amanda Holden?' Falling straight into the trap, I launched into a rant against the tabloid media, who I felt were obsessed with the seventeen-year-age gap. Before I knew what was happening, and despite Mark Owen's frantic pointing at the cameras, which were all zooming in on me, I was desperately slagging off the *Mirror*'s 3 a.m. Girls. 'Fuck the fucking fuckers...' I believe it began. When reflecting on my outburst in bed later that night, I could almost see Piers Morgan rubbing his hands with glee as he wrote the next morning's front-page headline: 'Who Is the Most Pathetic Man in Britain? Our Survey Says, "Les Dennis."' Note to self – take a leaf out of Jermaine Jackson's book and keep your mouth shut.

My conversations with the chickens were meant to be bits of comedy shtick that I thought would be amusing to watch. In hindsight it was a poultry routine too far and I looked like a bit of a loony. 'Do you guys ever go to bed and think, That was a good day – that was a really nice day?' I asked them, and, 'Do you think to yourself, Wow, I saw this chicken and she was gorgeous?' In my mind I imagined the sound of laughter, but in reality the producers were summoning the psychologists.

The way the show is edited would of course affect the way you were perceived. One afternoon Mark got his guitar out and sang the Verve anthem 'The Drugs Don't Work'. I am very suggestible and when I hear a song it will stay in my head for ages. At the end of that day's show, as the credits rolled and the theme tune struck up, the camera zoomed in on me alone in the Jacuzzi singing, ''Cos the drugs don't work, they just make you worse.' Of course, there was no footage of Mark's singalong in that show, and like everyone who saw it at the time, when I watched the episode recently, I thought I sounded like a man who was losing it.

The next time I saw Amanda was, in fact, onscreen rather than in the flesh. I came second in *Celebrity Big Brother*, so left the house an hour after Melinda Messenger and a short time before the winner, Mark. He is such a lovely guy he couldn't fail to win. In Chris Heath's book *Feel*, Robbie Williams often refers to the Tao of Owen. I know exactly what he means. He doesn't have a bad word to say about anybody. He survived the weird ten days as a reality-TV lab rat by laughing, making tea and constantly cleaning the house. By the time we sat down on the sofa to hear Davina's announcement of who the winner was, the house was cleaner than it had been when we'd first arrived. He had made beds, cleaned work surfaces and swept floors. If he'd had time to do the windows, he would have. As the last two housemates, we had been provided with a bottle of champagne and two glasses. As we sipped, Mark said, 'You're going to win, mate.'

'No,' I said. 'You definitely are.'

He wouldn't have it, though. 'When I've gone,' he said, 'will you do me a favour? Will you wash the glasses and put the bottle in the bin?'

He was obsessed!

Minutes later, though, it was me who exited as runner-up to meet Davina and the thronging crowd. After a quick catch-up with family and friends, noting Amanda was true to her word and was indeed absent, I was rushed into the adjacent studio for my post-eviction interview with Davina. She showed me my best and worst moments. I squirmed at some bits – the Forrest Gump-like sits on the bench, the agonising in the diary room, the chats with the chickens – and I laughed at the others. My bonding with Goldie (a friendship as unlikely as one between Hannibal Lecter and Mary Poppins) was hilarious.

'Right,' said Davina. 'You know Amanda is busy, but she has taped a message for you.'

My heart filled with dread – she couldn't even be bothered to do it live. Suddenly she was onscreen, not alone but with two of her *Cutting It* co-stars, Ben Daniels and Sarah Parish. Loving, supportive message for me, or blatant promotion for her new TV series? I wondered. *That* was my defining moment. As viewers watched me watch her jabber on about my amazing honesty, the words 'I love you and I'm proud of you' never crossing her lips, I came to the final decision that this charade of a marriage was over. I muddled through the rest of the interview and was then led off to face the national press.

Pat, my press agent, accompanied me, and I began to realise from her anxiety that perhaps my performance over the last ten days had garnered more derision and concern than admiration and laughs. All the questions seemed to be centred on when I was next going to see Amanda. As the call ended, it began to dawn on me that my stint in the house was not going to prove to be the popularity boost that I had hoped for. Perhaps, instead, it would turn out to be an exercise in how to end a career live on national television.

Amanda and I spoke on the phone, and she said she was not coming home on her one day off because she had an early start the following morning. 'I'm looking forward to seeing you in Bristol later this week, though,' she said. I was going off to Bristol to film an episode of *Casualty*.

I could hear the strain and distance in her voice, and decided that a decision had to be made there and then. 'Look, Amanda, let's stop pretending. We both know this has to end and we can't go on like this any longer.'

'Les, no,' she replied. 'This can wait until after Christmas.'

'No,' I said. 'I'm not going to play the happy couple so that your family's Christmas isn't ruined. In fact, I'm going to spend Christmas in Liverpool with our Marg and Tony. We both want this to end.'

The following Monday I did the two interviews I had agreed to do: one on *GMTV* with Fiona Phillips and the other with Richard and Judy, who were smashing. They had been out of the country while the show was on, so had caught up that day by watching a video. 'There's all this fuss about you having a breakdown,' said Richard, 'but I think you did great.'

'Yes,' agreed Judy, 'but if Richard went into the house, I'd divorce him.'

The world stopped as I seriously contemplated announcing on live TV that Amanda and I were going to do just that. I only stopped myself as I saw Pat, my press agent, out of the corner of my eye. She knew what I planned to do, as I had told her the minute I came out of my interview with Davina, and had advised me to be careful about blurting it. I suppose I knew that once Amanda and I made a joint announcement to the press, they would report that she had dumped me. Once again, I would be seen as the sad, jilted lover whose career and marriage were over.

Every day the tabloids would keep tally on how long it had been since Amanda and I had seen each other – 'It's now five days since Les came out and they remain apart.' The fact was, I was in Bristol working and she was in Manchester working. She did come down on the Thursday of that week and we managed to walk round a park in Bristol without any journalist knowing we had met up. Amanda again suggested that it was unfair to both our families to make a decision before Christmas. This time, though, I was adamant that this ridiculous charade had to end.

That weekend she got back to the house half an hour before I did. By the time I got there, I couldn't get through the gate for press. After being jostled and questioned as I tried to get into my own home, I felt angry and confused. That night when I walked the dogs a lone photographer got the brunt of my wrath as I tried to take his camera away from him, pleading to be left alone. The next day a very unflattering photo of me running at him made the papers.

Amanda and I shared the house for our last week together. I was working for Chris Evans's production company, co-hosting *Live With Chris Moyles* for Channel 5. Amanda was home from Manchester for the Christmas break and was making preparations for her family's arrival. On the Saturday, as the biggest Christmas tree I'd ever seen arrived, I packed a bag and left the house to stay with Andy G and his partner Sacha. On the Monday I went up to Liverpool to spend Christmas with my family, while Amanda stayed in the house with hers. Considering the on-off events of the last few years, in the end our separation was very undramatic. On 28 December we released a statement to the press saying that we had split for good.

While having supper with my friends Barbara and Cliff, I watched incredulous as there was a feature on us on ITV's *News at Ten*. Nina Nannar, along with various relationship pundits, examined and ruminated on the failure of our marriage. It was the holiday season and I realised that just as had happened when Dustin died, there was little world news, and so we were extra newsworthy. Time to get out of the country for a while, I decided. As Nina Nannar was uttering the words 'This is Nina Nannar in London for *News at Ten*' I was dialling my friend Paul Whittome, who was holidaying at his home in South Africa. 'Paul,' I said, 'remember you said I could come and stay at any time–'

'Get on a plane now,' he anticipated. The next day, as the front pages of the tabloids had me on suicide watch, I was in fact boarding a plane for Durban, with Andy G, who one paper would later describe as my 'ape of a minder'.

CHAPTER 26

South African Retreat

Andy and Sacha proved to be good and loyal friends. When I called and asked if he would come with me to South Africa for a couple of weeks, he hesitated for a moment and then asked, 'When?'

Expecting his reaction to be negative, I tentatively said, 'Er...the day after tomorrow.' It was three days before New Year. It was a lot to expect him to suddenly abandon Sacha and jump on a plane with me, but I heard him explaining it all to her in the background and then heard her say, 'Of course you must go. I'll be fine – I'll see my brother. It'll be great for both of you.' I wanted to reach down the phone and hug her.

I thanked Cliff and Barbara for their support and hospitality, and drove back to our Marg's. When I told her I was going to leave the country for a few weeks, she was delighted, agreeing that it was the best thing I could do right now. If I went back to London, I could expect a huge welcoming committee of photographers and staff journalists. New Year was always light on news and so

Primrose Hill would be swarming with them anxious to get shots of me looking 'suicidal'. In fact, the next morning the tabloids all had headlines like 'Showbiz Amanda Ditches Sad Les', 'Les Dumped' and 'Friends Fear for Sad Les'. Predictably, 'close friends' were quoted. Mike Reid was 'concerned' and, apparently, arranging a suicide watch for me. I've met Mike on a few occasions and he's a lovely bloke but he certainly wasn't a 'close friend' or someone who would be holding a vigil for me. He was probably as shocked as me to read such tosh.

Making a decision not to read any more, I packed my bag, hugged our Marg and Tony, and left their house. As I was walking towards my car, I remembered something. 'Shit,' I said to Marg, 'what about the party?'

'Don't worry,' she said. 'We'll still go. It'll be fine.' My family and Amanda's had all planned to get together for a New Year's bash in the same country house in Devon where we had celebrated Amanda's mum's fiftieth birthday. In all the commotion, I had forgotten about it. Amanda had flown off to Barcelona with the girls from *Cutting It*, and I was flying the next morning to Durban. The two people who had arranged the party were not going to be there, but were instead splitting and would never be together at a family party again. And that's what happened. The two families all spent New Year without us and, apparently, had a good night. Our Marg said everyone left the next day promising to keep in touch but knowing that they were unlikely to ever see each other again.

I drove back to London feeling desperately sad but, amazingly, calm. When you make that decision to give something up, there is, apart from the grief, an overwhelming sense of relief. However sad you feel when a relationship breaks down, you know that time and the healing process can only make things better. The limbo land that Amanda and I had been in since that awful day in 2000 was, at last, over. We could now pick up the pieces of our lives and move forward – but not together.

I decided not to go back to my house as it was still daylight. Instead, I travelled to Andy's and the first thing I did was give Sacha a big hug to thank her for allowing Andy to come with me to South Africa. Andy and Sacha had met in Los Angeles when he'd come out to get over his split with his wife, Ruby. In the drawer of their dressing table he had a small box where he had put his wedding ring. We got it out, and I removed the band from the third finger of my left hand and placed it in the box next to his. Brothers in divorce! As far as I know, it's still there to this day.

As soon as it was dark, we sneaked over to my house to pick up some summer shirts and shorts. The Christmas tree stood sadly in the window with no one to celebrate or enjoy it. We left quietly without being snapped and went back to Andy's.

The next morning Sacha dropped us at the airport and we headed quickly to the business lounge so as not to be noticed. We were, of course, and when we got to Johannesburg Airport, there was a line of photographers waiting. We boarded the short flight to Durban and I noticed that the guy in the isle seat opposite me was straining to hear my conversation with Andy. I leant over and said, 'Good morning. Which paper do you work for?'

'The *Mail*,' he replied, not even trying to hide it. 'We could take some shots of you here on the plane, if you like.'

'No,' I replied with a fixed smile, 'I think I'll give that one a miss.'

Clearly the papers were not going to allow me to escape. No more than they were going to let Amanda get on with her break in Barcelona. Because she had gone with the *Cutting It* girls, the tabloids went for a *Sex in the City* slant, saying that while lonely Les had fled to South Africa to bury his grief, she was living it up in a cool city, sipping champagne and enjoying a party lifestyle.

The press interest in the ups and downs of our marriage had

been absolutely extraordinary. Over the last few years of our relationship the media attention had been constant and baffling. It's not as if we were A-list movie stars. We were a couple who were on TV. Yes, there was the added interest that Amanda's affair with Neil had created, but even so, that would seem to me to be something of a curiosity only until the next morsel of showbiz gossip came along. For a newspaper to actually pay a journalist to follow me all the way to South Africa and then hang around to try and get the appropriate grief-stricken shot was bizarre and, frankly, absurd.

Andy and I were staying with my good friends Paul and Jeanne Whittome. Paul picked us up from the airport and, once we had dodged the photographers, drove us to their lovely home in Shaka's Rock, just north of Durban.

We had a couple of days relaxing round the pool, but it wasn't long before a press contingent was camped outside Paul's front gate. Notes would be sent up to the house offering exclusive deals for my story. Had I chosen to, I could, literally, have made hundreds of thousands of pounds during those mad few weeks.

Paul has a wonderful Zulu housekeeper, Gertie, who one day was offered a substantial bribe to sneakily take a photo of me by the pool. The provision of the deal was that I must look sad, preferably heartbroken. The Zulu people are honourable and extremely proud and so, of course, she refused and told Paul about the offer immediately. It seemed that the press were prepared to go to any length to get a story. Gertie had no idea why this pale, middle-aged man was getting such attention and even asked Paul if I was a gangster. To be honest, sometimes I wondered myself if I had committed some huge, horrific crime. But no, I wasn't a highly dangerous drug baron. I was, in fact, the host of a reasonably successful game show whose marriage to a reasonably successful TV actress had collapsed. The world seemed to have gone quite mad.

I tried my best to enjoy my time in this beautiful country, but of course I was grieving my marriage, so there were times, I'm sure, when Gertie could have got that profitable photo of me by the pool. It was New Year, a period for reflection at the best of times, but I didn't want to seem maudlin in front of my gracious hosts, who had kindly invited me out at the eleventh hour. On New Year's Eve there was a party at someone's house on the beach to bring in 2003. I went along and tried my hardest not to show my sadness. Midnight approached, and as I was resisting the urge to call Amanda to see how she was, a friend of Paul's came up to me. Paul Howell is a charismatic, colourful character who had been Margaret Thatcher's first Euro MP. He has a remarkable gravelly voice, not unlike that of Oliver Reed. 'Les,' he said, 'just a quiet word. The ladies have noticed that you're flying rather low.'

Now, I had never heard that expression before and didn't know that it meant my flies were undone! I thought he was telling me that people had noticed that my mood was somewhat subdued. So, instead of quietly zipping myself up, I tried desperately to show that I was OK and having a good time. What must they have thought as I beamed over at them, raised my glass in a toast, still with my flies undone!

Just after midnight I got a call from Amanda. She was as sad and reflective as I was. The papers were making out that she couldn't care less and was partying in a carefree, newly single frenzy. That's the way they wanted the story to be: me dumped, her the callous, heartless dumper. A marriage break-up is traumatic for both partners. Even when you know it's the best thing to do, it doesn't stop you from grieving. We wished each other a better new year – it couldn't be any worse than the old one – and said goodnight.

A couple of days later poor Paul Howell became an unknowing victim of the paparazzi. He had also been staying with Paul and Jeanne over the holiday and was due back at work in the UK on 2 January. He was having such a good time, though, that he decided to 'throw a sicky' and called his company to tell them he wouldn't be back until the following week. On 2 January Paul Whittome arranged a trip on a boat to spot dolphins. We were out on the ocean all afternoon but didn't see any dolphins. Little did we know that we were being spotted ourselves by the long lenses hidden on the beach. Of course, the next day, in the *Sun*, there was a photo on the front page of me looking reflectively out to sea. Unable to crop everyone else out of the shot, to show me as this sad, lonely figure, they had to leave the person next to me and that was a beaming Paul Howell. When he should have been at work, he was splashed across the front page of a tabloid paper having a great time in the South African sun. He got into terrible trouble when he returned and has only just about forgiven me!

Andy was a great support during those weeks away. We went on a game drive at the Phinda Wildlife Reserve, which was a wonderful experience. I couldn't concentrate, though, and would often glaze over as waves of grief hit me. 'You're not here, are you?' Andy would ask.

'Just thinking about stuff. Not looking forward to going back to London.'

'Well, don't. Stay here for a bit longer.'

I decided to extend my stay by a week. I knew I would have to go back and face the music one day, but not just yet. The needles on the Christmas tree would be dropping on to the wooden floor of the house that would now have to be sold. Also, the house in Norfolk that we now would never move into would have to go on the market. The developer I had bought it from had been very unsympathetic and refused to let me try to find a buyer before completion. I now had two huge financial millstones round my neck, and, on the work front, I was getting snow blindness from my diary. The only thing on the horizon was a short tour that I had arranged to do before I had gone into the *Big Brother* house. I wasn't relishing the prospect but knew that, if I cancelled, it would signal to the media that my breakdown was continuing. Once again the show would have to go on. Besides, Amanda and I would need to discuss divorce proceedings. Andy was right. All this could wait, at least for another week or so.

During the rest of my stay Paul and Jeanne did their best to entertain me, figuring that distraction would temper my grief. We went on a trip into the Natal farmlands to visit Jeanne's family farm. Her twin sister, Bridget, and her husband, Howie, were with us and one night we stayed at a beautiful colonial hotel with exquisitely furnished rooms. After dinner I went back to mine and felt so sad that I had no one to share it with. I would soon be fifty, with two failed marriages and a career that was seemingly in tatters. Being with two happy couples only served to highlight my situation, and alone in my room, I desperately wanted to speak to Amanda. I resisted and called our Marg instead. As always, she was a wise and compassionate listener who allowed me to cry and express my sadness. Thank God I had got my family back.

Family and friends are the ones you need at these times, and I was lucky to have both. I thanked Paul and Jeanne as I said goodbye at the airport. After a long flight the welcome sight of my lovely son, Philip, who was there to greet me with more hugs, brought the tears again. The first thing I did when I got back to the house was to throw out the Christmas tree. It was well after twelfth night and I hoped my run of bad luck was over. Onwards and upwards!

CHAPTER 27

The Girl Round the Corner

Upon my return from South Africa at the beginning of 2003, Amanda and I began proceedings for what we hoped would be an easy and hassle-free divorce. A complication arose, however, almost immediately. There are only two ways to obtain a quick divorce. One is to cite unreasonable behaviour and the other is to cite adultery. Both of our lawyers advised that unreasonable behaviour carried more stigma, and would mean that we'd have to give details of such behaviour which would then be readily available for the media to pick up. It was therefore suggested that we take the least defamatory option, adultery. Not long after my call with my brief, Amanda phoned.

'Les, you will have to let me divorce you for infidelity. You won't have to name anyone and it will help my reputation which I can't afford to damage any further.'

I laughed and then stopped when I realised she was serious. 'OK,' I replied. 'You never know it might help mine!'

Of course that is not what I thought at the time, but by then

I just wanted this ridiculous farce to end.

With Amanda's consent, while she was away in Los Angeles, once again pursuing the Hollywood dream, I got on with the business of selling the two homes we had. The threat of war in Iraq had affected the market and meant the St Mark's Square house pricetag would have to be reduced for a quick sale. Luckily, I managed to sell the one in Norfolk on the very day that I completed. I literally had the keys for less than twenty-four hours.

Not knowing what the future held, either professionally or personally, I decided to rent rather than buy a new property. I moved into a furnished house in Muswell Hill and put everything into storage. The saddest sound in the world is cardboard boxes and packing tape. It feels like your life is being boxed up and shipped out. At least there were fewer photographers in Muswell Hill, and for a while I could walk around Highgate Woods without someone popping out from behind a tree with a telephoto lens aimed at my face. Not for long, though.

Round the corner from the house in Primrose Hill is a small pub, the Queen's No. 1. It is owned by one of the village's most colourful characters, Tony Peters. Tony has his own table facing the door and sits there, holding court, looking like a cross between Don Corleone and Tony Soprano. His business is totally legitimate; he just looks like a gangster. Mind you, he does admit to having once been shot. A lot of the A-listers living in the area would often pop in for a pint. Jude Law, Johnny Lee Miller and Rhys Ifans knew they could relax because Tony respected their privacy and refused to allow the paps to take shots. During those weeks when lenses would be shoved against pub or restaurant windows in the hope of getting shots of me crying into my beer (one time I was drinking water with my friend Duncan Preston but photos appeared of me apparently drunk and heartbroken), the Queen's became a kind of safe house.

One evening in spring 2003 as I sat waiting in there for a Thai takeaway, I got chatting to two women at the bar. 'Hi, I'm Maxine,' said one, 'and this is Leoni.' They were both in the film industry and we got on well immediately.

'We're here on Saturday for Max's birthday. Why don't you join us for dinner?' Leoni asked.

'I will,' I said, and left with my curry.

On the Saturday evening I arrived with a couple of mates, Declan O'Dwyer, who had directed me in *Casualty*, and Justin. I decided not to go alone because the invitation had been so casual that I was unsure they would actually be there. They were, and they welcomed us and asked us to join their table. As I sat down, Leoni said, 'If you hadn't come, I was going to write to you and post it through your letterbox.'

'How do you know where I live?' I asked.

'My mum lives round the corner from you. That's my home when I am not in Spain.'

Within weeks Leoni and I were dating. Leoni lived and worked in Madrid, and Maxine on the Costa del Sol. One weekend I flew from London to Malaga and Leoni from Madrid. We had a lovely time together in Estepona and then drove up to the charming coastal town of Tarifa.

One day, as we lunched at a tiny restaurant outside the town, two blokes entered and immediately I knew they were journos. 'Hello, Les, we're from the *Sun*. You two look really happy. Care to give us the story?'

'No, guys. Thanks for asking, but we're on holiday. How did you find us, anyway?'

'Followed you up the coast. Your car is easy to spot.' Maxine had picked up the hire car so that we could travel incognito. The problem was, it was a lime-green Fiat Punto. We might as well have attached a banner saying, 'Les and Leoni on Tour'! The guys politely left us alone, and as we drove up to Rhonda, Pat called me to say there was going to be a story the next day. As I flew back to London, and Leoni to Madrid, the *Sun* carried the story 'Les in Love'. The pictures, taken on what we thought was a deserted beach north of Tarifa, looked like they'd been set up to prove that I was happy. I had to assure Leoni's mother that they hadn't been set up. The story was, at least, positive by suggesting that I had found love. Trouble was, we hadn't known each other long enough to be in love.

From then on the press would rush our relationship on faster than we could possibly keep up. It was insane. Reports that we were to marry, that I was to move to Spain and even that Leoni was pregnant hit the newsstands before we had had a chance to get to know each other. Journalists knocked endlessly on Leoni's mother's front door and looked for ex-boyfriends and schoolfriends to see if they could find out if she had a shady past. They quizzed the porter at her apartment block in Madrid and even went round her local bars and cafés with a photo asking people if they knew the girl because she was wanted by the police!

Almost every other day there were reports that my relationship with Leoni was over. The on-off speculation about my marriage to Amanda had been replaced by the on-off speculation about a relationship that was less than a month old. Every agony aunt in every newspaper wanted to give me advice about my love life. The fact that Leoni was in her early thirties didn't help. Carole Malone called me 'a silly old fool', and Vanessa Feltz suggested it was time I 'sought solace with a well-padded brunette fast pushing fifty'. Sometimes a cutting about you will make you laugh out loud. In the *Mail*'s 'Wicked Whispers' it said, 'Life for Les Dennis is hardly a bowl of cherries. Having suffered the indignity of his marriage break-up with Amanda Holden, Les has just endured further humiliation. Taking part in Comic Relief's celebrity egg and spoon race, he stumbled when his red nose fell off in mid-canter. Says fellow contestant Stephen Tompkinson, "One lady in the crowd shouted, 'Come on, Cheggers, sort it out!'"

Amanda called to tell me, before I read it in the papers, that she was seeing Chris Hughes. I can't pretend it wasn't a shock. Of course I knew she would be dating. What I didn't expect was that it would be the son of my long-term manager. The next call came from Mike, who seemed keen to let me know that he disapproved.

'Mike,' I said, 'it's none of my business. Amanda and I are divorcing and she is perfectly entitled to see who she likes.'

I did feel a bit odd, though. I had, as I have already said, known Chris since he was a boy. Life certainly throws you some curve balls.

CHAPTER 28

The 'We Love Les' Tour

That spring I went on the one-man tour I had arranged before *Celebrity Big Brother* and my break up with Amanda. The previous summer I had been on the bill at the opening of a new arts centre in Durham alongside performers as diverse as Ned Sherrin, Simon Callow, Bonnie Langford and Westlife. I had done twenty minutes stand-up and had absolutely loved being in front of a live audience again. It had reminded me of the reasons I had come into the business in the first place. I suggested to my agent, Mandy, that we should do a small-scale mini-tour the following spring. And that's what it would have been, had the events of the previous months not happened.

Now, of course, it was quite a different matter. I opened to huge press interest. Will he talk about *Celebrity Big Brother*? Will he mention his marriage break-up? It wasn't my finest hour. I opened in Swindon on a bank holiday Sunday and closed in Hunstanton on a wet Monday in June. It would have been better to have done it the other way round. 'It was a half-empty theatre in Swindon,' they wrote, though I prefer to use the 'glass is half full' analogy. Self-deprecation was seen as maudlin self-pity and I was savaged by the press. Some support, however, came from the unlikeliest of sources. The *Guardian*, feeling that the press reaction had been vitriolic and somewhat unjustified, got behind the show, promoting it with a large dollop of postmodernist irony as the 'We Love Les' Tour. Though it did little to help the business, it was a welcome boost to my battered ego and self-esteem. By the time I got to Hunstanton, I had a show I was proud of. I felt I could hold my head up high. If I had cancelled, the press would have said I was unfit to perform – that I was a broken man. Damned if you do, damned if you don't.

While holidaying in Spain a month or so later, the tide of my career began to turn. Within days of each other I got two really interesting and exciting job offers. David Jason was directing an ITV drama called *The Second Quest*, which was a follow-up to the successful *The Quest*. It concerned three men, played by David, Roy Hudd and Hywel Bennett, who reminisce about their adventures as friends in the 1950s. On a motorcycle trip to the Isle of Man they go to watch a Bathing Beauty Competition. I was asked to play the seedy, corrupt compère. The second job offer was to play Yvan in the national tour of the hit play *Art*. I had seen the original production in the West End and had adored it. Albert Finney, Tom Courtenay and Ken Stott had held the audience spellbound. After they finished their run, the producer, David Pugh, cleverly recast the play every three months, thereby bringing it fresh to the audiences every time. In various incarnations it starred the casts of *Cheers*, *Dallas* and, even, *The League of Gentlemen*. That autumn in 2003 it was to tour, beginning at the beautiful Harrogate Theatre. I said yes to both jobs and returned home excited that my work prospects had so dramatically improved.

Working with David Jason was a great honour and pleasure.

Like everyone, I had been a huge fan since seeing his early appearances in *Porridge*, *Open All Hours* and, of course, as the hilarious and touching Del Boy in *Only Fools and Horses*. He and Ronnie Barker were great friends, so I had met him on several occasions at Ronnie and Joy's summer garden parties. Then, at Bob Monkhouse's seventieth-birthday bash, Amanda and I had been on the same table as Ronnie and Joy, and David and his wife, Gill. David had commented that I hadn't touched my starter and that I seemed a little agitated. 'I'm one of the speakers,' I'd explained.

'Blimey, no wonder you're nervous. Ronnie, Les has to give a speech!'

'Oh, you poor fellow. Should have worn your brown trousers!'

Public speaking is daunting at the best of times, but to have to perform in front of such entertainment luminaries is totally nerve-racking. Worse still, I had to follow Denis Norden, who had been hilarious. As the laughter from Denis's last gag was subsiding, I approached the microphone, having been pushed forwards supportively by David and Ronnie, and said, 'Denis and I were talking before the show and Denis said he was extremely nervous. I said I wasn't at all, so we swapped speeches. Now, you've all heard how well I did, so, Denis, the best of luck.' It got a big laugh, but the biggest thrill for me were the nods of approval from two of the greatest comedy actors that Britain has ever produced.

On *The Second Quest* David was just as supportive. Actors make fine directors because they know what you are going through and can empathise. The shoot was a delight, and as I finished my last scene, he came running up to shake me by the hand. 'Well done, sir. All power to you. Good luck in everything you do.' It was another moment when I instantly wanted to phone my mum and dad. I called our Marg instead.

If I enjoyed working on *The Second Quest*, doing *Art* was an absolute joy. The play is about three old friends in Paris whose relationship hits crisis point when one of them, Serge, buys, at enormous expense, a totally white painting. Marc, whose taste in art is more traditional, is outraged at what he thinks are Serge's pseudo-intellectual pretensions. Yvan is the mild-mannered, easy-going one in the middle who thinks that Serge should be allowed to like what he likes. A huge row ensues, which is at times hilarious and extremely touching. The fuss about the painting is, of course, there to represent the complexities of male friendship.

That production brought me new, and strong, friendships with director Hannah Chiswick, producer Michael Harrison and, of course, my two co-stars. They were both actors whom I had enjoyed watching on TV in my youth. Notice I didn't say 'growing up'! They'd kill me, as they're not much older than me! Christopher Cazenove, I first remember watching as Charlie, the lovable rogue in the long-running series *The Duchess of Duke Street*. He would have enormous success in movies like *The Eye of the Needle*, *Three Men and a Little Lady* and as Blake Carrington's evil brother in *Dynasty*. John Duttine was marvellous in two other long-running series, *To Serve Them All My Days* and *The Mallens*.

To be working with two such distinguished actors was both a thrill and a great chance to learn. Thankfully, they're great blokes too. If three actors are on tour together and one is, either professionally or personally, difficult, it can be misery. As it was, we had a marvellous time. Our opening in Harrogate coincided with the opening of a stunning new Hotel du Vin in the centre of town. To help publicise both the play and the hotel, the management generously gave us rooms for free for the entire three-week run. During the run, John, who is a Yorkshireman, would give us guided tours of York, Haworth (Brontë country) and the Dales. In the evening we would do the play, which was an hour and twenty minutes without an interval. At the end, as the row subsided and their friendship was restored, the three characters sit there eating olives, a very funny, silent scene, until Marc says, 'Let's go and eat.' And that's what we did, every night.

One night when we were in Woking, Chris did the best ad-libbing I've ever seen in a play. The set was very simple. A white wall on which hung the painting, beautifully lit (I always got a kick out of watching an audience snigger at first and, slowly, over the course of the evening, come to appreciate its beauty), and three very different chairs are the only items to adorn the stage. The chairs represent the three men's personalities. Serge's is like one of those modern Barcelona chairs. Marc's is faintly baroque, and Yvan's is a somewhat worn, nondescript old armchair. In the scene where Yvan comes to see the painting for the first time, both he and Serge sit in their chairs and talk. As Chris sat, drink in hand, there was an enormous cracking noise and, his chair, with him in it, collapsed and fell to the floor in pieces. The audience, of course, laughed, but what were we going to do? The three chairs were integral to the play. As calm as you like, Chris rose and said, in his beautiful upper-class tones, 'It's all right. I've got another one in the kitchen.' As he sauntered off into the wings, I was thinking, Another one? We don't have another one. Why would we? Stage management wouldn't carry extra chairs in the unlikely event of one of them collapsing. Moments later, however, Chris returned with a red plastic bucket chair, plonked it down as if it was the most natural thing to do and, elegantly, sat down. By coincidence, my next line was 'Your place gets more and more monastic.' Chris, or rather, Serge, ad-libbed, 'Yes, it does rather, doesn't it!'

I love stories of actors having to get themselves out of sticky situations onstage. Comedians, of course, are used to chatting directly to an audience, but in a play there is the 'fourth wall' convention, meaning the audience has to be ignored. One night in *Me and My Girl*, when an actress didn't come onstage, I didn't know what to do. My instinct was to step forward and do ten minutes' patter but that would have broken the spell of the play. I tried to ad-lib some lines with the other actors, but they didn't want to know. Still the actress didn't appear. 'Where's my Sal?' I shouted, hoping Louise English was waiting in the wings. No. Two minutes felt like two hours and in desperation I shouted, 'But first, a song!' You have never seen a bunch of musicians move so quickly. David Beer, the MD, looked at me as if to say, 'What the fuck are you doing?' Luckily the actress, who had been talking in the wings, was at last pushed on and we were able to continue the scene.

Actors seem to deal with the situation with more composure. There is a story of a production of a drawing-room comedy where Sir John Gielgud, as a butler, flung the huge double doors open two pages too early. Realising, by the looks on the other actors' faces, his mistake, he said calmly, 'I'm awfully sorry. I thought it was a cupboard,' and promptly closed them again. Dame Edith Evans was in a play once where someone onstage dried up. When the prompt whispered the line to the actor, she shouted, 'We know the line, dear, but who the fuck says it?' My favourite, though, is the story Kenneth More told on *Parkinson*. He was in a play in which there was a murder in the final scene. As the tensions mounted, one actor pointed a gun at the other and shot him. One night the gun didn't go off and the two actors looked at each other as if to say, 'What do we do now?' Out of desperation, and in panic, the man with the gun simply kicked the other guy up the arse. 'Arrgh,' shouted the other, thinking on his feet, 'the poisoned boot!' and promptly died.

In the middle of the tour of *Art*, in October 2003, I turned fifty. I celebrated it with family and friends at the Hoste Arms in Burnham Market. My divorce papers came through and I bought a new house in Highgate. Life was moving on. I gutted the house and completely renovated it. It was a satisfying project, but when I moved in, in February 2004, I still felt un-rooted. My relationship with Leoni had come to an end, though I don't think any new relationship could have survived the constant press speculation and harassment. Although we split mutually, the headlines would once again paint me as the sad clown who had been dumped. I didn't feel at peace in the new house, either: a house is simply that, a house, not a home. By Easter 2004 I had been offered a ridiculous amount to sell it so, with no family ties, that's what I decided to do. Perhaps, I thought, if show business was slowing down for me, I could start a new career as a property developer. I seemed to have an eye for the right deals and doing houses up from scratch could be fun and creative, and could develop an artistic side of me I hadn't really explored before. Maybe a career change was what was called for.

Meanwhile, once again, I was homeless. My friend James Wilkinson, who, together with Justin had sold my house, invited me to share his flat. Apart from those weeks sharing with Dustin and Russell in the 1980s, I had never really flat-shared before. I had an absolute ball. In the past I had always been so busy working that I had never been able to do any of the things people do in the summer. I went to Wimbledon, a stag day out at Ascot and summer picnics at the Kenwood. It was great and very liberating.

One evening my friend, Jack, invited me to join his party at Kenwood to watch the Gypsy Kings. The Kenwood concerts are hugely popular events and thousands of people set their picnic blankets out overlooking the lake during the summer evenings and sip Pimm's and champagne as they listen to the music. I arrived to find Jack on his own in the middle of a huge plot he had reserved and where he had spread four blankets. As I joined him, the people around, who had squeezed their blankets into the limited available space, glared at us for being selfish.

'Jack,' I said, 'people are staring. I thought you had loads of friends coming.' The inherent embarrassment I had picked up from my dad was kicking in and I felt everyone looking at me.

'Relax,' he said. 'They'll be here. Anyway, it's me who put the blankets out so it's me they'll blame.'

'Yeah, but it's me they know off the telly. They'll think I'm being big time,' I argued.

As more of his friends arrived, I began to relax, and when the last two showed up, the hostile crowd forgave us completely.

'Here they come!' Jack said.

Making their way through the groups of picnickers, to my astonishment, came Paul McCartney and Heather Mills.

As the crowd spontaneously burst into applause at the couple doing something so openly public, I gawped open-mouthed as Paul came up and, pointing at me, said, 'Hey, I've seen you on the telly.'

'I've seen you too,' I mumbled back stupidly.

I spent the next three hours eating and drinking with a Beatle! Jack's wife, Dawn, is a mate of Heather's, so the girls all sat together and Paul sat next to me. 'Have some of Linda's "chicken",' he said, proffering a Tupperware container of vegetarian delights.

We had a lot in common. We'd been to the same schools in Liverpool, though at different times, and had lived in the same area. When I told him that I loved 'Here Today', the song he had written for John, he sang it to me. I was so excited but faintly embarrassed as people heard him warble to me 'I really loved you and was glad you came along'! We then sat harmonising to the Gypsy Kings as they sang 'Volare'. As the evening finished and Paul and Heather's driver arrived, they gave us all big hugs and left. It was a brilliant experience.

CHAPTER 29

After *Extras*

By the end of summer 2005 when I got that all-important call from Ricky Gervais, I knew that property developing would have to wait. The reaction to *Extras* from the public and the industry alike was extraordinary. Apart from receiving the best reviews of my career, I found that more and more young people were stopping me in the street to say how much they had enjoyed the show. Every time Ricky had a reaction he would ring me and tell me, which was very sweet. I suppose it's only in hindsight that I can see how much of a gamble it was to appear in *Extras*. If I'd got it wrong, it could have reinforced the whole 'sad, lonely Les' image. Instead, as I'd hoped it would, it showed that I could laugh at myself. It was a massive turning point and suddenly the phone began to ring again.

Producers at Endemol called me and asked me to come in to discuss a new game show for them. I spent a couple of weeks working it through with them and then did a pilot with a studio audience. It went well and they said they would let me know the outcome in a few weeks. Apparently, someone else was in the frame and it was between the two of us. After a month I got a call from Mandy Ward to say that the show had gone to Noel Edmonds. It was *Deal or No Deal* and would prove to be an enormous hit for Endemol, Channel 4 and, of course, Noel. For a day I was disappointed, but I figured that if I'd got it, I wouldn't have been able to carry on with my newly blossoming acting career. I mention it now because so often in interviews I'm asked if I turned the show down. It is because of the success and reinvention that *Extras* brought that I was even considered for it. That's what is so exciting about the entertainment industry: your fortune can change in a heartbeat.

There is always something unexpected round the corner. In a magazine interview to publicise a TV show I was doing, I was asked who I would most like to be stuck in a lift with. I said, 'Sir David Attenborough.' He has been a lifelong hero of mine. His passion and enthusiasm for the world we live in is so infectious and inspiring. There is one piece of film for *Life on Earth* that always makes me laugh out loud. Sir David is stuck in a cave somewhere in South America and thousands of bats are crapping all over him but he is filled with joy. 'Marvellous,' he exclaims, as more bat shit falls on to his trademark safari suit.

The day after my interview was printed, I got a call from the *Plant Earth* office at the BBC asking if I would like to join four other celebrities to make a film for the *Saving Planet Earth* series, which was being produced to create awareness about global warming. The producers wanted us to compete in the Lewa Marathon, in the heart of the Masai Mara region of Kenya. The run is one of the ten hardest marathons in the world and is set out across the Lewa Game Reserve. You literally run the course knowing that any of the big five could pop out of the bush at any time. I'm not a runner and I've got a dodgy knee, but this was an experience I couldn't miss, made all the more attractive by the fact that the five celebs would run in relay. The most I would have to run was five kilometres. So, along with Jeremy Edwards, Kelly Ryan, Michaela Strachan, John Culshaw and our enthusiastic coach and cheerleader, Ruby Wax, I spent a week camping out under the stunning Kenyan skies.

During the trip we visited a Masai village, I fed a beautiful baby rhino, called Lola, and, of course, we did the run. Determined not to let the team down, I blocked out the knee pain and ran my heart out. At every turn you could see, thankfully at a distance, elephants, giraffes and zebra. I couldn't help wondering, though, what Mike, our cameraman, would have done if a young male lion had jumped out and attacked me. Wildlife camera crews don't interfere with nature, so he probably would have carried on filming. Then, later, Sir David could have added the voiceover, in his commanding, unique style: 'After days without food, dinner at last. It is survival of the fittest and he's wisely gone for the weakest of the group. He's pounced on the ageing, limping, game show host who was struggling to keep up. As the cheesy grin becomes a grimace, he has done a great favour to the world of light entertainment!'

At the telethon to promote the series, I finally got to meet my hero. As the programme came to a close, I plucked up the courage to talk to him. Searching in my head for something to say, I mumbled, 'Sir David, we shared the same driver recently.'

'Oh, yes?' He smiled back. 'Ooh, what's his name?'

I couldn't remember either. 'Oh, thingy...what is it?' I babbled. And that's how it went on until Sir David pulled out a notebook full of names.

After looking in it, he shouted, 'Roger! How stupid of me to forget. He's a jolly good friend of mine.'

And that was it. My one conversation with the great man was nothing more than a joint senior moment about the name of a BBC driver. Watching him saunter away through the tropical hothouse at Kew Gardens, it was indeed like watching a majestic endangered species in its natural habitat. He is truly one of our great broadcasters and, if he ever retires, will be an extremely hard act to follow.

My personal life started to change for the better too. After Leoni and I had split, I had no real romantic connections in my life for over a year. I had a few dates and one in particular could have put me off dating for life. A woman I had asked out suggested we meet one Saturday evening in a quiet pub she knew in Fulham. She didn't want any fuss and thought I was unlikely to be recognised and talked to there. I arrived to find her already at the bar. She asked me what I wanted and pointed to a quiet table in the corner. 'Over there,' she said, anxious that I wasn't spotted by the barman. 'I'll get the drinks and bring them over.' She did and we sat and started that hideously difficult small talk that you have on a first date.

Then, from across the room, I heard a Liverpool accent. 'All right there, Les. How ya doing, lad?' I looked up to see a guy I didn't know.

'Ah, a fellow Scouser,' I said, politely. 'What are you doing here?'

'Just been to watch the Reds beat Fulham four-three, haven't we, lads?' Suddenly from the lounge bar there appeared ten to twelve Scousers in red scarves and hats.

'Good to see you,' I said, hoping the conversation would end there.

As I nervously turned to re-engage with my date a Kop-like chorus struck up: 'Les is on his first date. Les is on his first date, da, da, da, da.' As my face flushed to the colour of the scarves that were waving in the air, the chant changed to 'One Les Dennis. There's only one Les Dennis. One Le-e-e-s D-e-e-e-nis. There's only one Les Dennis!' With eyes pleading to the confused woman that this didn't always happen, and then to the guys to stop, my look turned to horror as the chant again changed to 'One Les Heseltine. There's only one Les Heseltine.'

Their behaviour was so good-natured, and funny, I began to laugh. 'How did you know that was my name?' I asked one of the lads.

'Pub quiz question last Thursday.'

I didn't get out of that pub without joining in with two choruses of 'You'll Never Walk Alone' and three of 'When the Reds Go Marching In'. Needless to say, it was my first and last date with that confused, embarrassed lady, but at least I laughed all the way home.

True romance comes when you least expect it. In November 2005 I agreed to host the auction at the Butterfly Ball at the Intercontinental Hotel on Park Lane. The event was organised by Sonya Sadler in memory of her beautiful, talented daughter, Laura Sadler, whom I worked with on her, and my, first film, *Intimate Relations*, and who had died so tragically when she fell from the balcony of her flat. Sonya is an amazingly strong woman and has worked tirelessly in Laura's memory to help young performers fund their training at drama college.

Having done my job with the auction, I settled down to enjoy the rest of the evening with friends. As the band struck up, I saw a tall, beautiful brunette in an elegant red dress walking across the room. I remember thinking, Wow! and that she must be making her way to the dance floor so was surprised when she stopped at our table.

'Hello,' she said. 'You did a great job. I hope you don't mind, and you're welcome to say no, but would you like to dance?'

'Oh, er, I'm not much of a dancer...but I'll give it a go,' I mumbled, and as she confidently offered her hand, I took it and walked with her on to the crowded floor.

We engaged in small talk, and as I proved I won't be queuing up to be a contestant on *Strictly Come Dancing*, a flashgun popped and caught us. My immediate thought was, Shit, here we go. That'll be all over the papers and they'll have us down the aisle before I even know her name.

The music finished. I thanked her and returned to my seat, thinking, She's lovely, but that's that. Ten minutes later she returned, photo in hand. 'One of the girls on my table bought it for me,' she said. 'It's a lovely photo and I thought you would like to see it?'

It was a good picture. It looked like we had been together for ever, not as if we'd just met. I didn't know what to say. 'Er, shall I sign it?' I asked, and then thought, You bloody idiot. What made you say that!

'Yes,' she replied, a little nonplussed. 'That would be...lovely.'

In automatic celeb mode I asked, 'Who's it to?'

'Claire.' She blushed.

And so the first photo of me and my lovely partner has 'To Claire. With love, Les Dennis' scrawled across it. Luckily it didn't put her off and we danced again, sat and chatted and I asked her out for dinner.

That first date, at a restaurant in Chiswick, led to another and we cautiously began a relationship. Claire isn't in the same business as me, which I think is one of the reasons our relationship works. Apart from that ridiculous photo signing, she doesn't allow me to let Les Dennis take over from Leslie Heseltine. Mine is a strange industry. As performers, we can get a little self-obsessed – 'Enough about me. Let's talk about you...What do you think of me?' Claire's career has, for many years, been in corporate human resources, and is now in business and life coaching, so although she doesn't coach me, she helps me to stay grounded. Sometimes that irrational fear of intimacy rears its ugly head, but when my hand slips out of hers in a crowded street, she will grab it and give me a look that says, very simply, 'You're not getting away with that!' With some matchmaking help from my friend Lino Carbosiero, who is a star hairdresser at the renowned salon Daniel Galvin in London, I asked Claire to move with me into the newly renovated house in Highgate.

Her introduction to my crazy world was a real baptism of fire. The first professional occasion she accompanied me to was *Radio Times*'s covers party. Every year *Radio Times* presents all the people who have appeared on their front cover with framed copies at a star-studded event. I was on the *Extras* cover, along with Ricky and the A-listers, so was invited to attend. Claire took it all in her stride, and for the first time in a long time, I felt relaxed to be at such an event.

Not long afterwards we went to the memorial service for Ronnie Barker at Westminster Abbey. Ever since staying at the same hotel as Ronnie and Joy in Barbados they had kept in touch. They came to see me in *Chicago* and always invited me to their lovely parties. Ronnie was a sweet, funny and thoughtful man. His love for Joy and his family was always supremely evident and something that I really envied. When he died, the world was a sadder place, robbed of the joyful laughter that he brought in abundance. The service was a fitting tribute and it was an honour to be there. Laughter rang throughout the hallowed walls of the abbey from the moment the minister lit 'four candles'. Ronnie Corbett's speech was moving and funny, and Peter Kay talked of his correspondences with Ronnie Barker. One day he had received a letter with a crest on the envelope and, when he opened it, realised it was from Slade Prison's famous inmate Norman Stanley Fletcher. Ronnie wrote to him in character, and Peter, thrilled, wrote back to him as Brian Potter from *Phoenix Nights*. As I listened to Peter telling the congregation about sending Fletcher a malt loaf with a file in it, I smiled with pride. I was partly responsible for their pen-pal relationship. A few years earlier, as Peter was first achieving his deserved success, I had seen him in London. 'The one person I'd love to send a fan letter to is Ronnie Barker. I idolise him,' he'd said.

The next day I rang Ronnie and told him.

'Who?' he asked. When I explained it was Peter from *Phoenix Nights*, he said, 'Oh, yes. He's very good. Tell him he can write to me, but not to ask for money!'

As the great and the good filed out of the abbey and made their way to the wake, I felt proud to have Claire on my arm.

Our courtship was not without its struggle. Claire is thirty-seven, so once again there is a substantial age gap. I no longer care what may be written about that, but for the first year of our relationship I felt emotionally frozen and took a long time to thaw out. After two failed marriages it was hard for me to truly fall in love and believe that we could have a future together. It seemed everyone around me, though, saw what a true and loyal woman she is before I allowed myself to see it, and thankfully Claire stood strong and had faith enough for both of us.

In summer 2007 I did my second season at the Edinburgh Festival. I had gone the year before with a new play, *Marlon Brando's Corset*, by Guy Jones, directed by Ed Curtis, that was a satire on celebrity culture, working alongside Mike McShane and Jeremy Edwards. I had a great time and so returned in 2007 with a very funny play, *Certified Male*. Written by Scott Rankin and Glynn Nicholas, it deals with the complexities of being male in the twenty-first century. The director of a company, Jarrad, played by Roger Aldborough, takes three of his executives, Alex, played by Glynn, Howard, played by Simon Gleeson, and McBride, played by me, away to a resort in Indonesia for a 'restructuring' weekend. By the end of the play, under possible threat of the sack, the three men are taught that life isn't all about work and that they should stop and smell the roses more. McBride almost drowns and has a kind of redemption when he realises how much he loves his wife and children. In the final scene Alex asks him, 'How did you get on at Baby Gap?'

'Good,' he replies. 'I got a blue one and a pink one, just in case.' He's going to be a dad again.

One Sunday evening, over dinner in Edinburgh, Claire handed me a bag saying, 'I got you a present.' I pulled out a small box on which she'd written, 'I got you a blue one and a pink one, just in case.'

That's my line from the play, I thought. Didn't get it. I turned the box over and it said, 'Baby Gap.' Still didn't get it. I opened it and there was a small babygro with 'I love my daddy' written on the front. 'Claire, that's lovely, but we shouldn't tempt fate...*What?*' Light-bulb moment. I got it!

We cried tears of joy. God willing, as you read these words, I will be a proud and loving dad again for the second time.

For a while I had been unsure that I wanted to have more children as I had been scared about being an older dad. I kept remembering that line in *When Harry Met Sally*: 'It's OK for men,' Sally says. 'Charlie Chaplin had kids into his seventies.'

'Yes,' replies Harry, 'but he was too old to pick 'em up.'

I knew how important it was to Claire, though, and as both our love and my confidence about the future grew, we had decided to start trying for a family at the beginning of 2007. We are now engaged and I couldn't be happier. Doing *Certified Male* in Edinburgh was a kind of epiphany for me. Playing that drowning scene every performance made me, like the character McBride, realise what I had, and wanted. I feel truly blessed. And anyway, Harry, seventy is the new sixty!

We both felt nervous yet excited telling Phil, who is approaching his thirties, that he was going to have a new sibling, but he was thrilled and excited too. He is already talking about all the things he wants to teach his new brother or sister.

I try very hard not to have regrets in life, but I remain

profoundly sorry for the way I treated his mum and for not being there for him when he was young. It has taken me some time to forgive myself for the mistakes I made all those years ago, but living in the past doesn't do anyone any good. By maintaining a good relationship with Lynne, I have been able to build a strong, loving and supportive bond with Philip over the years since.

This was particularly important a few years ago when Philip went through an incredibly diffiult experience. We were both able to be there for him and give him the support he needed. He and I went on holiday to St Lucia together. We had a great time, and with a few days to go he met a beautiful young St Lucian girl, Martina Flavien. After we got home, he remained in contact with her and went out to see her again. She then came over and they lived together. She was a funny, strong-willed young woman and Lynne and I both became very fond of her. When I was working in the Cole Porter musical *Kiss Me, Kate* in September 2004, Phil and Martina came to see it. The show is about a troupe of actors touring a production of *The Taming of the Shrew*. When Kate smacked Petrucio across the face, a voice in the auditorium said, clear as a bell, 'Ooh, that's a bit harsh!' It was Martina – she had never been to a theatre before and was so captivated and involved that she had shouted out. She celebrated her twenty-first birthday with us and adored the fuss that we, and, particularly Phil, made of her. When her Visa ran out, she returned home to the Caribbean with plans to come back.

As Phil and I were driving through Highgate on Maundy Thursday 2005, he got a call and I knew it was bad news. Martina had been hit by a car as she crossed the road to get bread and milk and was on a life-support machine.

'What do you want to do?' I asked Phil.

'I'm going out there,' he said firmly.

The next day he caught a flight to St Lucia and sat by

Martina's bedside with her family as they agonised over whether or not to turn off her life-support machine. In the end they didn't have to, as Martina slipped away naturally and peacefully. Lynne joined him at the funeral, where he was a tower of strength for Martina's family. As Lynne could be with him, I stayed in England, where I was playing at the Birmingham Repertory Theatre in *Neville's Island*. Once again, the show went on. This time, though, I felt it was OK. Phil needed to deal with the situation in his own way. His strength and compassion were truly inspiring. I have nothing but respect for the way he handled everything that Easter. I asked him whether or not I should mention Martina in this book and, without pausing, he said, 'Definitely, she would have loved it.'

I am glad Amanda has found happiness with Chris. They have started a family and I wish them everything they want in life. I recently read a poem about people coming into our lives for a reason, season or a lifetime – she was definitely a reason, and I can now look back and take from that relationship the lessons I was meant to learn. She and Sophie both helped me to reconnect with my biological family, and for that I am eternally grateful. It is great to have our Marg, Tony, Ken and Mandy back in my life, and going home to Liverpool to spend time with my family is now a great joy. As I write, the city has been celebrating its launch as the 2008 European Capital of Culture. I was very proud and thrilled to be part of the opening ceremony and look forward, with my fellow Scousers, to the forthcoming events and the exciting regeneration that is under way.

Time is a great healer and whatever anger I felt in the past about the failure of my second marriage has now disappeared. A couple of years ago I auditioned for an American sitcom for Touchstone TV and Elton John's company. It was based loosely on Elton's life and dealt with the day-to-day adventures of a flamboyant rock star and his devoted entourage. I was auditioning to play Max, the star's gay British valet. I got a recall and went just before Christmas to meet the writers and producers at Grouchos in Soho. Other actors had been recalled for various parts and I sat chatting for a while with Paul McGann, who was up to play the rock star. As he left, he bumped into another actor outside, and I could hear them talking. Shit, I thought, I know that voice. So would anyone who has watched *Bob the Builder*, *Men Behaving Badly* or any Homebase advert. It was, of course, Neil Morrissey. In four years I had never run into him, even though we only live a few miles apart. It's a small business, though, and I knew that one day our paths were bound to cross. I'd often wondered how I would react. Well, in a couple of minutes, if I wasn't called in for my audition, I was going to find out. He finished his chat with Paul, walked into reception, gave his name and glanced over to see who else was in. He looked at me and did a double-take. Like me, he was probably thinking, Oh, shit, but simply smiled and said, 'Nice to see you. I really mean that, by the way.'

And, you know, it was OK. I didn't want to punch his lights out. I didn't want to run away. We chatted politely and even laughed when we thought about how many photographers strolling round the streets of Soho would think that Christmas had truly come early if they could get this shot. The receptionist popped her head round the corner and, once she got over the shock of seeing us together, said, 'Oh, Les, they're ready to see you. Upstairs, first door on the left.'

'I've got a new club up the road,' Neil said, 'Hirst House. Pop in for a drink any time.' We looked at each other, and in unison both said, 'Probably not a good idea.' And that was it. We wished each other Merry Christmas and I plodded up the stairs for my meeting. Neither of us got a part. The pilot was made, but the show never made it to a series. Imagine, though, if we had both got the roles and had ended up working together. Now that would have been interesting!

When I had started out doing the clubs all those years ago, I had just wanted to entertain, to be a good and skilled performer. Over the years I got hooked on the attention and got sucked into that 'famous for being famous' syndrome. It cost me a lot of the truly valuable things in life and at times could have claimed my sanity. At my lowest points I blamed other people, particularly the press, but in hindsight, and through the catharsis of writing this book, I have come to realise that, like all addicts, the problem was my responsibility and I was in denial. My relationship with the media is now, I hope, much healthier. I know that press and publicity are important in my business, but I am more cautious about it involving my private life. Les Dennis is my work persona, but when I walk through my front door, I am I hope very much the Leslie Heseltine who grew up on the streets of Liverpool.

I am extremely grateful for the rich and varied career that I have. The thing that excites me most is the diversity of the work I am offered. One minute it'll be a concert performance of *South Pacific* with a seventy-piece orchestra and opera singers Alan Opie and Maria Ewing; the next minute I'll be voicing children's cartoon *Engie Benjy* with Ant and Dec. I'll go from doing a situation comedy by David Croft and Jeremy Lloyd, the creators of *Are You Being Served?*, and starring Wendy Richard, Ian Lavender and Philip Madoc, to a game show called *In the Grid* for Channel 5. I recently did an eighteenth-century *commedia dell'arte* masterpiece by Goldoni, *A Servant for Two Masters*. I was thrilled to be directed by the brilliant classical director Michael Bogdanov, whose ground-breaking production of *The Taming of the Shrew*, which I saw in 1978 at the RSC in Stratford, remains one of my favourite theatrical experiences.

I finished 2007 by doing my first pantomime in ten years. The previous Christmas I went to see my friend Bobby Davro in *Peter Pan* in Wimbledon. He was working with the brilliant

American actor Henry Winkler, who played the Fonz in the classic sitcom *Happy Days*. Bobby was having such fun working the audience that I decided I wanted to have another go. In a play, you work with a group of actors to create a world that the audience can become engrossed in. In panto, the audience is like an extra cast member and provides the comics with that instant fix of laughter and connection that they crave. So imagine how thrilled I was this year to share the stage at the Sunderland Empire with a true Hollywood legend, Mickey Rooney. He is the last of the great stars from the studio-led golden age of cinema. At the age of twelve, he played Puck in *A Midsummer Night's Dream* alongside James Cagney and Olivia de Havilland. He did dozens of musicals, including *Babes in Arms* in an unforgettable partnership with Judy Garland. He co-starred with Spencer Tracy in *Boys Town* and with Audrey Hepburn and George Peppard in *Breakfast at Tiffany's*. His credits go on and on. And here he was, with his lovely wife, Jan, making his panto debut in Sunderland at the age of eighty-seven. When he's interviewed, the question he is repeatedly asked is why he's doing it. The assumption is that he is broke and needs the money. It's not that. He has been performing since he was eighteen months old and show business is his lifeblood. For him, the show most definitely must go on. I felt privileged to sit with him in my dressing room every night as he regaled me with tales of Bette Davis, Errol Flynn, Fred Astaire and countless other Hollywood icons. Oh, the stories. But that's another book!

For me, the show has now been going on for over thirty-five years and I hope it continues for as long as I enjoy doing it. It all started with those black-and-white images of Jimmy Tarbuck on *Sunday Night at the London Palladium*. Thank you, Jimmy, for helping me believe that I could do it. The years working with Russ and his team were invaluable and extremely enjoyable. The partnership with Dustin was one of the most exciting periods of my career, and his untimely death came as we were only just starting to explore the boundless possibilities as a double act. It also robbed me of a friendship with one of the funniest and most charismatic men I have known and robbed him of the chance to enjoy the success he deserved and had worked so hard to achieve. He left me with a legacy that I have tried to live up to. If I hadn't been part of that extraordinary success, I wouldn't have been given the chance to host *Family Fortunes*, a show that kept me on TV for sixteen years. I am deeply indebted to him and still miss him very much.

Wanting to live out my mum's dream and impress my dad were major reasons for starting out on the path I did, and I would like to think that they would have been proud, although I'm sure my dad would have found some of the things that have happened in the last few years 'bloody embarrassing'. With the aid of that fucker hindsight, if I could do it all again, I would appreciate the time I had with them more and most certainly would have grieved their passing with more dignity and presence than I did at the time. It has, among other things, taught me that the show doesn't have to go on if something more important is happening in the wings. I can excuse myself and say, 'Thank you, ladies and gentlemen, you have been lovely, but I've got to go. Goodnight and God bless.'

Cue cheesy smile, music and closing credits!

Index